CW01151828

Julia Kristeva and Feminist Thought

JULIA KRISTEVA AND FEMINIST THOUGHT

Birgit Schippers

EDINBURGH UNIVERSITY PRESS

© Birgit Schippers, 2011

Edinburgh University Press Ltd
22 George Square, Edinburgh

www.euppublishing.com

Typeset in Sabon
by Servis Filmsetting Ltd, Stockport, Cheshire, and
printed and bound in Great Britain by
CPI Antony Rowe, Chippenham and Eastbourne

A CIP record for this book is available from the British Library

ISBN 978 0 7486 4089 8 (hardback)

The right of Birgit Schippers
to be identified as author of this work
has been asserted in accordance with
the Copyright, Designs and Patents Act 1988.

Contents

Acknowledgements	vii
Abbreviations	ix
Introduction	1
1 Kristeva and Feminism: A Critical Encounter	21
2 Crisis, Revolt, Intimacy	55
3 Corporeal Ethics: Between Violence and Forgiveness	87
4 The Singularity of Genius	115
5 Towards a Philosophy of Freedom?	145
Bibliography	175
Index	193

Acknowledgements

The ideas presented in this book began their life as part of a PhD thesis, and I wish to express my sincere thanks to my two PhD supervisors, Moya Lloyd and Iain MacKenzie. For their encouragement and support at various stages of this project I would like to thank Yvonne Galligan, Vincent Geoghegan, Kimberly Hutchings and John Thompson. Thanks are also due to my editor at Edinburgh University Press, Carol Macdonald. The research for this project was funded by the British Academy Small Research Grants Scheme (award reference no. SG090610), facilitating visits to the British Library and to the Hannah Arendt Zentrum at the University of Oldenburg/Germany. Oliver Bruns from the Hannah Arendt Zentrum and the staff at the British Library Humanities reading room were tremendously helpful in sourcing the material I needed for my research. I owe a big 'thank you' to the library staff at St Mary's University College, whose support went beyond the call of duty (they will know what I mean!). Thanks are also due to Damian Knipe from St Mary's Research Office and to the chair of the research committee, Gabrielle Maguire, for their support during crucial stages of the project.

Many of the arguments presented in this book have been 'tested' at various conferences, and I would like to thank all those who helped me to clarify my ideas, especially the participants of the Kristeva roundtable at the 2009 Manchester Workshops in Political Theory. I would also like to take this opportunity to express my gratitude to the two anonymous reviewers; their generous and useful suggestions have been very beneficial in improving the quality of my script. It goes without saying that the sole responsibility for its content, including any errors or omissions, lies with me. Finally, I want to acknowledge my biggest debt, to my partner Tom Hartley. His love and support sustained me throughout the duration of this project, and his encouragement helped me to get through the mundane and difficult aspects of the writing process.

Abbreviations

BS	*Black Sun*
Crisis	*Crisis of the ~~European~~ Subject*
CW	*About Chinese Women*
'Dissident'	'A New Type of Intellectual: The Dissident'
DL	*Desire in Language*
HA	*Hannah Arendt*
IR	*Intimate Revolt*
NMS	*New Maladies of the Soul*
NwN	*Nations without Nationalism*
PoH	*Powers of Horror*
Revolt	*Revolt, She Said*
RPL	*Revolution in Poetic Language*
'SM'	'Stabat Mater'
SNSR	*The Sense and Non-Sense of Revolt*
StO	*Strangers to Ourselves*
ToL	*Tales of Love*
'WT'	'Women's Time'

Introduction

> I don't consider myself a theorist of feminism. What little I wrote on women is empirical, dispersed, work in progress . . .
>
> (*Revolt*: 29)

> [E]mphasizing the singularity realized in exemplary works . . . is also a way of disassociating myself from feminism as a mass movement.
>
> (*Colette*: 404)

Few scholars can lay claim to being immortalised in a pop song;[1] that the Franco-Bulgarian literary theorist, semiotician and psychoanalyst Julia Kristeva can garner such admiration is testimony to her wide appeal and indeed to her cult status. Such a tribute, moreover, in no way diminishes her enormous scholarly achievements, and it is therefore without irony that she can be included among that small group of people that she herself refers to, rather disparagingly, as the 'Star Academy' (2009a: 20). Kristeva is much in demand as a speaker, and she has received many prestigious awards, including the Holberg International Memorial Prize and the Hannah Arendt Prize.[2] The output and scope of her work to date are staggering and still growing, stretching from early work on linguistics and semiotics, to literary theory, psychoanalysis, political philosophy, feminism and, in recent years, fiction. However, despite Kristeva's intellectual stardom and broad reach, she is a contested figure, especially within that area of critical thought that is the subject matter of this book: contemporary feminist theory. Exploring the reasons for feminism's diverse and conflicting responses to Kristeva is one of my aims, but I also want to establish Kristeva's significant contribution towards contemporary feminist thought.

Despite wide-ranging references to Kristeva's ideas within some sections of contemporary feminism, such as literary theory, film theory and aesthetics, their wider relevance for a feminist project is subject to much dispute, and it is fair to say that few other thinkers are as contested within feminism as Kristeva. Described by some of her critics as anti-feminist (Jones 1984: 56), unuseful for a feminist project (Fraser 1992b: 189), misogynistic and even proto-fascist (J. Stone 1983), she is celebrated by others as 'a brilliant feminist voice' (Zerilli 1992; see also Ziarek 1992; 2001). Such conflicting interpretations and assessments of her writings are compounded by her own ambivalence towards feminism, which ranges from a recognition of the importance of feminism's achievements, to a reluctance to subscribe to a feminist perspective (see Lechte and Margaroni 2004: 24), up to an occasional outright rejection of feminism as totalitarian.

The feminist reception of Kristeva's ideas, alongside her own treatment of feminism, has intrigued me ever since I first engaged with her work, and it is this interest that constitutes the background to my book; I wanted to make sense of the various readings, misreadings and productive rereadings of Kristevan ideas and their contribution to feminist thought. I also wanted to establish why, notwithstanding serious limitations in her thought, she is an important thinker to engage with, especially for anyone with an interest in feminism. This book is my contribution to such an engagement and it presents my critical appropriation of what I consider to be Kristeva's significant input into feminist theory, but it also reflects my discontent with her shortcomings in relation to feminism and politics. I will pay particular attention to Kristeva's relationship with the wider field of feminist political philosophy because it is this area of feminist thought that has been most reluctant to embrace Kristevan ideas. If feminism, broadly understood, is a project aimed at social and political transformation, then it is over the question of feminist politics, the agency of the female subject and the subversive capacity of Kristeva's conceptual tools that she has been most vehemently criticised. While I remain puzzled by her many hostile remarks about feminism, including her apparently ill-judged assertions regarding the nature, prospects and desirability of feminist politics, I am also attracted to her compelling critique of identity, her persistent emphasis on the centrality of embodiment to social and political life, and her concern for the fragility and precariousness of the subject.

As I want to demonstrate, feminism's conflicting accounts of Kristeva are as much the result of the ambiguity of her conceptual

Introduction

apparatus and her idiosyncratic understanding of feminism, as they are the product of a reading practice that does not sufficiently consider her fundamental ambivalence regarding all matters feminist. Yet, I want to suggest that it is paradoxically this conceptual ambiguity that facilitates a feminist appropriation of her ideas and that offers feminism a sophisticated conceptual apparatus to theorise issues of key concern to feminism, such as questions of embodiment, motherhood, sexual difference, ethics and prospects for social transformation. By remaining open to a plurality of interpretations, her writings facilitate an active misappropriation of Kristevan concepts for feminist purposes. It is this latter point that I advocate here: I want to show that Kristeva's conceptual tools, regardless of her position vis-à-vis feminism, can be utilised in the direction of feminist theory.

Kristeva's conceptual apparatus and her idiosyncratic understanding of feminism alone are not enough to account for her conflicting reception in feminism; neither does it suffice to charge her critics with a lack of intellectual generosity or with a misreading of her ideas. Rather, central to the understanding of the relationship between Kristeva and feminism is the way that her ideas epitomise the tensions and fissures in contemporary feminist theory. Kristeva's intellectual debts and her contribution to contemporary critical thought, including her insistence on the fluidity and instability of the subject, her displacement of politics and her critique of identity politics, have been broadly welcomed within those strands of feminist thought associated with post-structuralism or postmodernism. Likewise, feminists influenced by Critical Theory or by standpoint feminism have often been unsympathetic or even hostile towards Kristeva's work.[3] Thus, what is seen as a troubled relationship between Kristeva and feminism can only be understood if we examine how Kristevan ideas relate to wider debates within feminism, such as the controversy over the status of the female subject and her agency, her notion of the maternal body, the relationship between the feminine and women, the status of nature and culture, the debate over essentialism and, more widely, her views on feminist politics.

I already alluded to Kristeva's wider contribution to contemporary critical thought, and it is important to stress that the reception of her writings is not restricted to feminist scholarship. In fact, a burgeoning Kristeva scholarship is emerging that engages in sensitive and sympathetic readings of Kristeva's work, and that has already gone some way in establishing Kristeva as a thinker with feminist credentials.[4] Yet, it is her relationship with feminism that has occupied most of her commentators and that deserves renewed attention; of central importance to my discussion is the scrutiny of Kristeva's recent work, including her books on revolt and on the female genius, and her essays on Europe and freedom.[5]

While my overall emphasis lies with an exposition and critical analysis of Kristeva's recent writings and their significance for feminism, I begin with a brief sketch of some of the key debates within recent feminist theory. This is followed by a broad outline of Kristeva's intellectual heritage and position within the French intellectual scene of the 1960s and 1970s, and the dispute over so-called 'French feminism'. I conclude with a brief methodological reflection and with a summary of the chapter structure of my book.

Feminist Theory Today

As I indicated, feminism's heterogeneity and plurality constitute the point of departure for my analysis of the relationship between Kristeva and feminism. I further develop this aspect in Chapter 1, where I assess feminism's diverse reception of some of Kristeva's key ideas, such as her notions of the semiotic and the symbolic, and her discussion of the *chora* and the maternal body. For now, I want to map, albeit briefly, this heterogeneity and plurality, by attending to some of the debates and contentions within current feminist thinking.[6]

An emphasis on difference, diversity and plurality is often considered to be a key feature of contemporary feminist thought; however, it is fair to say that diversity and plurality have characterised feminism from its inception. Debates over the status of class or race in feminist thought, disputes over feminism's wider ideological attachments, manifested, for example, in the classification of feminism into liberal, Marxist and radical strands, and also questions of nationhood and nationalism, or of sexuality and morality, have structured feminism from its beginnings. To deny this conflictual history would amount to what Linda Zerilli calls 'a retroactive fantasy about the wholeness of political origins' (2005: 2). In a recent state-of-the-art article, Mary G. Dietz makes

Introduction

a similar claim for the diversity and plurality of contemporary feminism, describing feminist theory as 'a multifaceted, discursively contentious field of inquiry that does not promise to resolve itself into any programmatic consensus or converge onto any shared conceptual ground' (2003: 400). This absence of consensus does not seem to concern Dietz overly much; in actual fact, she sees it as a sign of the dynamism and vitality of contemporary feminist thought. A detailed exposition of the rich and diverse field of methodological, epistemological and ontological positions would lead me well beyond the scope of this book, but in order to aid the understanding of feminism's heterogeneous Kristeva reception, it is helpful to provide a brief sketch of the fault lines that make up contemporary feminist thought, and to evoke the wider context of the theory debates over the last thirty to forty years. Feminists' various positioning vis-à-vis so-called 'postmodernism' is frequently conjured up as a dividing line between different and opposing feminist camps (see, for example, the essays in Nicholson 1990); however, such an emphasis disguises a wider set of differences, shifting alliances and controversies, and it evades the nuanced and subtle positions put forward by many feminist scholars.

It is probably fair to suggest that the controversy over the question of the subject lies at the heart of these current feminist contentions. Disputes over the subject are not the exclusive domain of feminism, though; rather, they connect with wider discussions, pertaining to the idea that 'the individual' or 'the self' is not an unencumbered, stable individual, but is divided, decentred or subjected. This is not the place to track the origins of the debate over the subject or to expound on the subtleties and nuances of various critiques of the subject, informed, for example, by Foucault, psychoanalysis or Derridean deconstruction (see Williams 2001). Instead, I want to underline the manifestation of these discussions for feminist theory. The key reference for feminist discussions of the subject is the position taken vis-à-vis the term 'woman', which is considered to be the raison d'être of feminism, its privileged object of analysis and the rational underpinning of feminist politics. However, the term remains highly contested within feminism, in the first instance because there is no consensus as to who should be subsumed under the label 'woman'. Its inflection with race, class or sexuality, and the pursuit of exclusionary practices and strategies based on these categories has spurred major debates, splits and controversies. For example, the famous question, uttered in the nineteenth century by the African-American Sojourner Truth, 'Ain't I a woman?', has been taken up by late twentieth-century feminist thinkers to critique the idea of 'woman' based upon the racial exclusions that it performs (hooks 1984). Denise Riley (1988) deploys Sojourner Truth's exclamation to provide a critical genealogy of the term woman and its exclusionary practices that identifies the racial and cultural heterogeneity of women. Riley is at pains to stress that this genealogical critique of 'woman' does not advocate a feminism without women; rather, as she suggests, it points to a 'dangerous intimacy between subjectification and subjection': according to Riley, '"women" is a simultaneous foundation of and an irritant to feminism' (1988: 17; see also Butler 1990). This critique of the subject draws on what Dietz (2003) refers to as the politics of difference as much as it draws on the politics of diversity, two important and related strands within feminism that put forward a philosophical critique of the subject on the one hand, influenced, in the main, by psychoanalytic and post-structuralist thought, and a critique that draws on the intersection of gender with other identity categories on the other.

I have already stressed how feminism, defined as a project aimed at social and political transformation, is inherently political. Even though many debates within contemporary feminism seem highly abstract and are perceived to be of academic interest only, they are also intimately linked with feminism's political controversies and have impacted upon concrete concerns over policy. One such concern, which follows from the dispute over the subject, is the issue of female agency and feminist politics. At the heart of this concern is the question whether a critique of the subject can generate and sustain a feminist political practice, or whether feminism needs to define its agents in advance. The implications of either position seem far-reaching. Can feminism do without a clearly defined subject, or can it afford to leave the question of the subject open? What, on the other hand, are the risks that come with the notion of a pre-constituted subject? This debate between versions of a pre-constituted subject on the one hand and a decentred subject, or subject-in-process, as Kristeva calls it, on the other, has exerted an enormous influence, both directly and indirectly, on most other areas of recent feminist debate, and I return to it

Introduction

throughout the book. It is also directly linked to the seemingly intractable feminist controversy over essentialism. Often taken as a short-hand for a presumed set of shared characteristics, essentialism has served as a rallying call for feminist debates over sameness or difference, the question whether women, as women, possess a set of shared characteristics or features, and whether these features serve as the ground for a feminist ethics or for feminist politics. These features have been explained as both innate and acquired characteristics, such as an alleged capacity to mother, an innate non-violent relationship to the other, or the capacity to care. Because of its link with the question of the subject, the essentialism controversy has also had an impact upon the categorisation of contemporary feminism, where those feminist positions associated with difference or diversity are often seen as hostile to essentialist accounts, whereas feminist views presuming a unified subject have often been described – and decried – as essentialist.

The question of sexuality, its relationship to the body, and its linkage with that other central category of feminist thought, gender, has also occupied feminist theorists. An important element of feminist discussions over sexuality pertains to the question of sexual difference. Drawing on psychoanalysis and its narrative of the subject's alleged psychosexual development, sexual difference theorists, including Kristeva, provide an account of the development of the feminine (and by extension the masculine) that stresses the subject's complicated process of individuation in the framework of language, culture and the body. Critics of sexual difference point to the way that it entrenches the hegemonic binary of masculinity and femininity, and retains its attachment to biological notions of the body. Related to this charge is the feminist critique of the notion of gender, previously championed by feminists to refute naturalising accounts of women's status in society. As argued by Judith Butler, gender is only meaningful in a system of binary (hetero-)sexuality, where the terms of gender acquire their meaning as heterosexual.

The final key controversy that I want to draw attention to is the debate within feminism over the status of universality and its relationship to particularity. At the heart of this concern lies the feminist dispute over the politics of multiculturalism and its impact upon women's lives; it also pertains to the relationship between Western feminism, understood as a position articulated by and representing predominantly white, European, North American or Australian feminists, and its postcolonial feminist critics.[7] Highlighting these disputes, which evolve, in the main, around the intersection of gender with questions of race and culture, some feminists have sought to bring to the fore the racial blind-spots of contemporary feminist thought. In recent years, these debates have acquired a particular poignancy in the wake of 9/11 and the wars in Iraq and Afghanistan, challenging feminists to articulate and justify an adequate feminist response to what some perceive as part of a terrorist onslaught resulting from Muslim fundamentalist intransigence, while others see it as part of a wider colonial project that, despite its claims to liberate women, is deeply misogynistic and anti-feminist, and inherently racist.

I am conscious of the fact that this, necessarily brief, survey does not offer a comprehensive overview over the current field of feminist scholarship; neither can it do justice to the importance or complexity of the topics that I have addressed here. Its aims were more modest; it sought to identify some areas for discussion that correspond to many of Kristeva's recent concerns, and it hoped to illustrate the heterogeneity and diversity that define contemporary feminism and that come to mould feminism's diverse and heterogeneous reception of Kristeva's ideas. Indispensable to an analysis of Kristeva and feminism is also the way that her writings are located in specific intellectual, cultural and geographical settings. I turn to these contexts in the next section.

French Theory: From Tel Quel *to French Feminism*

The predominantly Anglophone nature of the feminist Kristeva reception should not cloud the significance of the intellectual atmosphere of her adopted country, France, for her work. Here it may be helpful briefly to recall her early intellectual development following her arrival in France, as this has contributed to the emergence of those very positions that later came to dominate the feminist reception of her work. Central to this development and to Kristeva's impact within the French intellectual scene and beyond, is her involvement with the journal and group *Tel Quel*. This story is by now well documented and has been told by Kristeva scholars, as well as by Kristeva herself (1984b).[8] A short synopsis should therefore suffice.

Introduction

Kristeva's arrival in Paris in December 1965 on a scholarship offered by the French Government paved the way for her involvement with *Tel Quel*, which played a formative role in her intellectual development. The *Tel Quel* group, established around Philippe Sollers, had an instrumental role in the theoretical debates, specifically in the promotion of the avant-garde; it also provided an early publication outlet, in the shape of the journal *Tel Quel*, for many of the figures that later became associated with French thought, such as Jacques Derrida and Michel Foucault (see Caws 1973; ffrench 1995; ffrench and Lack 1998). *Tel Quel*'s engagement with avant-garde literature, with Maoism and with psychoanalysis, amongst other areas, generated a series of highly influential writings that put forward a view of writing, broadly construed as production and as analogous to revolution. These themes, underpinned by *Tel Quel*'s wider theoretical perspectives, are largely reflected in Kristeva's early essays from the late 1960s and early 1970s, and they culminate in the publication of her famous *doctorat d'état*, *La Révolution du langage poétique* (1974a), whose first part is published in English as *Revolution in Poetic Language* (1984a).[9] As the Kristeva scholar Joan Brandt recently suggested, Kristeva's work is usually read through a feminist lens; such a reading, according to Brandt, neglects Kristeva's wider political agenda, including the political dimension of her involvement with the journal and group *Tel Quel*, and with *Tel Quel*'s political project (Brandt 2005; see also Sjöholm 2005). Brandt's insistence on the political dimension of Kristeva's ideas challenges a widespread perception of Kristeva's alleged lack of political concerns, said to be dominated by an 'aestheticizing bent' that values avant-garde aesthetic practices above political work (see Fraser 1992b: 187; see also Butler 1990). It also calls for a wider engagement with Kristeva's writings, above and beyond feminism. Indeed, *Tel Quel*'s engagement with theory and with avant-garde literature aimed at a political horizon has been highly significant to the formation of Kristeva's ideas.

Yet, it would unfair and also inaccurate to portray Kristeva as a blank slate inscribed by *Tel Quel* ideology. In fact, she was instrumental in shaping the direction of *Tel Quel* and, more specifically, in introducing some of the intellectual figures of Eastern Europe, such as Bakhtin, to a French audience (see Chapter 1). It is difficult to underestimate the significance of this aspect of Kristeva's œuvre, and it has deservedly received much scholarly attention.[10] Of interest to my discussion is a further point: already in her early writings on language, language acquisition and semiotics (or semanalysis, as she calls it), Kristeva subscribes to a Freudian framework that grows in importance as her writings develop. The full import of Kristeva's debt to psychoanalysis, as far as her reception within feminism is concerned, is revealed in some of her famous writings on women, such as 'Women's Time' (1979), 'Stabat Mater' (1977a) and *About Chinese Women* (1986). This aspect is of key significance, as it is at this juncture in the 1970s that the inception of 'French feminism', and Kristeva's association with it, originate. What, then, is 'French feminism', and how is Kristeva positioned in relation to it?[11]

The term 'French feminism', as distinguished from feminism in France, refers to a number of authors based in France who are loosely associated with psychoanalytic thought, especially in its Lacanian manifestation, and with Derridean deconstructive methods. However, 'French feminism' is a hotly disputed notion, not least because none of the three figures most commonly associated with it, Kristeva, Luce Irigaray and Hélène Cixous, is French-born. Yet the question of nationality or origin does not lie at the heart of the dispute over 'French feminism'. Rather, it is a dispute over the term and concept of feminism, the desirability of feminist politics, and the particular relation between notions of the feminine and women. Christine Delphy (2000), a critic of 'French feminism', has described it as an American invention, because its origin is said to lie in North America, especially in the literature departments of the academy (see also Moses 1998). It was in this academic and geographical environment, beginning in the mid-1970s, that a series of highly influential publications, mostly by North American feminist literary scholars, on recent theoretical developments emerging amongst sections of feminist groups in France, were generated.[12] This highly selective reception of 'French' ideas into the North American academy, focusing, in the main, on Lacanian and Derridean ideas, proved to be extremely open to forms of literary criticism already influenced by post-structuralist and psychoanalytic thought. However, as Christine Delphy has pointed out, this selective reception bore no relation to the experiences and conditions of feminism in France at the time; one should also add that this notion of a 'French feminism' accords a sense of

Introduction

coherence to the theories and ideas of its alleged practitioners that is not reflected in the self-understanding of those who are labelled with this term. Intriguingly, Delphy does not describe Kristeva's position as anti-feminist, but as pre-feminist. As she explains, some of the writers subsumed under the term 'French feminism' are not hostile towards feminism; rather, they do not address feminist concerns; with respect to Kristeva, she declares that 'Kristeva ... does not address the questions raised by feminism because she does not know what they are. Her only information about feminism is the kind of caricatures circulated by the media' (2000: 196). As I illustrated above, such hostility is emblematic for a particular reception of Kristeva's work, but it did not stop the widespread reception of her ideas, or those of 'French feminism', for that matter, which came to influence feminist thought beyond the confines of literary criticism and which prepared the ground for the articulation of many of the ideas which later generated the feminist contentions which I sketched above.

Kristeva's participation and position in feminist debates in France seem to have been, by all accounts, short-lived. What interests me here is not her engagement with the feminist movement in France, though. Rather, I want to pursue the impact of her writings on (Anglo-American) feminist thought, and to assess the wider potential of her thought for feminist theory. Several of her iconic pieces from the 1970s have come to influence the feminist reception of her work, and they continue to be influential to this day. This influence, as I discuss throughout this book, should be set alongside her ambivalence towards feminism, which she expresses frequently in her writings, and which poses a series of questions for the feminist Kristeva scholarship. For example, is it legitimate to judge her writings by feminist standards, especially since, as I have already intimated, it is difficult, if not impossible, to establish a set of shared criteria as to what constitutes feminism? Can a feminist aspiration be read into Kristeva, thereby neglecting her explicit wish not to be read in such a way? And finally, to return to my proviso, which feminist benchmark should be used to assess Kristeva? These questions, which have a direct import on the methodological and epistemological approach of this book, are addressed in the next section.

Reading Kristeva – Reading Feminism

The key substantive issue under investigation in my book is to appraise Kristeva's contribution to contemporary feminist thought, alongside an assessment of feminism's diverse and conflicting responses to Kristevan ideas. Drawing, in the main, on Kristeva's writings published in English since 2000, *Julia Kristeva and Feminist Thought* deals centrally with what may be termed 'the politics of reading'. As I have already intimated, the question of 'how to read Kristeva' can only be addressed by considering her fundamental ambivalence towards feminism, and by unpacking the ambiguities and inconsistencies of her conceptual tools. A recourse to interpretative methodologies and a close reading of Kristevan texts bring these ambiguities to the fore and illuminate the diverse reception of her ideas. However, it is in the nature of ambiguities that no conclusive interpretation of Kristeva's conceptual apparatus is possible; it is therefore unsurprising that the Kristeva reader operates in an intertextual space that allows for a variety of interpretations. As I demonstrate in Chapter 1, commentators have used different textual passages to inform their respective interpretation of Kristeva's texts. What looks like arbitrary choice between different hermeneutic practices may in fact be compatible with the methodological insistence on a 'surplus of meaning' (Ricœur), where texts and reading practices are open to a plurality of interpretations, beyond the control of the author, and where the elusiveness, contingency and indeterminacy of political concepts, as elements of language, allow for competing interpretative versions (see Freeden 2008). Such an approach facilitates an active misappropriation of Kristevan concepts for feminist purposes, even against the intentions of their author. It is this latter point that I wish to advance in my book, as I seek to demonstrate how Kristeva's conceptual tools, notwithstanding her own position vis-à-vis feminism, can be utilised in the direction of feminist theory.

Whether Kristeva can be read for a feminism that she tends to disavow is a crucial question. Despite her stance as a 'reluctant feminist', I want to argue that it is legitimate to do so. To begin with, Kristeva's writings have persistently addressed issues of relevance and interest to women, and I believe it is therefore legitimate to declare a 'feminist interest' in her work. The ques-

Introduction

tion of the permissiveness of a feminist appropriation of Kristeva leads to a further question, however. Considering my emphasis on feminist political philosophy, is it also legitimate to engage in a political reading of Kristeva's psychoanalytic theory? Moreover, should feminism turn to psychoanalytic theory, such as Kristeva's, in its attempt to illuminate the notion of the (female) subject (see Chapter 1), to articulate a feminist ethics (see Chapter 3), or to formulate a feminist politics (see Chapters 4 and 5)? Maria Margaroni (2007) further pursues the question of the legitimacy of such a transposition from psychoanalysis to political thought. Such a transposition, according to Margaroni, may be required if we want to make sense of the numerous challenges we are faced with today, but it needs to be mindful of the way these transpositions are read. As Margaroni claims, a simplistic transference of psychoanalytic concepts on to political processes raises serious problems, and she advises against the use of such analogies between political structures and psychic structures, suggesting that we proceed instead on the basis of a hermeneutics of complication that is mindful of the essentially separate spheres of psychic and social life. I am sympathetic to such a call for caution and I also acknowledge the necessity of a hermeneutics of complication, but I wonder whether such a caution circumvents the critical interrogation of the implicit political assumptions of psychoanalysis; thus, I advocate the need to challenge psychoanalysis for these assumptions, embodied, in particular, in distinctive normative conceptions of gender. Kristeva's own transpositions, between corporeal affect and signification, and between psychic and social life, I believe justify such a project.

The interpretative challenges, which the reading of Kristeva poses, are mirrored by a similar set of challenges that arises from the analysis of feminism's engagement with Kristeva.[13] How are we to assess the diverse feminist responses to Kristeva's thought? As I intimated above, Kristeva's ambiguities are partly responsible for the conflicting and diverse interpretations of her work. There is more to this, though, than an arbitrary choice between two (or more) opposing sets of reading practices and interpretations. As I outlined above, one of the substantive points of contention discussed in this book pertains to Kristeva's positioning vis-à-vis feminism, and to the reception of her work as 'French' theory within strands of Anglo-American feminism. Through a close reading of Kristeva's texts, I want to demonstrate that her reading of feminism is underpinned by a conception of feminism that is, on the whole, surprisingly unaware of feminism's plurality, and that constructs feminism as a monolithic and homogeneous theory and practice. A similar claim has been made by Kelly Oliver, who considers it 'an unfortunate irony that while Kristeva is concerned with difference and individuality, she denies the differences and individuality of multitudes of feminists writing and working all over the world' (1993a: 2). Such a denial, according to Oliver, is particularly regretful because she values Kristeva's challenge to traditional psychoanalytic theory and its usefulness for feminism. Instead, Oliver asserts, it has alienated many of her Anglo-American readers. Given feminism's plurality and diversity, Kristeva's reading of feminism is clearly out of step with the heterogeneous landscape of contemporary feminism, with its multiple and competing political projects, analyses and ontological commitments.

Finally, as I already intimated, key to my assessment of the feminist reception of Kristeva is feminism's own heterogeneity and plurality. I therefore take it as my task to make the wider political attachments and commitments of Kristeva's feminist readers explicit. This, I believe, is crucial if we aim for a better understanding of the reception of Kristeva's work within contemporary feminism. Moreover, as I already suggested, such an approach illuminates how Kristevan ideas, especially those elements of her work that stress the fluidity of the subject and that underscore a psychoanalytic perspective, generate anxiety within those sections of feminism that are attached to conceptions of a stable self and forms of agency based upon notions of a stable self. Developing this point, I want to suggest that the anxiety that Kristeva's work generates within sections of feminism attest to her commitment, broadly speaking, to post-structuralist ideas about the critique of identity and identity politics, her insistence on difference, and her psychoanalytically informed conception of the subject. This, as I argue, contributes substantially to a feminist project that seeks to connect the realm of the intimate with the political; besides, it illuminates her recent interest in conceptions of freedom, and the interrelated production of biography and politics. However, it is undermined by her evasion of a more serious investigation into the question of feminist politics,

Introduction

which she also fails to connect with her radical critique of the subject.

Structure of the Book

As I already suggested, the focus of *Julia Kristeva and Feminist Thought* lies with those Kristeva texts that have been published, in English, since 2000. However, for heuristic reasons, some context is necessary, and I provide this in Chapter 1. There, I stage an encounter between Kristeva and her feminist interlocutors, and I extrapolate some of her key concepts that have been particularly influential within the feminist reception of her work. These include her distinction between the semiotic and the symbolic, her notion of the subject-in-process, her engagement with psychoanalysis and her account of corporeality. This chapter is by no means a comprehensive analysis of Kristeva's overall œuvre, but I hope that it will be helpful to those readers who are new to Kristeva's ideas. Thus, while this chapter sketches familiar territory, the approach allows me to map the reception of Kristeva's ideas within the heterogeneous field that is contemporary feminism. The argument advanced in this chapter suggests that Kristeva's radical philosophical and psychoanalytic assertions, which draw on the notion of the heterogeneity, instability and fluidity of the subject, and which are underpinned by her celebration of singularity and plurality, do not translate easily into feminist perspectives. This disconnect is compounded by a dispute over the meaning of the feminine, its relation to woman/women, and its location within sexual difference. However, I also seek to appreciate Kristeva's emphasis on negativity, which, I wish to aver, contributes to the articulation of feminism as a critical practice.

Kristeva's writings on crisis and revolt are the focus of my discussion in Chapter 2. These topics, which underpin Kristeva's wider philosophical considerations, receive a distinctive attention in her work published since the 1990s. While one of my aims in Chapter 2 consists of a careful unpacking and interpretation of these writings, my particular interest evolves around two related themes that emerge from Kristeva's texts; these are the etymological link between crisis and critique and its potential for feminism on the one hand, and on the other, her notion of intimate revolt, described by some commentators as a 'displacement of politics', and its consequence for female revolt. Developing my argument from Chapter 1, here I will suggest that Kristeva's notion of the feminine, together with the importance she accords to a critical ethos, holds out the promise of establishing feminism as a critical project. A feminist scrutiny of these writings is only now beginning to emerge. Such work is crucial, however, because it can bring to the fore Kristeva's attention to issues of key concern to feminism, including the micro-political aspects of subjectivity and politics, the mutually constitutive realms of embodiment, psychic and social-political life, and the theorisation of female sexuality. Kristeva's writings, whilst not explicitly feminist in their aims or aspirations, constitute an important contribution towards a deterritorialisation of politics that stresses those intimate aspects of political life.

Kristeva's significant contribution to the field of feminist ethics, underpinned by her assertion of the centrality of embodiment to human life, is the subject of Chapter 3. I begin by considering Kristeva's insistence on heterogeneity and on alterity, leading to what I will call an ethics of traversal. A key section of this chapter revisits Kristeva's conception of a maternal ethics, which, as I demonstrate, has come to influence much of the critical reception of her work within feminism. Building upon her overall concern with corporeality and, more specifically, with the theory of the drives, I then proceed to consider the foundational role of violence in Kristeva's theory of the subject and its application in the context of conflict. This leads to my concluding section, on the notion of sublimation and forgiveness. As I will demonstrate in this chapter, I am broadly sympathetic towards Kristeva's ethical project; however, I will also argue that Kristeva's radical theory of heterogeneity and alterity, which informs her ethics, does not translate easily into feminist political efficacy. Developing my discussion from Chapter 1, I will also revisit some of my reservations regarding Kristeva's conception of the feminine.

Chapter 4 introduces Kristeva's recent writings on the female genius, focusing in particular on her work on Hannah Arendt and on the development of Arendtian themes in Kristeva's ideas. So far, this aspect of Kristeva's œuvre has not received much coverage in the critical commentary; hence, this chapter aims to provide a more detailed examination and discussion of Kristeva's work on Arendt, and seeks to initiate a feminist interpretation of

Introduction

these texts. I begin by attending to an exposition and assessment of Kristeva's Romantic heritage and its impact on the concept of (female) genius; I then proceed to discuss her engagement with Arendtian conceptions of narrative, life and rebirth, before considering the question of political bonds and its implications for feminist thought. I conclude with some rather tentative thoughts on a recent development in Kristeva's writings: namely, her engagement with the work of Simone de Beauvoir. Building upon Kristeva's insistence on the singularity and plurality of life, I want to suggest that her engagement with Arendt's ideas establishes the framework of a political philosophy that could, potentially, come to shape a feminist appropriation of Kristeva's work.

Chapter 5 further develops the reference points of Kristeva's political philosophy that I established in the preceding chapter, but asks a more specific question: how can we read Kristeva's philosophy of freedom as a feminist philosophy? And how does Kristeva's conception of freedom enhance feminism, understood as a political project? Drawing on an exposition and critical analysis of some of Kristeva's most recent writings, I critically interrogate the geopolitical and geophilosophical premise that underpins her discussion of freedom and that establishes Europe as a privileged space of freedom. Moreover, I assess this geopolitical element of Kristeva's discussion against the psychosexual and racial narratives that underpin her philosophy of freedom. I conclude by sketching the elements of a Kristevan feminist theory that is attuned to her critique of the subject, along with its emphasis on heterogeneity, alterity and fluidity, but that embraces more consciously and fully the potentially radical implications of her ideas.

Notes

1. The Norwegian band, The Kulta Beats, wrote a song entitled 'Julia Kristeva'. See www.thekultabeats.com/julia.php.
2. The Holberg Prize was established by the Norwegian Government to honour outstanding scholarly work in the arts, humanities and social sciences. Kristeva was the first recipient of this award in 2004. The Hannah Arendt Prize for Political Thought is awarded by the German Heinrich Böll Foundation. Kristeva was its recipient in 2006. A complete list of Kristeva's awards can be found on her web site at www.kristeva.fr/parcours.html.

3. I am conscious of the fact that these rather crude characterisations are not sufficiently attentive to the fissures that exist between and within different strands of feminism. For reasons of space I cannot do justice to this problem in this introduction; however, it is key to my discussion of Kristeva's reception within feminism and will be dealt with in detail in Chapter 1.
4. Recent important additions to the Kristeva scholarship include Beardsworth (2004a), Sjöholm (2005), Lechte and Margaroni (2004), Chanter and Ziarek (2005), and Oliver and Keltner (2009). A further book by Keltner, part of the Polity Press Key Contemporary Thinkers series, is forthcoming.
5. Kelly Oliver's *Reading Kristeva: Unravelling the Double-Bind* (1993) was the first monograph to engage with Kristeva's contribution to feminist thought.
6. For a useful overview see, for example, Dietz (2003). See also Lloyd (2005) and A. Stone (2007).
7. See, for example, Susan Muller Okin's essay, 'Is multiculturalism bad for women?', as well as the various responses to it (Okin 1999).
8. On the group and journal *Tel Quel* see, for example, ffrench (1995), ffrench and Lack (1998), and Caws (1973). For two recent accounts of Kristeva's intellectual beginnings see Brandt (2005) and Sjöholm (2005). See also her novel *The Samurai* (1992), a fictionalized account of the French intellectual scene of the late 1960s.
9. Parts B and C of *La Révolution du langage poétique*, which deal with avant-garde literature, have not been translated into English.
10. Several of Kristeva's early writings on language and literature can be found in *The Kristeva Reader* (1986) and also in *Desire in Language* (1980). For a useful overview see, for example, Becker-Leckrone (2005) and Bové (2006).
11. The critical literature on 'French feminism' and its relationship to feminism in France has grown substantially over the last two decades. For recent assessments see Gambaudo (2007b), Delphy (2000) and Moses (1998). The invention of the term 'French feminism' is often ascribed to Alice Jardine (see Jardine 1981; 1982). For older assessments see Spivak (1981), Burke (1978) and Marks (1978). Grosz (1989) and Cavallaro (2003) provide introductions to some of the theoretical debates in French feminism, while Duchen (1986) offers very useful historical context. Excerpts from Kristeva's writings are included in numerous readers and anthologies on French feminism. Some of the better-known texts include Fraser and Bartky (1992),

Introduction

Marks and de Courtivron (1981), and Moi (1992). See also Oliver (2000) and Oliver and Walsh (2004). Cahill and Hansen's recently published series on French feminists (2008) contains a volume on feminist writings on Kristeva.

12. The enormously influential and prestigious feminist journal, *Signs: Journal of Women in Culture and Society*, is closely associated with the advancement of French feminism. Kristeva features in the very first issue of *Signs* with an article 'On the Women of China' (1975), an extract from her *Des Chinoises* (1974).

13. My analysis of feminism's engagement with Kristeva occupies my discussion in Chapters 1 to 3. Given the relative recent publication of the texts under discussion in Chapters 4 and 5, there is as yet not much feminist material available.

1
Kristeva and Feminism: A Critical Encounter

I think feminists should have ... only the most minimal truck with Julia Kristeva.
(Fraser 1992b: 177)

Kristeva offers us a strategy of subversion that can never become a sustained political practice.
(Butler 1990: 81)

Julia Kristeva [is] one of the most brilliant feminist voices speaking today.
(Zerilli 1992: 111)

This chapter provides an exposition of Kristeva's key concepts and ideas, and sketches the diverse feminist responses to her work. Its aim is to map the fault-lines, both within feminism, and between Kristeva and feminism, that allow for an assessment of the turbulent relationship between Kristeva and feminism. As I already stated in the Introduction, such a task is complicated by feminism's heterogeneity and plurality; after all, which feminist principles and ideas should be used as a benchmark to gauge Kristeva's feminist credentials? It is further obfuscated by an ambiguity at the core of her conceptual apparatus and compounded by Kristeva's ambivalence about feminism. Is it not unfair, then, to seek answers to feminist questions in Kristeva's œuvre? My overall aim in *Julia Kristeva and Feminist Thought* is to demonstrate that feminists would benefit from an engagement with Kristeva's ideas. However, this assertion requires a further qualification; as I suggest in this chapter, Kristevan ideas do not translate easily into feminist thought, and where they do, they are bound to disappoint those feminist readers whose philosophical and political attachments are diametrically opposed to Kristeva's.

Taking the interlocking of the personal and the political as the central message of the feminist project, I want to suggest that one of Kristeva's most important contributions to contemporary feminist thought – indeed, to critical theory in general – lies in her persistent attention to the traversal between the personal and the political, affect and signification, body and meaning. This aspect of Kristeva's thought is a guiding thread of my overall analysis of her work that I begin to map in this chapter, where I sketch those elements of her work that have received considerable attention from her feminist readers. This includes an outline of her theory of language and the speaking subject, a discussion of her concepts of the semiotic and the symbolic, and with it, an assessment of the status of negativity. It will be followed by an overview of Kristeva's concept of the subject and its significance for feminism, a consideration of her psychoanalytic thought and a summary of her philosophy of corporeality.

Although this chapter sets out my interpretation of her work (I develop this further in the following chapters), my main focus is to provide exposition and context to Kristeva's key concepts and their reception within feminism. This emphasis is also reflected in the sources I have used, which include, in the main, some of Kristeva's early essays on language (1969a; 1969b; 1973a), her *Revolution in Poetic Language* (1984a) and her essays collated in *Desire in Language* (1980), as well as some of her essays and interviews from the 1970s and early 1980s that are widely read within feminism, including 'Women's Time' (1979) and 'Stabat Mater' (1977a; see also 1974b; 1977b; 1981).

I have already suggested that my discussion is selective in its focus on feminist political philosophy and its wider emphasis on questions of social and political transformation. This focus frames the range of my sources, which by and large neglects Kristeva's important writings on aesthetics, and it influences the selection of themes I have chosen to explore. These include an examination of the debates over agency, the notion of the feminine and its relation to women, the status of nature and culture, politics, and the maternal body.

It is perhaps not surprising that much of my discussion in this chapter is devoted to Kristeva's concept of the semiotic. As a quick glance through the critical literature reveals, it is with the notion of the semiotic that her work is mostly associated; it is key to an understanding of Kristeva's ideas in general and her reception within feminist debates in particular. The semiotic, identified by Kristeva as one of her core ideas (2002: 258–61),[1] encapsulates feminist aspirations towards social and political transformation; moreover, it alludes strongly to the embodied nature of subjectivity and politics. Whilst I briefly identify the wider-ranging deployment of the notion of the semiotic within Kristeva's œuvre, my focus lies with the exploration of the potentially transformative deployment of this concept; this, as I argue, plays a crucial role in the feminist readings of Kristeva and it exerts a strong influence on feminist discussions of fluid and decentred subjectivity. Building on my explication of Kristeva's ideas, which stresses their contribution to feminist philosophy, I proffer a critical interpretation of the readings that the notion of the semiotic has received in the feminist critical literature. This includes an analysis of the reception and deployment of Kristeva's notion of the subject-in-process within feminist writings. I also aver that the promising account of the concept of the semiotic for a theory of embodied subjectivity, and for a feminist project of political transformation, is undermined by Kristeva's ambivalent attitude towards feminism as a collective political project – in fact, towards politics in general. In order to rescue the semiotic for feminist philosophy and politics, I stress the negative dimensions of the semiotic, highlighting its Hegelian and Freudian connotations.

The Speaking Subject

As I intimated in the Introduction, *Tel Quel*'s mixture of theory, avant-garde literature and politics has been highly significant for the formation of Kristeva's ideas, especially the development of her theory of language, which provides the backdrop to her concepts of the semiotic and the symbolic. Her work on language is intrinsically linked with her key contentions about politics; as she herself suggests, it is aimed at the political horizon.[2] Moreover, her assertions about language acquisition prove to be central to her claims about the agency of the subject, including the subject's positioning within the wider social realm. An exploration of Kristeva's notion of the speaking subject serves as a useful path into her ideas, as it illuminates her discussion of subjectivity and of politics, and underpins her early work on language, culminating in the publication of *Revolution in Poetic Language*. This early work, developed in a critical encounter with the writings of the key figures of structuralism, post-structuralism, psychoanalysis and Marxism, is particularly important to a feminist interpretation of her work, because it sheds a light on her relationship with structuralism (I return to this point later) and on the role of agency.

Early on in *Revolution in Poetic Language*, Kristeva identifies two linguistic traditions, both highly influential during the 1960s, which, in her view, and notwithstanding substantial differences between them, share a series of problematic features. One is Saussurean structuralism; the other is the rationalist humanism of Generative Grammar. Both traditions, according to Kristeva, are void of social-economic and historical references (see also Kristeva 1973a), and they ignore how subject and language are shaped by bodily drives, unconscious desires and sexual difference. Crucially, following Kristeva's reading, they also fail to acknowledge the subject's agentic capacity for a transgressive practice.

It is important to note Kristeva's criticism of structuralism early on in my discussion, as her alleged adherence to structuralist positions has often been used to reject her work.[3] Arguing against structuralist formalism and rationalist, disembodied linguistics, Kristeva builds instead upon the ideas of the Russian linguist Mikhail Bakhtin, whose critical reworking of structuralist formalism exerts a strong influence on Kristeva's theory of language (see *DL*: 64–91). Bakhtin's notion of dialogism, which stresses the significance of context for the establishment of meaning, against the universalistic and ahistorical account of structuralism, and which emphasises the socio-historical dimensions of subject constitution, is particularly important to the development of Kristeva's ideas, and it allows her to articulate her critique of structuralism further. Dialogism also proves central to the formulation of the Kristevan concept of intertextuality: it indicates the existence of an other in language and in meaning, paving the way for Kristeva's theory of an ethics of alterity (see Chapter 3). It also underlines those dimensions of language that exceed formal meaning, pointing to Kristeva's use of the notion of the semiotic. Bakhtin's emphasis on heterogeneity has proven equally important to the intellectual formation of Kristeva, which she deploys to highlight two related aspects of language – the multiplicity of meaning and the operation of drives (see *RPL*: 17; *DL*: 92–123; 1973a: 28) – and which come to influence her account of the subject.

Equally important to the development of her theory of language is the notion of the 'speaking subject', which she borrows from the French linguist Emile Benveniste (1971).[4] His ideas further underpin Kristeva's concern with human agency and, in that sense, she is not, as some of her critics suggest, unambiguously anti-humanist but emphasises instead the historical, social and corporeal context of subject constitution and language. Kristeva utilises another element of Benveniste's ideas: the constitutive role of psychoanalysis, which proves to be indispensable for her early theories of language, and which becomes even more important in her work on the body, informed by the notion of sexual difference and the theory of drives (see below). The link with psychoanalytic models of language acquisition, in the wake of Lacan, proves to be of enduring importance to her account of subjectification.[5] In fact, Kristeva's ideas cannot be dissociated from psychoanalytic ideas (see also Gambaudo 2007a) and her adherence to psychoanalysis constitutes a key reference for her reception within feminism. As I discuss below, it is in particular her psychoanalytic decentring of the subject that places her firmly within the fault-lines of the 'feminist contentions' of the 1980s and 1990s (see Benhabib et al. 1995); it aligns her ideas with those positions in contemporary feminist theory that subscribe to a critique of the subject, a perspective that, as I indicated in the Introduction, has proven to be highly contentious amongst contemporary feminism. Kristeva's psycho-linguistic account of subject constitution, her concern with creativity and practice, and her assertion of the intersection of the psychic and social are captured in her notions of the semiotic and the symbolic. It is to these two concepts that I turn next.

The Semiotic and the Symbolic

One of Kristeva's key interests relates to the issue of signification, which she theorises with her notions of the semiotic and the symbolic. I already intimated that the semiotic, together with the symbolic, constitutes the conceptual core of Kristeva's theory of language and of subjectivity; the two notions surface, in various guises, throughout her writings, and they operate in a dialectical fashion, forming a signifying process during which the subject is constituted in and through language. Her linguistic account is mapped, in an intertextual fashion, upon psychoanalysis, where the stages of language acquisition mirror the stages of the child's psychic development. Thus, the terms 'semiotic' and 'symbolic' designate two different modalities of language; they also refer to two different psychic registers and they acquire gendered connotations, with the semiotic signifying the feminine/maternal and the symbolic representing the masculine/paternal.[6]

To stay with this developmental perspective, the semiotic designates, broadly speaking, the pre-Oedipal psycho-sexual phase and a corresponding set of expressions available to the pre-Oedipal child. Characteristic of this stage is a symbiotic mother–child relationship during which the child, dominated by bodily needs and as yet unable to control its drives, is sustained by the mother (*RPL:* 27). The child has not yet acquired formal language and communicates instead in echolalia, the gurgling and babbling noises of babies that resemble a musical, rhythmic sound and that lack sense, meaning and structure. Kristeva's presentation of the transition from the pre-Oedipal to the post-Oedipal stage, from the semiotic to the symbolic, is thoroughly Lacanian; the imposition of a formal syntactic structure, following the intervention of the phallus, paves the way for the child's entrance into the symbolic. Crucially, however, Kristeva departs from Lacan by stressing the semiotic's persistence as a subversive force within the symbolic; in this guise, it designates a modality of language that, like the pre-Oedipal language of the baby, lacks structure, rules and order. Linguistically, this absence of rules and order manifests itself in so-called glossolalia,[7] in psychotic discourse, as well as in music and in poetic language. Thus, Kristeva's notion of the semiotic encompasses 'pre- or translinguistic modalities of psychic inscription' (1987b: 5); it is captured via the idea of an other 'language' that transcends formal, coherent communication, whether in the form of the pre-Oedipal echolalia of the child, or in art or psychosis, and, hence not or no longer recognisable within symbolic discourse.

One manifestation of this other language that interests Kristeva's early work is poetic language; it forms the centrepiece of *La Révolution du langage poétique* (1974a), her exploration of the work of nineteenth-century French avant-garde writers such as Mallarmé and Lautréamont. In this book, Kristeva emphasises the interconnected production of subject and society, of psyche and language, and of language and of subject, a theme that also occupied *Tel Quel*'s avant-gardistic deployment of Marxism, including their interrelated approach towards aesthetics and politics (see Brandt 2005; ffrench 1995; ffrench and Lack 1998). Kristeva's discussion of poetic language, a term associated with Russian Formalism, draws again extensively on Bakhtin. Poetic language vocalises, like the echolalia of the baby, the materiality and sound of language;[8] it is rhythmic and musical (see also Todorov 1988), and it points to the heterogeneity of language and to the existence of a form of language in the margins of the symbolic (*DL*: 65). This exploration of signification in the margins is a leitmotif of Kristeva's work, brought to the fore in the attention given to notions of dissidence and singularity (see Chapter 4).

The importance of poetic language and, by extension, of the semiotic lies in the potential to initiate a 'revolution in language', based upon a transgressive capacity that is said to engender change in the subject and within society at large; it contains a focus on practice, derived from the semiotic's operation within the symbolic on the one hand, and its transgression and renewal of the symbolic on the other (1973a: 29). Kristeva's emphasis on practice encapsulates her critique of structuralism's neglect of the agentic subject on the one hand, and of the 'necrophiliac' rationalist philosophies of language on the other. Thus, she proposes a notion of the subject as open and fluid, equally indebted to semiotic processes and symbolic modes of signification. The influx of the semiotic is essential, as it generates, via drive energy, the possibility of symbolic exchange; without drive energy, meaning (and the symbolic) collapse. Furthermore, the subject's openness and fluidity do not preclude its engagement in (transgressive) practice; rather, it is the recourse to semiotic drive energy and the openness towards others that generate practice in the first place. To accuse Kristeva of succumbing to a structuralism that denies the subject any agentic capacity therefore neglects Kristeva's substantial departure from structuralism. Rather than precluding practice or agency, her account of the decentred subject puts forward a conception of agency that challenges notions of a willing, conscious subject. It pre-empts some of the key feminist controversies of the 1980s and 1990s that explore the question of female political agency, female solidarity and the feminist project of emancipation. Indeed, as I argue below, it is the (transgressive) practice of the subject that Kristeva celebrates, over and above symbolic agency. As I outline in the next section, central to this claim is Kristeva's appropriation of Hegel's notion of negativity, which denotes this moment of semiotic transgression and which gives the semiotic its subversive potential.[9] I further explore Kristeva's account of the decentred subject and its implications for feminism in the next two sections; in the remainder of this section I want to clarify her account of the relationship between the semiotic and the symbolic.

The semiotic can justifiably be claimed as Kristeva's original contribution to contemporary critical thought; it should be stressed again that, for Kristeva, the semiotic is only intelligible in relation to the symbolic, a term adapted from Lacan's work (see Oliver 1993a). Whilst she remains faithful to Lacan's linguistic interpretation of the symbolic, Kristeva also departs substantially from Lacanian ideas, proposing a re-evaluation of the semiotic–symbolic relationship. According to Kristeva, the symbolic, like the semiotic, indicates a dimension of language as well as a stage in the subject's psycho-sexual development. It is the stage of the post-Oedipal that characterises a particular modality of language and that displays formal rules, including syntax and grammar, aimed at conveying meaning. The child accesses the symbolic with the resolution of the Oedipal crisis, following the intervention of the paternal signifier, the phallus. It becomes initiated into the mirror stage and subjected to the intervention of the Name-of-the-Father. This development is complete once the child controls its bodily functions, sublimates drive energy and acquires language and culture. Furthermore, the symbolic, according to Kristeva, is initiated with the thetic break, Husserl's term that Kristeva applies to the subject's psycho-linguistic development. It indicates the break-up of the symbiotic mother–child relationship, leading to the assertion of a position or a thesis, essentially a negation,[10] the establishment of identity and of a subject–object relationship. Hence, the acquisition of subjectivity requires a distinction between subject and object; as Kristeva suggests, 'the *symbolic* – and therefore syntax and all linguistic categories – is a social effect of the relation to the other' (*RPL*: 29; italics in original).

The notions of the semiotic and the symbolic, and their at times inconsistent deployment in Kristeva's ideas, have generated much controversy and led to conflicting receptions of her work. Her critics read her, in the main, through a developmental lens that is mapped upon the psychoanalytic account of psycho-sexual development and that posits the semiotic as a subversive force, outside or before culture. More sympathetic interpretations, in a Hegelian vein, highlight the semiotic's disruptive and transformative potential in a socio-symbolic order defined as phallocentric. As I already suggested, Kristeva offers no conclusive account of the precise nature of the relationship between the semiotic and the symbolic; in fact, her characterisations are ambiguous and seem contradictory.

Early on in *Revolution in Poetic Language*, Kristeva classifies the relationship between the semiotic and the symbolic as dialectical. The two modalities, Kristeva claims, can only be separated for analytical purposes. Language consists of semiotic and symbolic elements, and their respective coupling characterises a particular type of language. Metalanguage, for example, such as mathematics and theoretical texts, displays a rigid, formal and logical structure, which indicates a predominance of the symbolic; poetic language, on the other hand, with its imitation of sound, its resemblance of echolalia and glossolalia, and its absence of a rigid structure, highlights a predominance of the semiotic (*RPL*: 24). Influenced by Freud's stages of psycho-sexual development, she proffers a developmental account, arguing that the semiotic precedes the symbolic, logically and chronologically (*RPL*: 41). This emphasis stresses the importance given to the non-symbolic, including the feminine, which becomes associated with the semiotic, and it may be read as her critique of the dominance that Lacan ascribes to the paternal-symbolic function and to masculinity. However, in the same text she contends that 'the semiotic that "precedes" symbolization is only a theoretical supposition justified by the need for description' (*RPL*: 68), while elsewhere she suggests that it is the symbolic that precedes the semiotic, logically and chronologically, asserting 'the logical and chronological priority of the symbolic in any organization of the semiotic' (1983: 34).

Kristeva's apparent inconsistencies pose serious challenges for the critical exegesis of her work, and they contribute substantially to the contradictory and often negative reception of her writings within feminism; it becomes impossible to adjudicate between a 'proper' and 'improper' reading.[11] I will illustrate the implications of these ambiguities for the feminist Kristeva reception below; for now, I want to consider the methodological implications. Perhaps surprisingly, not all of Kristeva's readers fault her for her inconsistencies; in fact, some commentators regard them as closely aligned with Kristeva's wider philosophical project. For example, Michelle Boulous Walker (1998) challenges what she terms 'one-sided readings of Kristeva [which] miss ... the importance she herself places upon keeping ambiguity alive in her work. Kristeva's texts refuse the simple binary logic that would settle the matter for all time' (1998: 124). While Kristeva's refusal to submit her argument to an identitarian logic may motivate her ambiguities (see also Oliver 1993a: 1), it certainly does not aid the scholarly exegesis of her work. Building upon Kristeva's wider concern with the fluidity and the precariousness of the subject, my own interpretation leans towards those readings of the signifying process that stress the dialectical entwinement of the semiotic and the symbolic. As I suggest in the next section, such a reading is further supported by Kristeva's positioning of the semiotic as a force of negativity. I begin by unpacking Kristeva's reading of negativity in *Revolution in Poetic Language*; I then discuss the reception of the semiotic in the works of two of her feminist critics, Judith Butler and Diana Coole.

Semiotic Negativity: 'Reading Hegel through Freud'

Kristeva shares with many contemporary critical theorists an enormous debt to Hegel, and Hegelian ideas obtain a particular importance for the understanding of her concept of the semiotic; as I already intimated, it is via her deployment of the Hegelian notion of negativity that the semiotic acquires its subversive quality. She also goes beyond Hegel, though, insisting on the need to supplement his dialectics with the Freudian theory of drives. How, then, should we understand negativity, and what is its relation to the semiotic?

Diana Coole (2000) traces negativity's deployment in those sections of Continental philosophy that are, broadly speaking, interested in questions of otherness. Negativity, according to Coole, defies the positive, reified and ossified structures that dominate society and that stress instead the radical, subterranean, transgressive and ultimately transformative forces that challenge the status quo. Coole emphasises negativity's critical dimension, and also, importantly, its affirmative and generative features. She regards Kristeva, whose discussion of negativity receives a chapter-length treatment in Coole's book, as one of the adventurers in negativity. This stress on negativity, as I already indicated, highlights an important theme in Kristeva's writings; here I want to suggest that it illuminates in particular the understanding of the semiotic, whose connotation with negativity is essential for an interpretation of this concept.

Kristeva establishes the link between negativity and the semiotic, and its importance to the formation of the subject, in *Revolution in Poetic Language*. Key to her discussion is the Hegelian impetus towards a productive rupture. She claims that semiotic negativity transgresses the symbolic order and, in doing so, generates a transformation associated with creation. As she suggests, '[W]hat remodels the symbolic order is always the influx of the semiotic' (*RPL*: 62). Thus, the semiotic interrupts, subverts and undermines the symbolic: for example, in the form of poetic language, music and parapraxes. It becomes a subversive force that, as I outlined above, provides the potential for political change and must be distinguished sharply from negation; whereas negation, the capacity to say 'no' that is associated with the thetic function and with judgement, is a property of the symbolic, semiotic negativity traverses and exceeds the symbolic.[12]

It does more, though. Given its dialectical coupling with the symbolic, the semiotic keeps the symbolic, and indeed the subject, permanently 'in process' (see next section). It is therefore crucial to reiterate that the semiotic does not function independently, but operates only through its dialectical articulation with the symbolic, producing language and subject. Hegelian negativity plays a central role in this process; it constitutes 'the liquefying and dissolving agent that does not destroy but rather reactivates new organizations and, in that sense, affirms' (*RPL*: 110), and it unsettles 'the immobilization of the thetic', thereby providing access for semiotic motility. Kristeva further utilises Hegel to account for negativity's role in the production of the subject as split or divided, or, in her words, 'in process' (see next section). Yet, because the Hegelian 'I', according to Kristeva, will eventually become unified, she misses in Hegel a more radical approach to the split subject that, moreover, could also take into account the materialist basis of subject constitution. Kristeva finds this materialism in Freud. Thus, Hegelian ideas can only become fully operable if read through the lens of Freudian materialism, which considers the operation of bodily drives (Rajan 1993: 221; see also below).

So far, I have traced the role of semiotic negativity in Kristeva's account of the subject. Given the semiotic's dual function, generating symbolic operations on the one hand whilst traversing it on the other, how does it function politically, or, as Diana Coole asks: 'How is negativity to be practised?' (2000: 62). In other words, how can it be translated into a feminist practice? This is a key question to be asked of Kristeva's theoretical apparatus and has divided her feminist readers; it will occupy me throughout this book. I begin to attend to this question in the next section, while in the remainder of this one I examine the reception of the semiotic in the critical literature, focusing on the work of Judith Butler and Diana Coole, two feminist thinkers whose work, like that of Kristeva, is influenced by ideas about negativity. As I intimated above, much of the interpretation of Kristeva hinges upon the way that her critics have conceptualised the semiotic-symbolic relationship. If we take into consideration the ambiguities in Kristeva's portrayal of the signifying process, which I sketched in the previous section, it is far from certain whether semiotic negativity is inherently subversive. This bears directly upon the interpretation of the semiotic as a force of negativity and, more specifically, on its ability to generate change and transformation. It should come as no surprise that Kristeva's conceptual ambiguity is reflected in the feminist critical commentary of her work.

One such critic is Judith Butler, whose own leanings towards the negative, including her Hegelian-inflected reading of French philosophy, as well as her important contributions to feminist debates over the last two decades, are worth considering in this context. Butler's ontological commitments, as well as her epistemological framework, overlap substantially with Kristeva's; like Kristeva, she is sympathetic towards ideas of the fluidity and instability of the subject. However, Butler raises fundamental objections against Kristeva's version of the subject; her critique turns on the semiotic's alleged subjection to the symbolic, which is said to posit the semiotic outside culture. In *Gender Trouble* (1990), Butler grounds her reservations about Kristeva's semiotic-symbolic distinction and, more specifically, about the positing of the semiotic as a subversive force in Kristeva's alleged adherence to Lacanian psychoanalysis in particular and to the structuralist distinction between nature and culture in general. She concludes that the semiotic cannot serve as a subversive force, because it is embedded in a symbolic law which inherently tames any challenge to its prohibitions (1990: 80).

Much of Butler's critique hinges upon her reading of Kristeva's presentation of the maternal body, which I examine below. For now, I focus on Butler's assessment of the semiotic-symbolic relationship. First, Butler asserts that the relationship between the semiotic and the symbolic is hierarchical, and she alleges that the symbolic assumes a hegemonic role in this relationship that makes it immune to challenge (1990: 80). Without specifying the nature of this symbolic hegemony over the semiotic, Butler contends, furthermore, that the semiotic is produced by the symbolic. In fact, any autonomy that the semiotic might possess, including its alleged subversiveness, is said to be derivative, conferred by the symbolic.[13] While Kristeva, according to Butler, proffers the semiotic as 'a perpetual source of subversion within the Symbolic' (1990: 79), she 'alternatively posits and denies the semiotic as an emancipatory ideal' (1990: 80). To claim the semiotic as a source of subversion is, according to Butler, self-defeating, and she declares Kristeva's political programme futile. Her overall assessment of Kristeva is epitomised in her claim that '[Kristevan] subversion becomes a futile gesture, entertained only in a derealized aesthetic mode which can never be translated into other cultural practices' (1990: 78).

While I share Butler's concerns regarding the developmental account presented by Kristeva, I would also suggest that her critique is not sensitive to Kristeva's, admittedly problematic, textual ambiguities. I already intimated that the semiotic-symbolic relationship could be read as mutually constitutive rather than developmental, with each element of the relationship generating and facilitating the functioning of the other. Hence, to suggest, as Butler does, that the symbolic configures the semiotic neglects the symbolic's dependence upon the semiotic, which manifests itself primarily through the inscription of drive energy into the symbolic (more on this below). Thus, without the semiotic there is no language, meaning or subject. A more fruitful way of utilising Kristeva's ideas has been proposed by Lechte and Margaroni; they suggest that the relationship between the semiotic and the symbolic is more accurately one of antagonism, which they describe as 'reciprocally deconstructive' (2004: 18), where each element of the signifying process puts the other under erasure. Such a reading is particularly attentive to Kristeva's concern with the precariousness and instability of the subject, captured in her discussions of melancholia and abjection, and it resonates with her more recent concerns with psychic suffering and crises (see Chapter 2). Butler's developmental reading of the semiotic-symbolic relationship fails to consider the generative function of semiotic negativity, as well as the deconstructive nature of the semiotic-symbolic relationship,[14] and she ends up neglecting Kristeva's important emphasis on the precarious and ambiguous nature of subjectivity, always under threat of dissolution. Besides, Butler misjudges, in my view, Kristeva's deployment of the notions of subversion and transgression. These are not consistently discussed in relation to politics or political transformation; rather, they refer in equal measure to Kristeva's interest in the subversive and transgressive nature of aesthetic and individualised practices that, given Kristeva's dialectics of aesthetics and politics, are aimed at the political horizon (see also Moi 1995: 171).

Notwithstanding my reservations regarding Butler's critique of Kristeva, the concerns expressed by Butler illustrate starkly why some feminists are so easily frustrated with Kristeva. A more sympathetic reading of Kristevan negativity is proffered by Diana Coole (2000), whose materialist interpretation of Kristeva's signifying process emphasises the drive basis of the negative; by tracing Kristeva's journey through Hegel and Freud, Coole stresses the dialectical articulation between the semiotic and the symbolic, between body and signification, and between aesthetics and politics. It is this latter aspect that, according to Coole, leads to a displacement of politics on to signifying practices and the psycho-cultural realm (see also Sjöholm 2005), culminating in what she considers to be Kristeva's postmodern politics. (I discuss the question of Kristeva's politics in Chapters 4 and 5.) Despite Coole's rather sober assessment of Kristeva's feminist credentials and interests, she considers Kristeva's equation between negativity and the feminine, and its subsequent 'gendering', as having useful implications for the articulation of feminist politics. Before I develop these themes further, I want to examine how semiotic negativity is crucial to Kristeva's account of the production of a subject-in-process. This politics of the subject, as I demonstrate in the next section, has shaped much of the feminist debate over the last two decades.

The Subject and Her Agency

The semiotic's transgressive capacities, which are indispensable to the generation of signification, reappear in Kristeva's articulation of the subject. This becomes possible because negativity, already contained within the subject, puts it 'in process'. Kristeva's emphasis on fluid subjectivity is part of a wider intellectual movement indebted to anti-humanist positions that has exerted a considerable influence within feminist thought. Feminist debates over the notion of the subject are at the heart of the so-called feminist contentions, between those who subscribe to a position of a coherent, unified self, and those who, variously influenced by psychoanalysis, post-structuralism and deconstruction, put forward ideas about a decentred, unstable and inherently fluid subject.[15]

Despite Kristeva's prominent association with notions of fluid subjectivity and, more specifically, with the idea of the 'subject-in-process', it is important to stress that not all feminists who position themselves within this tradition of fluidity subscribe to Kristevan ideas.[16] However, her notion of the subject-in-process figures prominently in feminist receptions of her work, which could be grouped, broadly, into three strands that comprise, first, those feminists who reject the notion of a subject in process altogether and instead hold on to notions of stable identity (see, for example, Leland 1992; Fraser 1992b); a second group of feminist scholars who subscribe to notions of fluid subjectivity but either criticise (Cornell 1991) or reject the Kristevan version of the subject (see Butler 1990); and a third group, who build upon Kristeva's ideas, which they utilise to stress the heterogeneity of the subject, its relationship with alterity and its attention to difference (see, for example, Oliver 1993a; Ziarek 1992; 2001). Before I map this critical engagement with her ideas, I want to take a close look at Kristeva's writings on the subject. As I demonstrate here, whilst I am broadly sympathetic towards Kristeva's conception of fluid subjectivity, I have two reservations. First, building on Cornell (1991; see also Cornell and Thurschwell 1987), I am concerned by Kristeva's slippage between the notion of the feminine and her subscription to sociological concepts of gender; second, I aver that her insistence on the fluidity and instability of the subject is missing in her at times stinging critique of feminism and (feminist) politics.

The articulation between the semiotic and the symbolic, as we have seen, does not just configure language; it is also constitutive of the subject. The subject remains indebted to both notions of the signifying process, oscillating between them. Kristeva refers to this unstable subject with her notion of the 'subject-in-process', a concept with three related connotations. First, it highlights the fluidity of the subject; contained within this claim is a rejection of fixed subject positions and an emphasis on the subject's oscillation between the semiotic and the symbolic. The second connotation plays on the double meaning of the French original, 'sujet-en-procès', translated as the 'subject on trial' or 'subject before the law'. Here, Kristeva emphasises the importance of the paternal law for the constitution of the subject, as well as the subject's transgression of the law. Finally, 'subject-in-process' indicates how the subject is implicated in a practice, the process of signification, which, in turn, is aimed at a transgression of the law.

The idea of a subject in process is mapped in *Revolution in Poetic Language* (see also Kristeva 1973b), but I want to draw on a well-known interview with *Psych et po*, a prominent and controversial group within the feminist scene in 1970s France (see Duchen 1986; Moses 1998), which proved to be highly influential for the feminist appropriation of Kristeva (Kristeva 1981). Explaining her emphasis on the fluidity of subjectivity, which characterises the concept of the subject-in-process, she rejects fixed notions of 'man' and 'woman', and deploys the semiotic's negative characteristics to outline a fluid female subjectivity. Given the importance of this aspect to Kristeva's overall theoretical argument, as well as to her reception within feminism, it is worth quoting her at length:

> The belief that 'one is a woman' is almost as absurd and obscurantist as the belief that 'one is a man'. I say 'almost' because there are still many goals which women can achieve: freedom of abortion and contraception, day-care centers for children, equality on the job, etc. Therefore, we must use 'we are women' as an advertisement slogan for our demands. On a deeper level, however, a woman cannot 'be'; it is something that does not even belong in the order of being. It follows that a feminist practice can only be negative, at odds with what already

exists so that we may say 'that's not it' and 'that's still not it'. (1981: 137)

Despite Kristeva's attachment to what might be termed a 'strategic essentialism' (Spivak 1988) that recognises the important political achievements of feminism, she stresses, in the main, her underlying radical critique of identity. As Kristeva further suggests, the operation of the negative, and the avant-garde practices associated with it, 'dissolve identity', challenging those theories that proclaim fixed categories of male and female. This assertion raises three issues that are central to Kristeva's account of the subject and to her configuration of feminist politics: first, her stress on the plurality of women, a claim which comes to inform her refutation of feminism as a form of totalitarian identity politics (see Chapter 4); second, her insistence on the precarious nature of the subject, including its oscillation between a semiotic and a symbolic mode of signification; and finally, her openness regarding the nature of feminist practice, emphasising the critical aspect of feminist practice (see Chapters 2 and 5). Offering an account of the female subject that is strongly reminiscent of Simone de Beauvoir, 'woman', for Kristeva, is forever in the process of becoming. Thus, there is no essence to 'woman', leading Kristeva to assert, moreover, the singularity and plurality of women. It is this assertion, at least, that should put to rest some of the concerns over Kristeva's alleged essentialism.[17] It is with the French original term, "unes femmes", that she captures this plurality and singularity of each woman which, furthermore, undermine unitary notions of 'woman'. The assertion of the plurality and singularity of women is indeed a leitmotif of Kristeva's vision of a new generation of feminism that guides her critique of existing feminist movements (see Chapters 4 and 5). However, as I illustrate now, her rejection of the alleged totalitarianism of feminism, as much as her particular deployment of psychoanalysis, tends to undermine the feminist implications of her radical critique of the subject. I want to unpack this further, by drawing on one of Kristeva's most famous essays, 'Women's Time' (1979).

In this essay, Kristeva presents a narrative of feminism that is mapped upon a temporal sequence of three generations of feminism. According to Kristeva, feminism's first generation, broadly conceived as egalitarian feminists, fought for the achievement of equal rights, including reproductive rights and freedoms for women. Feminism's second generation, which could be labelled difference feminists, were mainly concerned with women's difference from men, and with their positioning vis-à-vis power and a socio-symbolic contract defined as masculine. It should be stressed that Kristeva acknowledges the achievements of both generations of feminism, but she criticises them for their articulation of forms of collective politics that she rejects as totalitarian and at odds with the singularity and individuality of each woman. She faults the first generation for seeking to gain acceptance in the existing social-symbolic contract by emulating the masculine, at the expense of the feminine (and a denial of sexual difference), whilst the second generation is said to have sought refuge in feminist utopias and counter-societies that equally failed to address questions of plurality (a denial of female plurality). Given her criticism of the previous two generations of feminism, Kristeva envisages a third generation, which celebrates difference over unity, and which seeks to tap into the semiotic potential that women are said to possess.

One could plausibly argue that Kristeva's vision of a third generation overlaps with many positions put forward by those feminists who subscribe to notions of a decentred subject and who employ the idea of the indeterminacy of the category 'woman' (see, for example, Riley 1988). Moreover, as I already suggested, this heterogeneous subject-in-process is not void of agency, drawing instead on semiotic and symbolic modes of inscription. Yet these positions, as Riley has argued, have generated a profound anxiety amongst some feminists who, Riley conjectures, fear that a critique of the subject may erode the self-identity of women and of feminism as a political project (1992: 121).

I have already declared my sympathy towards positions like Riley's, and indeed Kristeva's; however, the critique of the subject still leaves open the question of how it translates into (feminist) political agency. As Noëlle McAfee articulates it, '*Can the subject-in-process be an effective political agent?*' (2000: 19; italics in original). This question has indeed been taken up by Kristeva's critics, who, for various reasons, denounce the effectiveness of (her version of) the decentred subject. Nancy Fraser, for example, grounds her critique in Kristeva's Lacanianism, which she charges with being ahistorical and atemporal. She rejects what she refers to as 'the subject of the symbolic' as an 'oversocialized conformist', while the semiotic subject is said to be posited beneath culture and society; its radical negative agenda, furthermore, cannot effectively pursue the kind of reconstructive and collective agenda that Fraser considers essential to the project of feminism (1992b: 189; see also Leland 1992 and Meyers 1992). As we have already seen, Judith Butler, albeit positioned in a different philosophical tradition to Fraser – in fact, one that, like Kristeva, draws on notions of fluid subjectivity and the critique of the subject, is also highly critical of what she perceives as Kristeva's alleged Lacanian narrative, leading her to reject Kristeva's psychoanalytic account of the decentred subject.

If the question of the female subject constitutes one area of discontent, it is the question of (feminist) politics that has also troubled many of Kristeva's feminist readers (see also Chapters 3, 4 and 5). Yet not all commentators take issue with Kristeva's notion of the decentred subject, which has been welcomed by some feminists as a relief from essentialist and repressive notions of identity. Kelly Oliver, for example, highlights how Kristeva's critique of identity is indispensable to a notion of feminism attuned to the idea of difference, including a difference already located within the subject (Oliver 1993a: 14; see also A.-M. Smith 1998: 24). Drucilla Cornell and Adam Thurschwell (1987) also provide a largely sympathetic assessment that stresses in particular the disruptive quality of the negative and its anti-essentialist potential for feminist politics. Like Coole, Cornell and Thurschwell subscribe to a philosophy of negativity that endorses the disruptive-affirmative potential of the negative; they also abide by Kristeva's articulation between negativity, the semiotic and femininity, establishing the feminine as a force of subversion within a phallogocentric symbolic order. Yet, they diagnose a problematic slippage in Kristeva's writings, pertaining in particular to her celebration of motherhood (see Chapter 3), from the notion of a subversive feminine to a sociological conception of women. This slippage has indeed plagued Kristeva's ideas, re-introducing an essentialist account of 'woman' into her ideas that runs counter to her anti-essentialist philosophical intentions. It points to a key dilemma in the feminist reception of Kristeva's writings; her philosophical ideas and critique are not easily mapped upon her statements on politics, leading many of her feminist readers to abandon her work. The question of the subject and politics, as it emerges from Kristeva's psychoanalytic and philosophical account, evades its direct translatability into the language of political philosophy, even though they are not irreconcilable. As I already suggested, politics, for Kristeva, is displaced into the realms of aesthetics and art (see Coole 2000; Sjöholm 2005), and into a more profound concern with the realm of the intimate (see Chapter 2) and with ethics (see Chapter 3). For many of her feminist critics, this disjuncture between Kristeva's philosophical ideas and her views on the subject, agency and politics is further compounded by her deployment of psychoanalysis, which I turn to in the next section.

The Dutiful Daughter? Kristeva, Psychoanalysis and Feminism

Kristeva's persistent adherence to psychoanalysis is doubtlessly one of the major contributing factors for her contentiousness within feminism; this is true even for those feminists otherwise sympathetic towards fluid notions of subjectivity. As we have already seen, the charges against Kristeva range from a fundamental critique of her subscription to psychoanalysis,[18] to a more specific critique of her engagement with Lacan's ideas. This critique taps into a more widespread feminist discontent with psychoanalysis.

Feminism's engagement with psychoanalysis is marred from the beginning by a dispute over the value of psychoanalysis for feminist thought and practice, which evolves around the alleged a-historicism of psychoanalysis, its misogyny and its biologism, all of which are said to contribute towards a discursive constitution of essentialist accounts of gender and the subjugation of women. It is the structuralist aspect of psychoanalysis, in particular, embodied in its adherence to the notion of the Oedipal family, with its relating elements of castration fear and penis envy that has proved to be particularly contentious with feminism. Others point to a misogyny, rooted in the positioning of women as inherently inferior to men, and to the way that bodily organs, specifically the penis, are elevated to the status of key signifier. And yet, some feminists also began to explore the usefulness of Freudian thought to an account of women's subordination, to the representation of femininity in society, and to the internalisation of misogynistic norms by women. Juliet Mitchell's work (1990; 2001) proved to be groundbreaking in this respect, and her claim that Freud's texts should be understood descriptively, not prescriptively, exerted an enormous influence on the reception of Freud within wider feminist thought.

Mitchell's thought also proved to be crucial in another respect; together with Jacqueline Rose (Mitchell and Rose 1982), she helped to introduce the thought of Jacques Lacan into English-speaking feminism. Lacan's work, as I already suggested, has been enormously influential for the development of 'French feminism' and for the ideas of Kristeva. However, this proved to be a double-edged sword for the feminist reception of Kristeva, given the contested status of Lacan within feminism, specifically his stress on the paternally coded symbolic order. It is because of this perception that Kristeva has been described as one of Lacan's 'dutiful daughters' (Grosz 1990; Gross 1986; Braidotti 1991); the depiction is meant to diminish Kristeva's feminist credentials, but neglects her substantial reworking of and departure from Lacan, reflected, for example, in the importance she accords to the role and function of the semiotic, the feminine and the maternal. This is not the place to assess Kristeva's relationship with Lacan further (see Kristeva 1983); instead, I want to use this section to present a brief sketch of those themes that, in my view, are instrumental to the feminist engagement with Kristeva and more widely to feminist thought in general. These are her account of identification, her treatment of kinship matters, and her writings on sexuality.

I already intimated that Kristeva maps her account of the signifying process upon the psychoanalytic narrative of gender acquisition. Combining Freudian premises with Lacan's emphasis on language acquisition, Kristeva claims that the subject emerges as a result of language acquisition and of entrance into the symbolic. Following Lacan, boy-child and girl-child acquire language differently and take up different positions in the linguistically structured symbolic order. Girls' psycho-linguistic development connects them to the semiotic and positions them on the periphery of the phallogocentric symbolic order. I alluded above to the fact that language, according to Kristeva's psychoanalytic framework, emerges as a result of the break with the maternal object, which only boys can fully accomplish, a prerequisite for entry into the symbolic and for language acquisition. Due to girls' difficulty in separating from the mother and their cultural compulsion to identify with her, they remain connected to the maternal semiotic. Whilst women are not barred from speech or symbolisation, they remain under constant threat of psychic disintegration, engaging in a life-long battle with the paternal-masculine symbolic. This also clarifies women's relationship with the semiotic. Women's attachment to the semiotic does not preclude access to the symbolic, a claim sometimes made by Kristeva's critics (see, for example, Gross 1986: 131); rather, they oscillate between the semiotic and the symbolic.

I already argued that Kristeva's deployment of psychoanalysis, despite its commitment to heterogeneity and a 'subject-in-process', generates a gendered order where femininity cross-checks with women. This, however, does not follow conclusively from Kristeva's account. Indeed, as we have seen, sexed positions, for Kristeva, are not rigid, and either sex can, potentially, assume either of the two sexed positions. Masculinity, for Kristeva, is not barred for women, and neither is femininity necessarily barred for men. As Kristeva asserts, '"man" is in "woman", and "woman" is in "man"' (1981: 140). It is the link with the semiotic and the symbolic that defines femininity and masculinity respectively. Thus, neither masculinity nor femininity is defined in relation to a given biological body, but in relation to the subject's position in language.[19] Moreover, Kristeva's assertion, that the dialectical relationship between the semiotic and the symbolic is constitutive of the subject, and that the subject is indebted to both semiotic and symbolic processes, implies that any subject position is, ontologically, unstable. Through her emphasis on dialectical negativity, Kristeva endorses the fluidity associated with subjectivity and she stresses the instability of identity. Situating herself within the context of French post-structuralism, Kristeva asserts that '[o]ur work fought against [identificatory thinking], producing instead a vision of man and his discourse that is ... clearly anti-identificatory' (1996a: 259). It is the transgressive capacity of the semiotic which subverts stable forms of subjectivity and puts the subject 'in process'.

Yet identification is also at the heart of psychoanalysis, and central to Kristeva's further discussion is the idea of a melancholic identification (1989a). Following Kristeva's psychoanalytic assumptions, the normal route to femininity forecloses an identification with the father and requires instead a (melancholic) identification with the mother. However, female melancholia is countered by *jouissance* which, potentially, protects women from the workings of the death drive. Still, father-identification is not completely impossible for women. Access to the symbolic and sublimatory activity are difficult, though not impossible, for women to achieve. As Kristeva asserts, 'shifting to the symbolic order *at the same time* as to a sexual object of a sex other than that of the primary maternal object represents a gigantic elaboration in which a woman cathexes a psychic potential greater than what is demanded of the male sex' (*BS*: 30). Indeed, once women separate from the mother, they are capable of producing symbolic discourse and, thus, of overcoming melancholia. In this way, women engage in a balancing act between their attachment to the maternal-semiotic and a yearning for the Law (1977a: 175).

Thus, even though women are under a cultural compulsion to identify with the mother, Kristeva concedes that father-identification is possible. Such an identification, however, is pathologised, and she describes father-identified women as 'Electras', 'militants in the cause of the father, frigid with exaltation – are they then dramatic figures emerging at the point where the social consensus corners any woman who wants to escape her condition: nuns, "revolutionaries", even "feminists"?' (1974b: 152).[20] Key to the process of identification is the subject's relationship with embodiment, and it is to this aspect that I turn in the next section. As I will argue there, it is with her emphasis on the body that Kristeva makes a significant contribution to contemporary feminist theory.

Body Matters

Although Kristeva's discussion of the maternal body has divided feminist assessments of her work, it is also fair to say that embodiment constitutes a leitmotif of practically all of Kristeva's writings, informing her work on language, psychoanalysis, women and foreignness. Her persistent attention to body matters offers a radical challenge to the dualistic Cartesian mind–body hierarchy and a rejection of the 'somatophobia' of Western philosophy (see Spelman 1982), that disembodied understanding of human experience that, furthermore, associates women with the body and men with the mind or reason, and that disqualifies and abjects women from the realm of the properly human. Even though Kristeva has at times been criticised for failing to give due recognition to the corporeal implications of sexual difference (see Boulous Walker 1998), a more generous interpretation may highlight how Kristevan corporeality cuts across sexual difference. In this respect, and notwithstanding the attention she gives to women's bodies, it would also be misleading to reduce her account to a theory of women's bodies. Rather, Kristevan embodiment, couched in a psychoanalytic narrative that is based upon the Oedipal family drama, is played out along an axis of sexual difference, where embodied masculinity and femininity develop differently, constituted as a result of the workings of the drives, the acquisition of language, and the intervention of the phallus (see also Chapter 2). Thus, over and above her writings on maternity and her notion of abjection, which has been taken up more broadly within feminist debates on aesthetics, art and film, Kristeva's important contribution to the formulation of a corporeal philosophy consists in the notion of a body-in-process that paves the way towards a corporeal ethics (see Chapter 3) and that I will map briefly here.

I already stressed the semiotic's operation within language; it is equally imperative to highlight its centrality to the generation of embodiment. In fact, Kristeva's opening argument of *Revolution in Poetic Language* is that the body is implicated in the process of signification, a contention that affirms the link between body, language and psychic life. As Kelly Oliver points out, part of Kristeva's project is to bring the speaking body back to signification (1993a: 3). Kristeva's criticism, directed against what she terms the 'necrophiliac philosophies of language', should thus be read alongside her refutation of disembodied notions of subjectivity and signification (see Grosz 1990: 80). Whilst she leaves unexplored the assertion of the primacy of the somatic dimension of embodiment, she is concerned with the issue of body constitution, the establishment of a 'body proper' (*RPL*: 27), and with the implication of bodies in the process of signification. Early on in *Revolution in Poetic Language*, she connects the body with language and the psyche, with the constitution of the subject in a theoretical framework informed by psychoanalysis, and located in the social structure of capitalism.

Crucially though, the body is not a passive surface, subjected to social and historical inscription; it displays 'somatic agency' (Coole 2005), engaging in a practice that rejuvenates society, and that moves with and transgresses, through the operation of negativity, the social structures of capitalism, which in turn attempt to hinder this 'body-in-process'. In times of change or crisis, when political revolutions coincide with a revolution in language, subject and body are implicated in such change and the dynamic quality of body and subject come to the fore (*RPL*: 15; see also Chapter 2). It is important to highlight this facet of Kristeva's work, as it stresses the constitutive role of the body in the creation, sustenance and also transgression of systems of representation.

However, socio-historical factors alone do not account for the constitution of the body. As we have already seen, they require a materialist foundation, which Kristeva finds in psychoanalysis and which provides her with two interlinked approaches to the body: the Oedipal family, with the mother's body as a central reference point on the one hand, and the theory of drives on the other.[21] The heterogeneous drives, channelled, ordered and directed by the protagonists of the Oedipal family, point the body in distinctive directions, in accordance with psychoanalytic injunctions of gender normativity.[22]

Drives also discharge the transgressive negativity that is essential for the emergence of language and for the rejuvenation of the symbolic, and that Kristeva, as I outlined above, associates with practice. This assertion also allows for a further revision of Butler's critique of Kristeva (Butler 1990). Questioning the nature of the dialectical relationship between the semiotic and the symbolic, Butler wondered whether the semiotic owes its subversive potential to the symbolic. Equipped with Kristeva's theory of the body, we can now re-emphasise the symbolic's dependence upon the drive energy transmitted by the semiotic. Even though the symbolic configures semiotic transgression, it can only do so because of the semiotic discharge into the symbolic. In the absence of drive energy, meaning, and thus the symbolic, collapse. To remain with Butler's critique for a moment, in *Gender Trouble* (1990) she challenges Kristeva's assumption of a pre-constituted body, unaffected by socio-cultural inscriptions, and she criticises Kristeva's association of the semiotic with the maternal body and its embeddedness in the functioning of the drives operating in the pre-Oedipal body. This assertion, however, fails to consider Kristeva's dialectics between the semiotic and the symbolic, including the workings of negativity in the constitution of the symbolic on the one hand, and of the ordering of the semiotic by the symbolic on the other. If Butler's critique requires some modification, if not a reversal, in the light of Kristeva's discussion of drives and of the body, it also allows for a clarification of Kristeva's use of the term 'dialectic'; it is not resolved in a Hegelian 'Aufhebung', but oscillates permanently between semiotic drive energy on the one hand, and symbolic ordering on the other, both of which are dependent upon one another. It is thus essential to acknowledge the corporeal dimension of the semiotic *and* the symbolic.

Yet it is the maternal body that receives particular attention from Kristeva and that attracted much feminist commentary. She theorises the maternal body via the concept of the *chora*, a notion she borrows from the *Timaeus* (Hamilton and Cairns 1999), Plato's narrative of the creation of the universe that defines the *chora* as a nourishing and maternal space, or receptacle, which he opposes with a paternal principle and a child principle (48b–52d). Plato's *chora* already precipitates the emphasis on the maternal developed by Kristeva. In *Revolution in Poetic Language*, she introduces the *chora* as a 'non-expressive totality formed by drives and their stases in a motility that is as full of movement as it is regulated' (*RPL*: 26), while she defines it elsewhere as 'a matrix-like space that is nourishing, unnameable' (*NMS*: 204). The *chora* is not yet subject to the symbolic, but it is regulated by social and natural constraints, such as family structure, culture and sexual difference. As a mother–child totality, it is already implicated in the Oedipal triangle and becomes subject to the intervention of the phallus: 'social organisation, always already symbolic, imprints its constraints in a mediated form which organises the *chora* not according to a law (a term we reserve for the symbolic) but through an *ordering*' (*RPL*: 26–7; italics in original).

Kristeva continues that it is the mother's body that mediates the symbolic law, and that therefore becomes the ordering principle of the semiotic *chora* (*RPL*: 27). This association between maternal body and *chora* has received much comment from her feminist readers. More hostile interpretations regard the *chora* as a metaphor for the uterus, a view which confirms the critics' perception of Kristeva's essentialism and her association of the maternal body, and of women more generally, with the pre-symbolic and pre-cultural (see J. Stone 1983: 42; see also Butler 1990, Huffer 1998). Others stress the function of the *chora* as a metaphor for the symbiotic link between mother and child (see Grosz 1992: 195; Gross 1986). Such a spatial interpretation of the *chora* should be complemented, according to Margaroni (2005), by the *chora's* temporal function, as that which lies prior to the intervention of the phallus and the Name-of-the-Father. In that respect, the *chora*, together with the semiotic, represents the challenge to the symbolic, located on the side of the feminine that, moreover, articulates the beginning of the ethical encounter with alterity (see Chapter 3). Via the *chora* as a maternal space, Kristeva theorises the maternal body as the child's first point of reference. The drives and their satisfaction – in other words, the child's dependence upon the mother for its physical and emotional well-being – connect the body of the child to that of the mother (*RPL*: 27–8). Yet, in spite of this symbiotic relationship, which supports the child's fragmented and undifferentiated body image, the ambiguity and contradictory aims of the drives imply that the pre-Oedipal body is already split (*RPL*: 27). Hence, the danger of bodily disintegration and thus the need for bodily boundaries are a constant concern (see below).

The fault-line between nature and culture, which informs Kristeva's deployment of the *chora* as well as the feminist responses to it, returns in her discussion of the pregnant body, which Kristeva characterises in the following way:

> Cells fuse, split, and proliferate; volumes grow, tissues stretch, and body fluids change rhythm, speeding up or slowing down. Within the body, growing as a graft, indomitable, there is an other. And no one is present, within that simultaneously dual and alien space, to signify what is going on. 'It happens, but I'm not there.' (*DL*: 237)

It should come as no surprise that Kristeva's emphasis on the absence of the female subject during pregnancy has invited commentators to suggest that Kristeva's pregnant body is a body without a subject and, hence, a body without agency (Gross 1986: 131). This denial of agency, as I indicated previously, chimes strongly with the wider critique of Kristeva's alleged neglect of women's agency, and it also relates closely to the contested status of nature and culture in her thought. Yet despite this allusion to women's 'absence' as a subject during their pregnancy, Kristeva does not associate pregnancy with nature; rather, pregnancy is positioned on the threshold between nature and culture, conceptualised as one of those borderline experiences that Kristeva posits as dialectical. As she argues,

> [t]hrough a body, destined to insure reproduction of the species, the woman-subject, although under the sway of the paternal function (as symbolizing, speaking subject and like all others), [is] more of a *filter* than anyone else – a thoroughfare, a threshold where 'nature' confronts 'culture'. (*DL*: 238; italics in original)

Is it so easy to dismiss the concerns of her critics, though? As Boulous Walker (1998) has pointed out in her broadly sympathetic assessment, there is something in Kristeva's texts, despite her intentional ambiguities, that remains stubbornly attached to the notion of women as evacuated from the realm of the symbolic. Boulous Walker traces this attachment to Kristeva's discussion of the avant-garde, but it is also apparent in some of her more brusque comments about female embodiment. For example, in her essay 'A New Type of Intellectual: The Dissident' (1977b), Kristeva evokes the subversive dimension of the semiotic, and with it the subversive function of the intellectual and the avant-garde writer as examples of two figures who draw on the subversive potential of the semiotic. Women are also included in Kristeva's consideration of dissidence, but this specifically female dissidence is embodied 'simply through being pregnant and then becoming a mother' (1977b: 297). Taken together with a further claim, in the same text, that '[a] woman is trapped within the frontiers of her body and even of her species' (1977b: 296), this makes for uncomfortable reading.

Kristeva returns to her consideration of the nature–culture threshold with her discussion of the nursing body, which turns the mother into 'a strange fold that changes culture into nature, the speaking into biology. Although it concerns every woman's body, the heterogeneity that cannot be subsumed in the signifier nevertheless explodes violently with pregnancy (the threshold of culture and nature)' (1977a: 182–3). What is more, the nursing maternal body does not solely belong to the mother, but, as I already outlined, forms a symbiotic *chora* with the child:

> My body is no longer mine, it doubles up, suffers, bleeds, catches cold, puts its teeth in, slobbers, coughs, is covered with pimples, and

it laughs. . . . But the pain, its pain – it comes from the inside, never remains apart, other, it inflames me at once, without a second's respite. As if that was what I had given birth to and, not willing to part from me, insisted on coming back, dwelled in me permanently. One does not give birth in pain, one gives birth to pain. (1977a: 167)

Yet, the child's symbiotic relationship with the mother and the maternal body comes to an end; separation from the maternal body is necessary for the emergence of the subject. Key to understanding the idea of separation is Kristeva's concept of abjection.

While the origins of the concept of abjection go back to her discussion of rejection (see *RPL*: 147–64), it is in *Powers of Horror* (1982a) that Kristeva, influenced by anthropological work on pollution (Douglas 1966), introduces the notion of abjection. With the notion of abjection, Kristeva further challenges assumptions of a coherent body that highlights her concern with the fluidity of the subject – in other words, her claim that bodies are not coherent, but split, and that they oscillate between the semiotic and the symbolic; abjection also underscores the threat to its integrity. Initially located in the process of subject constitution, it induces the separation of the child from the parents, in particular the cutting of the symbiotic link with the mother, and the establishment of the child's tentative bodily boundaries. Abjecting the parents, the child develops its bodily awareness, transforming the fragmented 'body-in-bits-and-pieces' into a coherent whole. The child also transforms its relationship with bodily excrements; previously experienced as pleasurable, they are now subjected to feelings of loathing and disgust. While the abjection of bodily excrements and of the parents establishes its sense of bodily boundaries, these, however, are continuously undermined by the persistence of those bodily fluids and bodily organs that excrete the abjected bodily stuff. The subject thus engages in a continuous struggle with the transgression of bodily boundaries. This disregard highlights abjection's paradoxical nature; whilst it is necessary in order to obtain a sense of bodily, and indeed psychic, integrity, this sense of integrity is deceptive, as boundaries are crossed and violated, beyond the control of the subject. The illusion of stable and clearly demarcated boundaries, whether morphological or indeed social, can only be maintained at the price of the temporary, and essentially futile, exclusion of that which is considered as not belonging to this body. Although the abject points to the subject's lack of autonomy with respect to his or her bodily affairs, it is paradoxically only through the abject that there is a subject at all. Moreover, it is important to distinguish the abject from the other transgressive force, the semiotic; whereas the semiotic rejuvenates the symbolic, the abject undermines and threatens the symbolic. Hence, with the notion of abjection Kristeva highlights her concern with the vulnerability and precariousness of the subject, which Kelly Oliver refers to as the dark side of the subject (1993a: 62); abjection threatens the integrity of the subject's corporeal boundaries, while it is also constitutive of the subject.

To emphasise the ambiguity of abjection, Kristeva defines abjection as what 'disturbs identity, system, order. What does not respect borders, positions, rules. The in-between, the ambiguous, the composite' (*PoH*: 4). She illustrates abjection through the example of food loathing and the sensation of disgust at certain smells or foods, and also feelings of disgust at the thought or sight of bodily secretions: blood, excrements, vomit, mucus; of corpses. However, despite abjection's connotation with bodily waste, it does not represent a lack of cleanliness or health; Kristeva's concern with abjection is thus not a 'mania for cleanliness . . ., a "housewife psychosis"' (J. Stone 1983: 45). Such a claim points to a fundamental misunderstanding that fails to recognise abjection's ambiguity and hovering on the borders.

The concept of abjection has been deployed by some commentators to account for the constitution of the social body, and to explain misogyny, homophobia, racism and anti-semitism: in short, practices of oppression that draw on the abjection of those groups who are seen as a threat to the boundaries of the social or political body (see Young 1990).[23] What, though, is its relationship to women? Is abjection gendered? Like much of Kristeva's work, *Powers of Horror* is not immediately feminist and it does not explicitly deal with gender issues. Abjection, and the simultaneous horror and fascination of abjection, are experienced universally; they emerge following the separation from the parents and the establishment of psychic and bodily boundaries that facilitate the development of ego and superego as psychic agencies (see also Lechte 1990: 158). Highlighting the universality of abjection, Judith Still avers that associating abjection with the maternal is an attempt to 'tidy up' the Kristevan text (Still 1997: 224). She

Kristeva and Feminism

challenges, in particular, Kelly Oliver's claim that abjection is a struggle to separate from the maternal body (1993a: 56). Against Oliver, Still draws on Elizabeth Grosz's analogy between the semiotic, the maternal *chora* and the abject (Grosz 1989), which is said to avoid the connotation of abjection with (empirical) women, and specifically with mothers, drawing instead on the feminine's critical and subversive capacity, beyond its association with binary conceptions of gender.

Yet, Kristeva's discussion, including her account of the feminine and of abjection, remains open to different and contradictory interpretations. According to Kristeva, it is the fear of women, which is said to have its basis in women's reproductive capacities, that is turned into phobia and leads to the abjection of women and to the association of women with the abject (*PoH*: 77). Moreover, as Kristeva claims,

> the relation to abjection is finally rooted in the combat that every human being carries on with the mother. For in order to become autonomous, it is necessary that one cut the instinctual dyad of the mother and the child and that one become something other. (1996a: 118)

This 'fascinated rejection' is captured with the notion of abjection. However, as I already indicated, women cannot unambiguously reject the mother; instead, they identify with her, by becoming mothers themselves. The centrality of motherhood to Kristeva's œuvre will occupy me again in Chapter 3, but in the next chapter I will take a closer look at Kristeva's writings on crisis and revolt. This discussion, as I hope to demonstrate there, will add to my assessment in this chapter, which focused, in the main, on the dispute over the female subject and her constitution, the question of her agency, and the controversy over her alleged subversive capacity. Developing my journey into Kristeva's ideas further will also allow me to broach a further question that is of crucial interest to feminism: this is the question of feminist politics and its location in Kristeva's recent, psychoanalytically informed, ideas on revolt.

Notes

1. In the same essay, Kristeva posits as her other core ideas intertextuality, abjection and foreignness/strangeness.
2. A comprehensive assessment of Kristeva's linguistic ideas and their contribution to literary theory can be found in Becker-Leckrone (2005). See also Bové (1983; 2006).
3. See, for example, Nancy Fraser who accuses Kristeva of subscribing to a 'quasi-Lacanian neostructuralism' (1992b: 186). For a more cautious assessment of Kristeva's engagement with structuralism see Kearney (1994).
4. It should be added that Kristeva's work on language is also influenced by Barthes and Jacobsen; however, I cannot consider their influence within the context of this book.
5. As I argue below, Kristeva does not uncritically adopt a Lacanian perspective. In fact, much of her conceptual apparatus is a critical response to perceived shortcomings in Lacanian theory.
6. In a recent essay, Kristeva claims that the distinction between the semiotic and the symbolic has no political or feminist connotations, and is merely concerned with meaning (2004a: 204–5).
7. According to David Crystal (1992: 11), glossolalia consist of few predictable, structural units lacking systematic word or sentence meaning.
8. See also Kristeva's recent discussion of Colette's sensuous style of writing (2004c), which receives a book-length treatment as part of Kristeva's genius trilogy (see Chapter 4).
9. It also provides the subject with *jouissance*, the Lacanian concept that designates an unidentifiable capacity for enjoyment that lies outside the realm of the symbolic and defies control, definition and representation (Lacan 1998).
10. Negation – that is, the position of a thesis – should not be confused with (semiotic and transgressive) negativity.
11. I do not share Anne-Marie Smith's endorsement of Kristeva's 'conceptual coherence' (1998: 4).
12. The idea of traversal is also key to my discussion of Kristeva's ethics (see Chapter 3).
13. Although otherwise more sympathetic towards Kristeva's ideas than Butler, Jacqueline Rose also queries the semiotic's alleged subversive potential, arguing that '[t]he semiotic can never wholly displace the

symbolic since it relies on that very order to give it its, albeit resistant, shape' (1993: 43). Of course, one should equally stress that the symbolic can never displace the semiotic.
14. Intriguingly, Butler entitles her chapter 'Kristeva's Body Politics', without taking much account of the corporeal dimension of the signifying process and the generative function played therein by the semiotic.
15. Many of these ideas are articulated in the contributions to Nicholson (1990). See also Butler and Scott (1992), and Benhabib et al. (1995).
16. For an outline of the different versions of the subject-in-process in contemporary feminist thought see Lloyd (2005).
17. However, as I argue further below, her philosophical anti-essentialism is undermined by her adherence to the psychoanalytic narrative of gender identity, which, despite Kristeva's efforts to the contrary, does not resolve the tension between her insistence on plurality and singularity, and the psychoanalytic injunction of gender normativity.
18. As Eleanor H. Kuykendall states, 'Kristeva's ethics of linguistics is not, finally feminist . . . in that it is avowedly Freudian and leaves no place for a feminine conception of agency' (1989: 181).
19. And in relation to the signifier phallus, where 'having the phallus' refers to masculinity and 'being the phallus' to femininity. See Lacan (1993: 289–90).
20. This pathologisation of the father-identified, or phallic, woman also underpins Kristeva's depiction of the figure of the lesbian, a point that has been taken up in queer readings of her work (see Butler 1990; Cooper 2000).
21. I return to a discussion of the drives in Chapter 3, where I consider the role of the death drive in the generation of violence.
22. Following Freud, Kristeva defines the drive as 'a pivot between "soma" and "psyche", between biology and representation'. The somatic or biological facet of the drive is itself implicated within the social; as she declares, 'what we understand by biology is – drives and energy, if you wish, but always already a "carrier of meaning" and a "relation" to another person' (*NMS*: 30). I consider the ethical dimension of Kristeva's intercorporeal account in Chapter 3.
23. See McAfee (1993) and Moruzzi (1993) for a consideration of abjection in the context of the nation and migration. See also Butler (1990; 1993), who employs Kristeva's concept of abjection in her discussion of sexuality.

2

Crisis, Revolt, Intimacy

[H]appiness exists only at the price of a revolt. None of us has pleasure without confronting an obstacle, prohibition, authority, or law that allows us to realize ourselves as autonomous and free.

(*SNSR*: 7)

In the previous chapter, I alluded to the pivotal role of the idea of crisis in Kristeva's early work. As I intimated there, *Revolution in Poetic Language* discusses how the crisis of modernity displaces political revolution on to a revolution in signification and into the field of aesthetics more generally. Her 1980s trilogy, which comprises her book on abjection, *Powers of Horror* (1982a), her book on love, *Tales of Love* (1987a), and her book on melancholia, *Black Sun* (1989a), delves further into the topic of crisis; however, instead of attending to the working-out of crisis at the wider social and political level, Kristeva's writings take an inward turn, which manifests itself in her concern with the psychical symptoms of individual crises, and which are conveyed in the individual's suffering in the face of familial and social problems. A more systematic treatment of this topic can be found in Kristeva's recent writings, beginning with *New Maladies of the Soul* (1995) and continued in the volumes of *The Powers and Limits of Psychoanalysis*.[1] It is in this latter work that she develops the link between crisis and revolt more fully (see also Kristeva 2000c); as I outline in this chapter, her emphasis now lies with the assertion of the unfolding of a crisis of Western societies, coupled with modern Man's curtailed ability to generate meaning and engage in representation. Furthermore, these crises, according to Kristeva, produce specific types of psychic illnesses, which she refers to as 'new maladies of the soul' (this is also the title of her book from 1995). As a path out of crisis, Kristeva proposes the need to re-establish a lost European tradition of revolt (see also Chapter 5) that can restore the capacity for representation.

Julia Kristeva and Feminist Thought

Like most of her other writings, Kristeva's texts on crisis and revolt are not obviously recognisable as feminist; they do not explicitly address feminist concerns or offer feminist solutions (although comments on feminism are interspersed throughout them). This absence of a feminist sensibility is also reflected in the critical commentary. Recent works, notably several of the contributions to Chanter and Ziarek (2005) and to Oliver and Keltner (2009), as well as recent monographs on Kristeva, have given this issue some attention (see in particular Gambaudo 2007a; see also Beardsworth 2004a; Sjöholm 2005). However, feminist analyses of this work are only now beginning to emerge (see, for example, Ziarek 2005). Such work is crucial, however, because it can bring to the fore Kristeva's attention to issues of key concern to feminism, including the micro-political aspects of subjectivity and politics, and the mutually constitutive realms of embodiment, psychic and social-political life. Described by commentators as a 'displacement of politics' – Kristeva herself refers to it as 'intimate revolt' – this emphasis should also entail an analysis of Kristeva's theorisation of female sexuality and of the specifically female prospects for revolt and transformation. Hence, these writings, whilst not explicitly feminist in their aims or aspirations, constitute an important contribution to a deterritorialisation of politics that stresses the intimate aspects of political life.[2]

The importance that Kristeva accords to the idea of crisis is underscored by a more fundamental assertion that also informs her recent writings and that further aids, in my view, a feminist appropriation; this is the connection she establishes between psychic and social life. This aspect has recently been emphasised by Sylvie Gambaudo (2007a), who formulates a compelling case in favour of such a cultural reading of psychoanalysis, by suggesting that Kristeva's œuvre makes an important contribution to the understanding of recent socio-cultural changes in gender relations, specifically as they pertain to parenting. Kelly Oliver's work illustrates how Kristeva's psychoanalytic thought can be utilised in a more specifically feminist direction (Oliver 1993a) and to account, more broadly, for what Oliver terms a psychoanalytic social theory (2004; see also Margaroni 2007). As I suggested in the Introduction, such a use of psychoanalysis generates its own set of challenges: for example, is it acceptable to deploy psychoanalytic terms and concepts for an analysis of gender relations if, as I sought to demonstrate in the previous chapter, psychoanalysis has been dismissed by many feminists for its complicity in the production of misogynistic discourses on gender? Moreover, can a psychoanalytic discourse provide feminism with the tools to explain unequal gender relations and to articulate ideas for a feminist project of political and social transformation, a feminist revolt? We have already seen that a widespread feminist response to this challenge consists in abandoning psychoanalysis altogether (see Chapter 1). However, against such as a rejection, I want to advocate a more nuanced engagement with Kristevan psychoanalysis because it offers, in my view, an insightful account into the interrelated production of psychic, social and political life that could be read, against the grain, in the service of a feminist project aimed at transformation.

Therefore, this chapter fulfils two functions. I want to demonstrate, first, that Kristeva provides feminism with a very helpful account of the intersection of psychic and social life. This contribution, useful overall, is, however, undermined by her reluctance to embrace more fully the political dimension of revolt, and in doing so, fails to address explicitly the prospects for political transformation that emerge from her thought. In essence, her response to the psycho-social causes of crisis is a predominantly individual or, as she calls it, intimist, one that does not connect the two more fully. This is somewhat paradoxical, as it tends to downplay her insistence on the socio-genetic origins of crisis at the expense of a psycho-genetic account. Central to my further discussion will be the question of the connection between feminism and revolt: is feminism, for Kristeva, a form of revolt? And if not, can Kristeva be utilised for a feminist conception of revolt? This requires a critical assessment of her emphasis on the intimate sphere and her apparent endorsement of individualised accounts of revolt. As I argue here, these ideas cannot be understood outside the context of her social analysis. Moreover, mapping out the feminist implications of this work, I want to suggest that her writings on revolt should be interpreted in conjunction with her most recent publications on the female genius (see Chapter 4). I want to begin this task by providing an exposition of Kristeva's key ideas on crisis and revolt. This will be followed by an examination of the role accorded to the feminine in these recent texts.

Crisis, the Society of the Spectacle and the New Maladies of the Soul

According to the philosopher Simon Critchley, the theme of crisis is a leitmotif of contemporary philosophy that is both intrinsically and etymologically linked with the self-awareness of philosophy, especially in its Continental manifestations. The importance accorded to crisis is evident, Critchley argues, in the circuitous undertaking of philosophy, which offers a critique of the present on the one hand, while basing this critique upon its diagnosis of the crisis of society on the other (Critchley 1999: 12).[3] Even the most cursory survey of Kristeva's writings will recognise that she belongs to this philosophical tradition. Stressing this aspect of Kristeva's work also underpins a central argument of Sara Beardsworth's analysis of Kristeva's writings (2004a). Beardsworth conceptualises Kristeva's ideas as a philosophy of modernity that offers a response to the problem of nihilism, a philosophical concern that occupied the writings of, amongst others, Nietzsche, and that emerged in response to the decline of religious certainties and the subsequent uncertainty faced by modern Man. Focusing on Kristeva's 1980s trilogy, Beardsworth contends that at the core of Kristeva's thought lies the diagnosis of the loss of loss; therefore, her concern with meaning, authority and its collapse must be positioned within the wider context of nihilism and its treatment of loss.

If philosophical concerns frame Kristeva's wider discussion, it is psychoanalysis that informs her concrete analyses of the problem of crisis (see Gambaudo 2007a). Even though this psychoanalytic response is primarily a therapeutic one, it is also part of a philosophical tradition that seeks to offer an answer to the crisis that is modernity. Kristeva argues as much when she asserts that 'psychoanalysis is determined as much by philosophical preoccupations as it is influenced by its own scientific sources' (*IR*: 144). I return to this theme below, where I ask how women are inscribed in this circuitous discourse of 'crisis-of-modernity' and 'modernity-as-crisis'. For the moment, my interest remains with the emergence of Kristeva's account of and her answer to crisis.

I previously indicated that the crisis evoked by the onset of modernity informs Kristeva's understanding of human interaction and leads to her engagement with that other theoretician of

Crisis, Revolt, Intimacy

the crisis of modern Man, Freud. Thus, whereas *Revolution in Poetic Language* could be described as a philosophical reflection on crisis and on the role of aesthetics, albeit one already informed by psychoanalytic categories, the work Kristeva has published since the 1980s takes a distinctly psychoanalytic and therapeutic turn, addressing the individual manifestations of this crisis, which she experiences in the psychoanalytic encounter with her patients. I already mentioned her 1980s trilogy, whose main foci, on love, abjection and melancholia, engage with the subject's suffering in the face of crisis. Here I want to draw attention to *New Maladies of the Soul*, where Kristeva illustrates at length the emergence of new patients who suffer from a society that no longer provides an adequate outlet for representation.[4]

New Maladies of the Soul constitutes a departure in more than one way, though. For one, it has been described as instituting a shift from an Oedipal to a narcissistic framework (Gambaudo 2007a; Beardsworth 2004b: 126). With this shift, Kristeva accounts for the crisis in authority, specifically a decline in the authority of the paternal function, which, as Gambaudo avers, is generated by changes in the structure of modern parenting (see also Chapter 3) and which leaves the subject with no outlet for revolt (more on this below). It also introduces a new gender narrative vis-à-vis the question of suffering. Whereas *Black Sun*, for example, draws extensively on the subject of female suffering, experienced as female melancholia, and whereas earlier work stressed the paradoxical nature of maternal suffering (which, as we have seen in the previous chapter, is always offset by *jouissance*), *New Maladies of the Soul* introduces a set of new patients who emerge from across the gender divide. What they share is a suffering triggered by the crisis of paternal function, which, as we have seen, is said to correspond to wider changes in social life, such as changes in the structure of parenting.

Given her psychoanalytic emphasis, Kristeva's key interest lies in an exploration of the implications of this crisis for psychic life and, more specifically, for psychic well-being. In order to pursue this further, I want to turn to some of the psychoanalytic ideas that underpin Kristeva's discussion of revolt and that she discusses in *Revolt*.

Following Kristeva's focus on the interrelated production of the psychic and the social realms, the origin of crisis cannot just be found in society. Rather, as she discusses at length in *New Maladies of the Soul*, individual suffering is also the product of a crisis of authority in the familial realm, where the place of the paternal remains vacant. The first part of the book presents at length several case studies of her patients that are said to display these symptoms. These include mainly an inability to form connections or bonds with others and, crucially, an inability to form representations. However, due to the widespread nature of these individual malaises, Kristeva concludes that they are experienced at a collective level. Declaring that we live in a culture of melancholy, Kristeva asserts that melancholia is not merely the expression of individual suffering, but a wider cultural symptom. Reflecting on the geographical and national context of her work, she observes these symptoms in particular in France, a country that in her view suffers from national depression (see also Chapter 5).

I already alluded to a potentially profitable reading of Kristeva's work at the intersection between psychic and social life.[5] *New Maladies of the Soul* brings this traversal between the psyche and the social to the fore, by demonstrating how wider social trends intersect with the functioning of the Oedipal family, and how together they spark off a crisis of the subject. Before I comment on this further, I want to introduce a central reference point that underpins Kristeva's discussion of these new maladies of the soul and that makes a frequent appearance in her work, but receives scant detailed analysis; Kristeva's writings on crisis, and indeed her work on revolt, are informed by Guy Debord's situationist analysis of the society of the spectacle (Debord 1994).

Broadly speaking, Debord's work is an attempt to couple aesthetic practices with transformations in everyday life and, informed by a critique of consumer society and of the attempts of (left-wing) organisations, challenges the dominance of late-modern capitalism that is said to stifle creativity and rebellion.[6] As I mentioned above, Kristeva does not provide a comprehensive engagement with Debord's ideas; rather, they are invoked, at various points, as a metaphor for crisis and its manifestations, to the point where the title of Debord's book, *The Society of the Spectacle*, acquires the status of a theoretical concept in Kristeva's discussion of the crisis of contemporary society. What, then, does this crisis consist of, and how and why does it generate the kinds of patients that I alluded to briefly at the beginning of this section?

Crisis, Revolt, Intimacy

According to Kristeva, the dominance of a media society, with its spectacles and theatricalisation, combines with economic deprivation as a result of neo-liberal policies to form a crisis that grips Western societies.[7] In this crisis, individual suffering, resulting from a lack of ideals, including a decline of paternal authority, conjoins with the effects of socio-economic deprivation, such as unemployment and poverty (2000b: 55). The outcome of the cultural crisis of the society of the spectacle culminates in a new world order, which is said to normalise and to corrupt (*SNSR*: 5). As Kristeva avers, 'the normalizing order is far from perfect and fails to support the excluded: jobless youth, the poor in the projects, the homeless, the unemployed, and foreigners, among many others (*SNSR*: 7). Intrinsically connected with this crisis, and part of what Critchley refers to as the circuitous argumentation of Continental philosophy (see above), is a curtailed ability to revolt, which endangers what Kristeva regards as an older European tradition of revolt. As she suggests, 'the very notion of culture as revolt and of art as revolt is in peril, submerged as we are in the culture of entertainment, the culture of performance, the culture of the show' (*SNSR*: 6). Building further on Debord, Kristeva claims that the image, the media, trivialisation and theatricalisation have usurped individual and public imagination, resulting in a weakening of the imaginary and a decline in the capacity for representation. The excluded are left with images and regressive ideologies, culminating either in the spread of psychic illness or in aimless rioting and violence (*SNSR*: 7).[8] Kristeva's thesis is an intriguing one, and it would be worth while examining it further. However, my focus lies elsewhere; rather than further investigating her assertions drawn from her reading of Debord, I want to pursue the implications that build on her diagnosis.

Overall, Kristeva's diagnosis of contemporary society is a rather pessimistic one (see also Gambaudo 2007a: 189), and one is left wondering whether a way out of crisis is possible at all. Yet, as I hope to show in the next section, despite her pessimism, she holds on to the idea of revolt, asserting that the capacity for revolt is not completely lost and can be restored. Thus, paradoxically, and in spite of the infringement of crisis upon the capacity for revolt, only revolt presents a solution to crisis. This idea is more fully unpacked in Kristeva's writings on revolt, specifically in *The Sense and Non-Sense of Revolt* (2000a), where she further maps her understanding of crisis and revolt. It is also there that she sketches three related responses to crisis; these include a psychoanalytic-therapeutic response, an aesthetic response and a philosophical response.

From Crisis to Revolt

One of Kristeva's privileged responses to crisis, which I discuss in Chapter 5, is the practice of critique (see also Brown 2005), but for now I want to return briefly to the relevance of Debord, whose situationist response to the society of the spectacle consists of a series of strategies that seek to disrupt the routine of a society in the thrall of consumer capitalism. Such strategies include the deployment of ludic elements, eroticism, *dérive* and *détournement*.[9] These elements of a strategy of revolt are considered to contribute ultimately to the downfall of the capitalist system of production and reproduction. Elements of this situationist strategy of revolt can also be detected in Kristeva's writings (and, more broadly speaking, in Lacanian conceptions based upon *jouissance*). Yet, Kristeva's answer to the problem of crisis ultimately is not a ludic or situationist one, but draws instead upon psychoanalytic insights. The details of this response occupy me in the remainder of this chapter, where I attend to the notion of revolt, as it is presented in *The Sense and Non-Sense of Revolt* and in *Intimate Revolt*.

It may be intuitive, especially in a book concerned with the feminist appropriation of Kristeva's ideas, to expect an exploration of the conditions, prospects and strategies of political revolt. Yet the kind of revolt envisaged by Kristeva is not primarily associated with politics or with political transformation, even though she begins *The Sense and Non-Sense of Revolt* with the intention to 'evoke the current political state' (*SNSR*: 1). In fact, any link between revolt and politics is tentative; following her concern, since the 1980s, with individual well-being, she emphasises instead the necessity to restore psychic life, and to re-establish the capacity for intimate sensory experiences that allow for a reconnection between discourse and affect. In this respect, her work on revolt evokes her criticism, articulated two decades earlier, of feminism's first and second generations; she charges the first generation for its attempt to gain access to the paternally coded symbolic order, at the expense of the maternal-feminine, while she faults the second generation for its alleged efforts at establishing a feminist counter-culture that turns its back on the symbolic. Translated into the language of political philosophy, Kristeva's criticism is aimed as much at attempts located in the wider landscape of civil society, whether they attempt to overthrow existing institutions via political violence, or whether they enter and engage with the existing institutional network of formal democracy (1977b). As I will suggest in the next section, Kristeva's revolt performs what Diana Coole, as well as Cecilia Sjöholm, has described as a displacement of politics that focuses its attention on to the private and micro-political or, as Kristeva refers to it, the intimate realm (see Coole 2000; Sjöholm 2005).

Kristeva justifies her seemingly non-political account of revolt via a series of etymological expositions of the term that, at least on the surface, resemble Hannah Arendt's similar use of etymology in her discussion of revolution (Arendt 1963); unsurprisingly, aim, focus and result differ substantially. Unlike Arendt's, Kristeva's discussion does not focus upon revolt's political connotations. In fact, as I have proposed, the idea that politics is, at least potentially, antithetical to the possibility of revolt lies at the heart of her argument. Inspired instead by her reading of Freud and also of Proust (1996b),[10] she proposes an interpretation of revolt as remembrance and return. This, as I want to suggest, also requires renewed attention to her use of negativity and of the concept of the semiotic. In *The Sense and Non-Sense of Revolt*, the first volume of the revolt series, Kristeva identifies three constellations of revolt that are said to be logically independent but psychologically interdependent. These are revolt as the transgression of prohibition; revolt as repetition, working-through and working-out; and revolt as displacement and games (*SNSR*: 16). All three, according to Kristeva, are essential elements of a Freudian conception of revolt, and they are said to facilitate the subject's return to its unconscious, but it is the second element that Kristeva favours in particular. Building upon her assertion of the alleged loss of a culture of revolt, Kristeva surmises that this loss cannot be regained by embarking on a project of political rebellion. The capacity for rebellion is contingent upon the existence of authority; in other words, it requires an obstacle that can be transgressed. Such authority, however, is in decline, and hence there is no obstacle, no prohibition or authority left against which we can rebel. What is required instead is the reconstitution, with the help of psychoanalysis, of the psychic imaginary, of sublimation and of a balance between drive and language. It is through this inward turn, or turn towards the intimate (see below), that psychoanalysis plays a central role in the re-establishment of a culture of revolt.

For now, I want to remain briefly with *New Maladies of the Soul*, where Kristeva further outlines the role of psychoanalysis. As she states, to rectify individual suffering, we need to restore the capacity of individuals to rebuild their psyches, 'to create a space for an "inner zone" – a secret garden, an intimate quarter, or more simply and ambitiously, a psychic life' (*NMS*: 27). Psychoanalytic therapy is central to the restoration of psychic life, but she also broadens its function, and devotes most of her second volume of the revolt series, on intimate revolt, to it. Thus, in the wake of *New Maladies of the Soul*, Kristeva further develops her account of crisis, most prominently in her volumes on revolt (2000a; 2002; 2005b). In fact, these books could be read quite profitably as an answer to the questions that emerge in *New Maladies of the Soul*, and I turn to an exploration of their key themes in the following sections.

I already alluded to Kristeva's claim that a culture of revolt previously existed within European societies. Such a culture of revolt is necessary, according to Kristeva, for psychical and social well-being, as it provides an outlet for the pleasure principle, and she is at pains to assert the 'necessity of a culture of revolt in a society that is alive and developing, not stagnating. In fact, if such a culture did not exist, life would become a life of death' (*SNSR*: 7). While this general endorsement of revolt and its alleged benefit for psychic well-being informs Kristeva's wider concerns, she identifies society's margins as a privileged location for revolt, because it is there, according to Kristeva, that the drive or change is said to be generated (1996a: 45). Conceptually, her celebration of marginality (and a permanent one at that) resonates strongly with her concept of the semiotic; the semiotic, along with the feminine, is a metaphor for marginality whose transgressive capacities rejuvenate the symbolic and engender change (see Chapter 1). Kristeva also offers a sociological account, which identifies those groups who, as I alluded to above, are excluded by the society of the spectacle, as the agents of this change. Taken together, they constitute a fairly heterogeneous group, consisting of artists, the unemployed, young people, immigrants and so on. Unfortunately, Kristeva does not develop this further, leaving open any questions regarding the specific nature of revolt, the formation and exercise of collective agency, or the relationships between the different elements of the marginalised. Moreover, it would also be interesting to ask why revolt emerges at the margins; in other words, whether marginality constitutes a privileged position in the generation of change.

While these questions remain unanswered (in fact, they are not posed by Kristeva), it should be stressed that her celebration of marginality (as we will see in Chapter 5, her preferred term in her more recent writings is 'singularity') reverberates more widely with her previous writings on dissidence, and with the intellectual and aesthetic creations associated with dissidence (1977b). Two conclusions can be drawn from this. First, Kristeva's notion of revolt is not primarily aimed at the political horizon and cannot easily be translated into collective revolt – for example, in the form of feminist activism; instead, it is closely linked with aesthetic practice (2000b: 80–1) and with psychoanalytic experience, aimed at providing an outlet for the drives. Kristeva is at pains to detach the term 'revolt' from its exclusively political connotations (2000b: 99).[11] As she states, in her introduction to *The Sense and Non-Sense of Revolt*, she wants to evoke the current political state, characterised by a lack of revolt; moreover, she promises not to evade the problem of politics, but to approach it 'from a bit of a distance' (*SNSR*: 1). Yet, this promise is never kept, and the connection between politics and revolt is, at best, tentative and, at worst, severed at the expense of politics.

It is easy to see how the charges raised against Kristeva's earlier work, including the doubts over her political usefulness and her contribution to feminism, are confirmed by such a reading of her most recent writings. For Kristeva, revolt seems a solitary experience, aimed at providing an outlet for the drives. There are passages in Kristeva that describe politics as part of the problem, even though she stresses the importance of politics and indeed of political struggle. (I return to this below, with respect to feminism.) In a sense, psychic well-being precedes the capacity or even desirability of political engagement. Hence, it also follows that the step between revolt-as-return and revolt-as-politics is not a necessary one.[12] Yet, revolt is necessary and possible.

There is a second aspect to Kristeva's discussion of revolt, which I develop further in Chapter 5; this is her insistence on questioning and on permanent inquiry and critique. In her recent work, Kristeva asserts, following in particular her reading of Hannah Arendt, the need for questioning, and thus for psychoanalysis as a discourse of 'permanent inquiry' (*IR*: 236) where questioning becomes the 'quintessential mode of speech in analysis' (*IR*: 236). Such an approach provides Kristeva with the link between psychoanalysis, as the epistemological and therapeutic device, the permanent questioning and critique, and revolt as return. It is to this last point that my attention turns in the next section.

Beyond the Phallus? Female Sexuality, Oedipus and Revolt

We have already seen that Kristeva's concept of revolt carries a series of related connotations that aim at the psychoanalytic and the aesthetic, as well as the philosophical horizon. Here I want to look more closely at some of the psychoanalytic ideas that underpin her writings on revolt. Of particular interest to my discussion is her reformulation of Freudian conceptions of sexuality, as this, I believe, illuminates her work on revolt and establishes its connection with the feminine. It also allows for a fuller development of the potential cross-fertilisation between her writings on revolt and their possible contributions to feminist thought (see next section). In order to develop such a reading, I will consider the psychoanalytic narrative of revolt. However, this also returns me to a question I asked in the previous chapter: namely, whether the ethos and practice of psychoanalysis is antithetical to the idea of revolt. In other words, I want to ask whether psychoanalysis is a conformist enterprise, or an enterprise of revolt. To understand Kristeva's insistence on the role of psychoanalysis in the re-establishment of a culture of revolt more fully, it is therefore necessary to examine how she conceptualises the function of psychoanalysis, and what role she imagines it to fulfil in revolt.[13]

I already intimated that Kristeva refers to psychoanalysis as a questioning and critical practice (I develop this more fully in Chapter 5). She vehemently opposes normalising and conformist interpretations of psychoanalysis, most strongly articulated in her critique of ego psychology, which she accuses of stifling the negative, and with it, the openness, fluidity and precariousness of the subject. This is not to say that Kristeva wants to put the subject in crisis; in fact, as I stated above, an important concern of her work, especially in the 1980s trilogy, deals with the challenge of providing subjects with some form of psychic stability. However, this emphasis on stability can only ever offset a suffering psyche out of joint. Thus, instead of ego psychology's attempts at shoring up the stability of the subject, Kristeva advocates a form of psychoanalysis that brings to the fore the subject's suppleness and openness. This openness manifests itself in the figure of the analysand as much as in the figure of the analyst, leading Kristeva to proclaim that analysis must result in 'a state of perpetual rebirth' (*IR*: 233), while the 'analyzed subject . . . must be a subject in revolt' (*IR*: 237).[14] Hence, the methods deployed by psychoanalysis, as well as its goal, must aim towards this rebirth-in-revolt, returning the subject to its unconscious and on to a journey back through its own (pre-)history.

Unsurprisingly, the issue of sexuality is central to Kristeva's psychoanalytic discussion of revolt. In Chapter 1, I sketched Kristeva's psychoanalytic version, influenced by Freud and Lacan, of the girl-child's incomplete route into the order of law and language. Here I want to pay attention to Kristeva's recent discussion of female sexuality and the ensuing prospects for revolt. As Kristeva states, girls and women, by necessity, position themselves in relation to the phallus, language and the symbolic order, but this positioning is ambiguous, informed by a female irony that recognises the illusory nature of the phallus. This female ambiguity and irony vis-à-vis the phallus and the symbolic order also shed some light on the question of women's oscillation between the semiotic and the symbolic, a question that has occupied Kristeva's feminist critics and that has led some to claim – wrongly, as I suggested in the previous chapter – that Kristeva denies women access to the symbolic order. Female irony, furthermore, is indicative of women's constitutive psychic bisexuality, which engages in an inscription into the social order with 'aloof efficiency', described by Kristeva as a 'critical and ironical capacity' (*SNSR*: 103).

In order to understand Kristeva's theory of female sexuality more fully, it is helpful to recall briefly some of Freud's key assertions on the development of female sexuality, which he developed over a period of more than two decades.[15] Crucial to his discussion, but also to Kristeva's appropriation of his work, is the consideration given to the girl-child's positioning vis-à-vis the Oedipus complex, specifically her self-'discovery' as a castrated being, and her ambivalent relationship towards her parents. As is well known, Freud asserts that the little girl's path towards mature adult sexuality undergoes a more complex process of differentiation and development than that of the little boy. In essence, this is due to the social, psychic and familial compulsion imposed upon the girl, who has to change both object and aim of her initial affection: the mother. While the little boy accomplishes this infantile trauma by transferring from the mother to another woman – that is, from one female object to another (Kristeva refers to this as 'Oedipus 1'), the 'normal' route to femininity requires the girl to switch both aim and object, away from the mother and on to a male object of love (Kristeva calls this 'Oedipus 2'). Yet, despite this Oedipal injunction, girls rarely complete this process successfully, which accounts, according to Freud and Kristeva, for the more frequent display of bisexuality in women.

If the girl, following Freud's narrative, cannot or does not accomplish the requirements imposed upon her by the incest taboo – that is, the prohibition on the mother, she seems additionally burdened by her restricted ability to revolt against the father and, hence, against authority. The boy, on the other hand, along with his brothers, does not suffer the same fate. As outlined by Freud in *Totem and Taboo* (1998a), a text Kristeva invokes repeatedly, the sons wage a revolt against the father, which results in the replacement of the authority of the father with the totemic symbol (and thus to a restoration of authority). Female revolt, as I proposed in the previous chapter, is more likely to perform an inward turn, experienced, in the main, in the frequent display of female melancholia (see also Chapter 3).[16]

Whereas Freud's narrative of revolt ends with the brothers, Kristeva develops his story to account for a form of female revolt that she locates in women's constitutive bisexuality and in their ambiguous position vis-à-vis the phallus and the order of law and language. Two central elements inform this narrative; these are her assertion of the universal applicability of the Oedipal injunction, notwithstanding its concrete modifications (more on this below), and phallic monism. With Freud, Kristeva insists on the universal application of the Oedipus complex as the structure that frames the child's entrance into the order of law and language. While she alludes, too briefly, to the fact that the concrete manifestations of the Oedipus complex may differ, thus hinting at a potential departure from the traditional heterosexual family structures (see Chapter 3), she firmly holds on to the notion of a triangular, universally applicable structure. Unfortunately, Kristeva does not develop this point further, and hence one can only speculate on how she would envisage a non-heterosexual Oedipality, or how the masculine and the feminine would be distributed in a non-heterosexual context. Such a discussion could have presented an interesting addition to recent debates on kinship structures, located at the intersection of feminism and queer theory, which have challenged the position of the heterosexual family.[17] Moreover, such a queer reading of sexual difference may have led to a welcome deconstruction of the foundational binary of masculinity and femininity, which haunts theories of sexual difference and which acquires its meaning in the context of the heterosexual matrix intrinsic to the configuration of the Oedipal constellation. While Kristeva does not pursue these questions, it is worth mentioning that her 'concession' regarding the viability of a non-heterosexual Oedipality constitutes a welcome departure from her previously expressed view, that the absence of the father carries the danger of psychosis in the child (I return to this aspect in Chapter 3).

She also posits, secondly, the operation of what she refers to as phallic monism: that is, the universal application of the phallus as a reference point for the development of both male and female sexuality. However, despite the universal operation of Oedipus and phallus as structural reference points for the development of female and male sexuality alike, there emerge substantial differences in the sexual individuation of boys and girls, and in their entrance into the symbolic order. It is at this juncture that the difference between 'Oedipus 1' and 'Oedipus 2' comes into play. Oedipus 1, as I already intimated, articulates the prohibition of the child's incestuous desire for the mother; its 'law' obtains universal applicability in so far as both boy-child and girl-child must submit to it. Oedipus 2, on the other hand, is an injunction against the girl-child and a prerequisite for the development of a 'normal' female sexuality, requiring her to change her desire from the maternal object on to a man.

While Kristeva, as we see below, will map an alternative path towards female revolt, she leaves unchallenged the main premises of Freud's narrative. These include, as mentioned, her insistence on the universality of a triangular Oedipal structure and of the necessity of phallic monism. She also does not question the implicit normative content of sexed positions. As Judith Butler (1990) has stated, the meaning of masculinity and of femininity can only become intelligible within a wider normative framework of heterosexuality, where desire is channelled into a heterosexual direction, and where gender emerges and is continuously reaffirmed by the articulation of such heterosexual desire. Moreover, bisexuality, which, according to Kristeva, is most prominent amongst women, can only be understood inside this 'heterosexual matrix', as an oscillation between heterosexuality and homosexuality.[18] While such a 'queer' reading of Kristeva would lead me beyond the scope of this book, it is, I believe, a necessary challenge to any feminist interpretation that leaves unquestioned the notion of sexual difference, and of the binary between masculine and feminine (see also Cooper 2000).[19] For now, I want to return to an immanent reading of Kristeva, by attending further to the implications that follow from her story of female sexuality.

The openness of the psyche, which raises the prospect of a variation from the normal route to adult sexuality, generates a series of potential implications that can follow from women's constitutive bisexuality. Key to these options is women's respective positioning vis-à-vis the phallus. While an acknowledgment of the illusory position of the phallus risks the descent into depressive regression, this risk is outweighed by the danger and disadvantage that follow a denial of psychical bisexuality, and with it a denial of the illusory, an identification with the phallus and the emergence of the female paranoiac.

What, though, happens to women beyond depressive regression and paranoia? If women's position vis-à-vis the phallus is illusory, what are the implications for revolt? Are women also beyond the phallus? Kristeva denies this, insisting again on a phallic monism: that is, on the universality of the phallus. However, girls' and women's position towards the phallus differs substantially from that of men, and it is due to this differential position that the prospect for feminine (though not feminist) revolt emerges. Much has been made of the gendering of Kristeva's categorical distinction between the semiotic and the symbolic, and about women's position in the symbolic order. As we have seen in the previous chapter, this has been a key issue of contention in the reception of Kristeva's ideas, leading to accusations that she condemns women to a position outside the symbolic and, hence, outside intelligibility. Without making an explicit reference to these debates, Kristeva takes up the central issue in *The Sense and Non-Sense of Revolt*, where she outlines women's position vis-à-vis the phallus. She suggests that women recognise what she describes as the illusory nature of the phallus, allowing them to inscribe themselves into the social order – that is, the symbolic – while at the same time remaining removed from it. With reference to Hegel's quip about women being the eternal irony of the community, Kristeva characterises it as an 'aloof efficiency' (*SNSR*: 101–2). In *Intimate Revolt*, she develops this point, locating the source of women's irony and aloofness with respect to the symbolic order in their 'sensory intimacy' (*IR*: 5), providing them with the capacity to develop a questioning attitude that she sees as the hallmark of revolt (see also below and Chapter 5). Thus, for Kristeva, women's psycho-sexual development, culminating in a constitutive bisexuality, equips them with an attitude of revolt, what I will call an ethos of revolt. Their capacity to engage in revolt, however, is contingent upon their ability to engage with their constitutive ambiguity: that is, their bisexuality. The main threat to this capacity is the essentially futile attempt to hang on to phallicism, which is rooted in the denial of bisexuality. The consequences of such denial stretch from the benign to the dangerous, and they are key to informing Kristeva's views on feminist politics. As she suggests, identifying with man's phallicism generates female paranoia, embodied in the figure of 'the boss, the director, or virile lesbian, partisans of power in all its more or less dictatorial forms' (*SNSR*: 102).

It is not difficult to recognise in this last claim an assertion already encountered in her earlier work – for example, in her essay, 'Women's Time' (1979), where she diagnoses and criticises paranoid investments that, in her view, lie at the bottom of any political involvement, including feminism ('WT': 203). I return to this point in the following section, as it is crucial to the assessment of Kristeva's conceptualisation of feminism. But they can also have more serious implications, and Kristeva illustrates this by introducing, early on in her chapter on female sexuality, three case studies of women suffering from such an adherence to the phallus, an 'unbearable phallicism' (*SNSR*: 96).

Because of Kristeva's caution with regard to women's alleged phallicism, it is difficult to see how her account of female bisexuality, and its corresponding link with female revolt, could translate into a strategy for feminist political practice. For one, her account of female sexuality, especially her insistence on phallic monism, sits oddly alongside her equally forceful insistence on female plurality. How can such a post-phallic plurality emerge from the universally experienced stages of psycho-sexual development? In other words, how do we get from monism to plurality? As I intimated in the previous chapter, this is a serious challenge for any feminist theory informed by psychoanalytic categories and it is one that Kristeva does not answer adequately or satisfactorily.[20] Kristeva's account raises a further challenge. It is difficult to imagine how women's privileged position vis-à-vis the phallus, their 'aloof efficiency' and irony, could translate into the language of political philosophy. How does such an account accommodate concepts such as agency, solidarity, citizenship or justice? This challenge has recently been taken up by Ewa Ziarek (2005), who seeks to utilise Kristeva's narrative of women's ironic relationship with the symbolic for the possibility of an ongoing transformation of the symbolic.

Ziarek locates the capacity for a transformative practice, which is said to emerge from irony, in the emphasis accorded to contestation (see also Chapter 5). While she criticises Kristeva for a series of limitations, specifically her alleged focus on aesthetic and religious manifestations of revolt, which, according to Ziarek, are stressed at the expense of working out the political logic of revolution, Ziarek also brings to the fore what she considers to be of value in Kristeva's discussion of feminine revolt. In what, then, does this consist? Her point of departure is the work of Frantz Fanon, and more specifically Fanon's critique of Jean-Paul Sartre's treatment of the relationship between the universal and the particular in Sartre's preface to Fanon's book, *The Wretched of the Earth* (2001). In this short text, Sartre (2001) is said to perform a feminisation of the excluded particular, embodied in the figure of the Black man, whom he tasks with abandoning his racial particularity and with adopting the position of the universal, untainted by racial particularities. Against Sartre, Fanon takes up this challenge by engaging in an interpretative act of reversal that feminises the universal, which he sees embodied in another figure of particularity, Europe. (I return to this discussion of universality and particularity, and of Europe, in Chapter 5.) Developing this contamination of universal and particular that is said to follow from Fanon's account, but connecting it now with Kristeva's discussion of revolt, Ziarek suggests that the feminisation of the particular can be reversed into a feminine ironisation of the universal (2005: 58). Kristeva, in her view, performs such a reversal by adding to Freud's story of the rebellion of the sons, which stresses the gaps and fissures opened up by female (bi-)sexuality. Central to Kristeva's discussion, and considered by Ziarek as the key contribution to working out the political logic of revolution, is the feminine emphasis on irony. The feminine points to the illusory nature of the law and of authority. As Ziarek suggests, 'feminine logic is associated with the ironic adherence and non-adherence to this new form of authority, and with the refusal of the fetishistic fixity of symbolic and psychic protections against the finitude and the contingency it offers' (2005: 69). She concludes by stating that feminine ironisation takes place 'when the excluded, feminized particular lays claim to universality through identification with the new form of paternal authority. This ironic play with illusion . . . opens the symbolic to ongoing transformation' (2005: 69) (see also Chapter 5). Kristeva herself underscores this crucial aspect in an interview where she states that:

> the woman is a stranger to the phallic order she nonetheless adheres to, if only because she is a speaking being, a being of thought and law. But she keeps a distance vis-à-vis the social order, its rules, political contracts, etc., and this makes her sceptical, potentially atheist, ironic and all in all, pragmatic. I'm not really in the loop, says the woman, I'm staying outside, I don't believe in it, but I play the game, and at times, better than others. (*Revolt*: 93)

It is difficult to imagine how such a focus on irony is said to generate a transformation of the symbolic, or how it can be translated into a feminist political practice. For example, it remains unclear whether and how female irony replaces, displaces or transforms the symbolic. Ziarek herself concedes that Kristeva's conclusion may seem banal. Moreover, as Ziarek has demonstrated, while Kristeva's insistence on the ironic posture of the feminine generates a nuanced and sophisticated account of revolt vis-à-vis the symbolic, beyond phallicism and psychosis, it is not at all clear whether this relates exclusively to women. Furthermore, what remains unspoken is whether this feminine ironisation of the law can relate in any way to a feminist reformulation of it. Kristeva herself does not address this, and one can only surmise whether her references to the feminine refer specifically to women or whether they articulate, more broadly, a feminine heterogeneity that is said to be a feature of both men and women.

Notwithstanding these reservations, I want to suggest that the value of Kristeva's account of female irony for feminism lies in its emphasis on the critical, open and contestatory practices associated with revolt, which connect with her earlier assertions about feminism. Recall that Kristeva, in her famous interview with *Psych et po* (1981), identifies feminism as a practice of the negative, leaving intact the heterogeneity of the female subject and the fluidity of the subject-in-process (see Chapter 1). As Ziarek points out, by stressing the illusory nature of the law and of authority, the feminine ironises the claim to an impossible fullness, and in doing so reveals a gap between the particular and the universal. As she suggests, 'the estrangement of revolutionary illusions maintains the conflicting relation between the particular and the universal, and, in doing so, sustains the culture of revolt' (2005: 74); in fact, it may even, as Ziarek intimates, dissociate the universal from paternal authority. It is thus in this gap between the universal and the particular, and in the continued opening of this gap, that the promise of a Kristevan politics of futurality lies. (I discuss this in more detail in Chapter 5.)

This returns me to the question that I alluded to briefly in my discussion of crisis. As I intimated there, the notion of crisis is intimately linked with that of critique. I therefore want to suggest that one of Kristeva's key contributions to contemporary feminist thought, albeit possibly unintended, is her insistence on critique, contestation and questioning. As I already stated, feminism as a political project aimed at social and political transformation is deeply embedded in this nexus of crisis and critique. The birth of feminism constitutes a twofold response, to the crisis of a modernity blind to gender injustices and as a critical response to this crisis.

In her insightful historical study of French feminism and its engagement with the notion of the rights of man, Joan W. Scott (1996) uses the framework of paradox to assess feminist practice. She suggests that feminist agency is paradoxical because it is constituted by a universalist discourse, that of individualism, which at the same time evokes particularity through the idea of 'sexual difference' in order to naturalise women's exclusion (1996: 16). To make sense of feminism, Scott suggests, requires a reading for paradoxes, looking at internal tensions and incompatibilities and engaging in a technically deconstructive way, both of which sit uneasily within a linear historical narrative and teleology (1996: 16). Clearly, this has implications for the way we assess Kristeva. As we have seen in the previous chapter, her narrative of the temporality of women is also uncomfortable with the notion of a linear history of progress. Moreover, women's agency, and more specifically their capacity for a transgressive practice of revolt, is in an uneasy relationship with some feminist narratives of female agency. Yet, returning to the idea of a hermeneutics of complication that positions Kristeva at a series of thresholds (Margaroni 2007; 2009), we are left with the fact that Kristeva does not provide us with easy answers. As I discuss in more detail in Chapter 5, where I examine her notion of singularity, Kristeva's reservation about forms of collective agency, including feminism, complicates a fuller engagement between Kristeva and feminist thought, despite her repeated acknowledgement of the achievements of feminism.

There is a further aspect to this. As I argue in the next section, by introducing her notion of the intimate to the realm of revolt, Kristeva opens up further avenues for theorising the political as a displacement activity. I have repeatedly stressed Kristeva's ambiguous relationship with feminism as a political movement. Her writings on revolt, which stress the intimate dimension of revolt, and the marginal attention given to feminism in these writings which focus, in the main, as we have seen above, on male figures, seem to suggest at first glance that there is not much to be gained for feminist purposes.

'Tiny Revolts': The Intimate

In the previous chapter, I suggested that the assertion of an interconnected relationship between psychical and social processes of transformation is a key feature of *Revolution in Poetic Language*. The thesis advanced in Kristeva's books on revolt reiterate this earlier assertion, as they, like *Revolution in Poetic Language*, explore the psychic potential for revolt in a society that Kristeva, building upon Debord, diagnoses to be in crisis. However, developing the ideas that she introduced in *New Maladies of the Soul*, Kristeva stresses a further aspect of the crisis–revolt nexus with her concept of the intimate and of intimate revolt. Examining the scope for a psychic life, against the restrictions imposed by symbolic and social injunctions, and by the degenerate trends associated with the society of the spectacle, is, as we have already seen, a leitmotif of Kristeva's work. She develops this in detail in *Intimate Revolt*, the second book of her trilogy on revolt. I want to begin with a brief exposition of her main arguments, before examining more closely its implications for feminist thought. What I want to suggest is that, in addition to the 'unfaithful' feminist appropriation of *The Sense and Non-Sense of Revolt*, which, as we have seen, exposes the illusory nature of paternal authority, Kristeva's emphasis on the intimate opens up further avenues for theorising feminism. These avenues emerge, I want to suggest, in the intertextual space between the intimate and revolt, and they develop feminism's own emphasis on intimate and private realms. (I propose a distinction between the two below.) However, despite Kristeva's allusion to the political horizon of (intimate) revolt, she does not fully develop its potential implications; it is this task that occupies me in this section and that I continue in Chapter 5.

In the opening chapter to *Intimate Revolt*, the second volume of the revolt series, Kristeva specifies, in a theoretically more rigorous way than in *The Sense and Non-Sense of Revolt*, what she considers to be the key issues for an account of revolt. Just like *The Sense and Non-Sense of Revolt*, *Intimate Revolt* is not a feminist book; despite alluding to the role of women and the feminine in revolt, and some general and brief comments about feminism, which I discuss below, there is no specific or detailed engagement with women or with gender issues. Nevertheless, I want to suggest that the two *Revolt* publications have an – albeit indirect – bearing upon theorising gender and the role of feminism as a transformative political project, a project of revolt. What, then, are the key assertions of *Intimate Revolt*?

Already in *The Sense and Non-Sense of Revolt*, Kristeva alludes

Crisis, Revolt, Intimacy

to the possibility of a non-political, intimate form of revolt. She develops this idea further in *Intimate Revolt*, where she provides a more philosophical grounding of her assertion of the crisis of modern Man, above and beyond her deployment of Debord's concept of the society of the spectacle that I discussed previously. This philosophical grounding turns on the development of philosophical thought since Hegel, and it considers the emergence of nihilism in modern thought that I referred to at the beginning of this chapter. As I outlined there, it is this nihilism problematic, coupled with the challenges of contemporary society, which constitute the crisis, and which curtail the prospect for revolt.

Two arguments are central to the further development of Kristeva's account. First, revolt, Kristeva avers, challenges the stability of the subject, emphasising instead its fragility and precariousness. As Kristeva declares,

> [t]he permanence of contradiction, the temporariness of reconciliation, the bringing to the fore of everything that puts the very possibility of unitary meaning to the test (such as the drive, the unnameable feminine, destructivity, psychosis, etc.): these are what the culture of revolt explores. (*IR*: 10)

This challenge to unity also links her recent work on revolt with her earlier revolutionary writings, which stressed (semiotic) negativity, disruption and instability (see Chapter 1). In this respect, this recent stress on fragility, precariousness and the negative also requires, I believe, a qualification of those positions that accentuate a rupture between an early, revolutionary Kristeva of the 1970s, and the Kristeva of the 1980s who is said to consider more strongly the need for stability, and with it, to lay more emphasis on the symbolic. While the *Revolt* publications highlight the need for psychic well-being, and hence require the stabilising function provided by the symbolic, they also underscore the importance of fluidity that keeps the subject in process and thus alive.

It is this rediscovery of negativity, or rather a more fully reconciled account of rupture and stability, that, in my view, makes Kristeva's writings on revolt interesting for a theory of politics and, by extension, for feminist theory. Such a suggestion, however, requires further justification, given that the explicit emphasis of *Intimate Revolt*, on the intimate, seems counter-intuitive to the idea of a politics. Towards the end of the first chapter of *Intimate Revolt*, Kristeva asks whether intimate revolt is the only possible form of revolt (*IR*: 12). The focus of *Intimate Revolt*, as well as the implicit assumption contained in *The Sense and Non-Sense of Revolt*, seems to affirm this question. Yet, I want to argue for a wider deployment of the concept of revolt which encompasses the political and which, again, reconnects Kristeva's recent understanding of revolt with her earlier conceptualisation of politics. As she contends:

> [I]t is not exclusively in the world of action that this revolt is realized but in that of psychical life and its social manifestations (writing, thought, art), a revolt that seems to me to manifest the crises of modern man as much as the advances. Yet as a transformation of man's relationship to meaning this cultural revolt intrinsically concerns public life and consequently has profoundly political implications. In fact, it poses the question of another politics, that of permanent conflictuality. (*IR*: 11)

What this 'other politics' will look like, and what its implications for feminist theory are, will occupy me in Chapters 4 and 5. For now, I want to examine more closely Kristeva's emphasis on the intimate.

As we have already seen, Kristeva's general concern, at least since the 1980s and expressed in a more pronounced way since the 1990s, lies with the psychic well-being of the individual. I have already stated that it is driven by a cultural pessimism, including a lack of faith in the atoning capacities of contemporary art, and in the capacity of political projects to provide an adequate response to the crisis. Yet, despite the apparent non- or a-political connotation of the intimate, it is important to stress that individual crises are not merely the product of a private or privatised family drama; rather, they are embedded in and also generated by the social world and its manifestations, most recently through the spectacle, a decline of authority and the law. Psychoanalysis has a key role to play here, although Kristeva is at pains to stress that psychoanalysis is no cure for wider social ills, but can only ever work effectively at the individual level. Still, it shores up the individual against the onslaughts of the spectacle and other crises of contemporary society, by restoring the individual's psychic life. It does

Crisis, Revolt, Intimacy

so by reconnecting the drives and affects with discourse, allowing the suffering patient to restore his or her imaginary and to begin the process of representation anew. This alone, according to Kristeva, establishes the capacity for happiness, and it is in this sense of the term revolt, as a return to the unconscious, that Kristeva's concern with revolt should be understood.

Connecting her broader ideas on crisis and psychic life with her recent work on revolt, she investigates the possibilities of an intimate revolt. As I already suggested, the bond between revolt and political transformation is rather tentative and fragile. In its place, Kristeva advances the linkage between revolt and return, or rather, revolt as return, where through revolt we can facilitate an immersion into our archaic past – that is, into the unconscious – in order to restore a psychic healing and life that is, in Kristeva's view, necessary. Yet, her apparent turn from politics towards the intimate is paradoxical, as it is through the emphasis on the intimate that the future can be secured: 'we will have to re-turn to the little things, tiny revolts, in order to preserve the life of the mind and of the species' (IR: 5).

Intimate revolt, or maybe more correctly a revolt towards the intimate (in the sense of turn or return), also underscores Kristeva's emphasis on the connection between drives and signification, language and affect, body and psyche. One could plausibly link these recent insights with her foundational categorical distinction between the semiotic and the symbolic; if the two are out of joint, the subject suffers. However, a permanent equilibrium or balance may not be possible either; in fact, it is the return to the unconscious (and hence to the negative) that invigorates and facilitates a process of rebirth. Thus, in accordance with Kristeva's concern with individual psychic well-being, it is not surprising that the intimate obtains such a prominent position in her recent work. Curiously, though, as I want to suggest, this focus on the intimate prepares the way for Kristeva's more recent concern with political philosophy. In fact, as she proposes early on in *Intimate Revolt*, (intimate) revolt has political implications, posing the question of 'another politics' (*IR*: 11). (I deal with this aspect in Chapter 5.)

The intimate, or rather the restoration of the intimate, seems to occupy the space of resistance against the onslaught of the society of the spectacle. This also implies that psychoanalysis can shore up the individual's resistances against an oppressive social hegemony.

Yet what does this mean for the way that the psychic and social are connected? And where does this leave the concerns over the transpositions from psychoanalytic theory and concepts to social and political theory? The answer to this question, as I already suggested, depends upon the way we conceptualise psychoanalysis. For example, Butler's critical engagement with psychoanalysis depends upon the way that the (gender) norms of psychoanalysis contribute to the normative constitution of the subject. Translated into her Foucauldian terminology, it means that, as she suggests, the conceptual apparatus that establishes us as subjects is pervaded by power (1990). For Butler, the prohibitions and the 'incitements' of psychoanalysis operate as part of the social world; therefore, to posit a realm of the psyche as independent of the social is a ruse of power (1997). Despite Kristeva's frequent allusions to the intersection of the psychic and social world, it is not fully developed nor, I suspect, recognised.

Is there a role for women in this intimate revolt? Kristeva seems to suggest this, when she stresses the 'sensibilities and passions', or more generally, a 'sensory intimacy', coupled with the capacity to ask questions (see Chapter 5) that some individuals, including women, bring to life. Yet this female capacity is severed from the possibilities of the feminist practice; in fact, it seems only to develop fully after the time of feminism:

> I am convinced that after all the more or less reasonable and promising projects and slogans the feminist movement has promulgated over the past decades, the arrival of women at the forefront of the social and ethical scene has had the result of revalorizing the sensory experience ... The immense responsibility of women in regard to the survival of the species – how to preserve the freedom of our bodies while at the same time ensuring the conditions for better lives for our children? – goes hand in hand with this rehabilitation of the sensory. (*IR*: 5)

The theme of intimacy has recently received some attention in the critical commentary on Kristeva. Keltner's treatment of the subject (2009a), in her contribution to a recently published edited collection on Kristeva's work (Oliver and Keltner 2009), offers a helpful explication of the concept of intimacy in Kristeva's writings, tracing its emergence and development in Kristeva's recent thought.[21] The backdrop to Keltner's analysis is Hannah Arendt's thought, which serves as a contra-point to Kristeva's delineation of the intimate. Keltner positions Arendt's diagnosis of the loss of the public space, and of politics more generally, in the modern world, which, according to Arendt, sees the intimate move centre-stage, against Kristeva's assertion of a loss of intimacy in the modern world. This loss of intimacy, as we have seen, can only be recuperated by restoring the connection between affect and language. Keltner's questions aim at political theory, and while she concedes that Kristeva's concern for intimacy, and indeed her writings more generally, do not meet the requirements of political theory proper, she nevertheless sees this concern for politics emerge in Kristeva's attention to difference, to the feminine and to marginalised groups. It is there that, according to Keltner, the need to reinscribe the intimate into politics is established. Furthermore, it is this emphasis, according to Keltner, that makes Kristeva's contribution to social and political thought so distinctive, even though it condemns politics to futurality.[22] As I already suggested, this emphasis on futurality is indeed a key feature of any account of politics that draws on Kristevan ideas. It is coupled, moreover, as I argued, with the emphasis she accords to the practices of contestation, questioning and critique, and it is at this juncture that feminism, as a critical practice, overlaps with Kristeva's concern.

The theme of corporeality, as I also intimated in Chapter 1, constitutes an essential part of such a dialogue between Kristeva and feminism, and this aspect is taken up in a further contribution in the same book, by Cecilia Sjöholm (2009), who emphasises intimacy's link to corporeality and sensuality. In particular, she contrasts the Kristevan conception of the intimate with the common demarcation of the public and the private (she illustrates this mainly through reference to Habermas), stressing the protective function of the intimate. More specifically, she posits the intimate as the domain of singularity (2009: 191), and in that respect, like Keltner, establishes Kristeva's contribution as an important corrective to a political theory that lacks attention to corporeality and sensibility. A central element of Kristeva's discussion of intimate revolt, as I have demonstrated, is its return to the unconscious; such a return provides the subject with the capacity to establish, or re-establish, connections with others. Hence, in addition to its psychoanalytic dimension, the intimate obtains further significance as an ethical category. It is to this aspect that I turn in the next section.

In conclusion, as I sought to demonstrate in this chapter, Kristeva's writings on crisis and revolt establish a close connection between the realm of the social and the intimate via their concern for the suffering of contemporary individuals. This suffering, as we have seen, occurs in the face of what Kristeva considers to be fundamental changes in wider society and which she captures, building upon the work of Guy Debord, with the idea of the society of the spectacle. While Kristeva alludes to the wider social reference points of this crisis, her concern is primarily with the well-being, or suffering, of the individual.

Furthermore, I suggested that despite the absence of an explicit feminist sensibility, Kristeva's writings on crisis and revolt resonate with wider feminist concerns. The persistence of a gendered narrative, intrinsic to the psychoanalytic ideas deployed by Kristeva, facilitates a feminist critique of her texts. Building on feminist work that criticises the gendered and heterosexist assumptions of psychoanalysis, I took issue with Kristeva's deployment of psychoanalysis. In its place, I advocate a more attentive reading of the operations of social norms in the generation of psychoanalysis. Moreover, while the wider references to the possibility of a political revolt or transformation are missing in her work, I suggested an appropriation of Kristeva's emphasis on the intimate that draws on her displacement of politics.

It is paradoxically around the idea of the intimate that a convergence becomes possible, because it is there that a feminist focus on the 'art of living' or on the politics of everyday life emerges. Moreover, as I suggested, the connection that Kristeva makes between the practice of revolt and the practice of questioning and critique is an essential component of feminism's self-understanding as a critical theory and practice, which I termed Kristeva's ethos of revolt. I will return to this aspect, which is so crucial to Kristeva's most recent work, in the final chapter. In the next chapter, I will explore how this crisis plays itself out in the field of ethics.

Notes

1. The academic literature commonly references these volumes by their individual titles, *The Sense and Non-Sense of Revolt* (2000a) and

Intimate Revolt (2002). These two volumes encompass three French texts, *Sens et non-sens de la révolte* (1996), as well as *La révolte intime* (1997) and *L'Avenir d'une révolte* (1998), the latter two of which are published in *Intimate Revolt* (2002). A further volume of the revolt series, *La Haine et le pardon* (2005), will be available in English from Columbia University Press in 2011. See also the collection of interviews in *Revolt, She Said* (2000b).
2. This also includes Kristeva's claim of a crisis of paternal authority and her wider reflections on parenting. On these points see Gambaudo (2007a), who provides an assessment of Kristeva's work on crisis, above and beyond her reception within feminism.
3. On the etymological link between crisis and critique see also Brown (2005). In Chapter 5 I discuss how Kristeva's answer to crisis is related to the practice of critique.
4. The idea of representation is central to Kristeva's thought. It entails the transmission of drive energy and affect, generating symbols and signification. The issue of representation takes on a particular significance in her writings on women and motherhood.
5. I explore this theme further below, where I question Kristeva's reading of Oedipality. See also Margaroni (2009) on the notion of crossroads.
6. To discuss the details and merits of Debord's work would lead me beyond the scope of this book. Moreover, it is not my intention to assess the validity or accuracy of Kristeva's engagement with Debord's ideas. Rather, I want to contextualise this aspect of Kristeva's thought. For a recent assessment of Debord and situationism see, for example, Clark and Nicholson-Smith (1997), McDonough (1997), Raunig (2007), D. Smith (2005) and Wollen (1989).
7. Kristeva also avers that the decline of religion and, more generally, of the realm of the sacred is one of the main contributing factors to society's contemporary crisis. I want to stress that she does not envisage, as some of her critics have claimed, a return to religiosity. Rather, she laments that, with the decline of the sacred, modern Man has lost his or her inner space. The role and function of religion or, more generally, of spirituality has been usurped by the society of the spectacle.
8. In Chapter 3 I will connect this with a discussion of violence.
9. According to Smith (2005), situationist strategies promote playful, ludic or erotic elements that seek to disrupt, decontextualise and

reappropriate the social order: for example, through the practice of drifting through urban spaces (*dérive*) or the relocation of objects into new contexts (*détournement*).

10. Kristeva engages with the idea of return, with respect to Marcel Proust's writings, in her book on Proust (Kristeva 1996b).
11. In this respect, Kristeva's account differs substantially from Arendt's notion of revolution, despite the similarities in their respective etymological methodology and a concern with crisis. For Arendt, revolution is captured in collective action; its sole purpose is freedom, and the establishment of institutions which guarantee freedom. See my discussion in the next chapter.
12. As I discuss below, this facet of her writings is also linked to her dislike of political movements.
13. My discussion draws in particular on Chapters 4 and 5 of *The Sense and Non-Sense of Revolt* (see also Kristeva 2001c; 2004b; 2004c: 404–19).
14. The theme of birth or rebirth is also a central aspect in Kristeva's discussion of Arendt. See Chapter 4.
15. In her discussion of female sexuality in *The Sense and Non-Sense of Revolt*, Kristeva draws on several of Freud's texts. See Freud (1994a; 1994b; 1997; 1998e).
16. Freud, in 'Mourning and Melancholia' (1998b), refers to this inward turn as a 'psychic constellation of revolt'. I will consider the wider question of the role of murder and of violence in the next chapter.
17. For a critical interrogation of the role of Oedipus in the formation of kinship see Butler (2000a).
18. One may also ask, with Butler, after the meaning of bisexuality and its relationship with heterosexuality. See also Butler's alternative reading of the phallus in *Bodies that Matter* (1993).
19. For a deployment on Kristeva for transgender theory see Maur (no date).
20. In Chapters 4 and 5, I outline how feminist theories 'beyond the subject' that draw on Arendtian categories attempt to answer this problem.
21. According to Keltner, Kristeva's use of the term intimacy can be traced back as far as her *Powers of Horror*, even though, as Keltner points out, the meaning and use of the term remain somewhat opaque.
22. I questioned above whether Kristeva's notion of revolt can be translated into the language of (feminist) political philosophy. The same

question could be asked of the concept of intimacy. As I suggest in the next chapter, although she remains removed from political concerns, narrowly defined, her concept of intimacy ties in with wider discussions on intimate citizenship, especially as they pertain to what might be termed 'the art of living'.

3

Corporeal Ethics: Between Violence and Forgiveness

> [T]he issue of ethics crops up wherever a code (mores, social contract) must be shattered in order to give way to the free play of negativity, need, desire, pleasure, and jouissance, before being put together again, although temporarily and with full knowledge of what is involved.
>
> (*DL*: 23)

Kristeva's focus on representation, including her writings on art, constitutes an important component in the feminist Kristeva reception that I alluded to previously. One would expect her works on ethics to have a similar impact, but it is somewhat puzzling to compare the prominence of her ethical thought in the Kristeva scholarship with the relative neglect in the wider field of feminist ethics. For example, two of her best-known and highly influential essays, 'Stabat Mater' (1977a) and 'Women's Time' (1979), both of which articulate distinctive conceptions of the feminine and of the maternal, do not feature extensively in the field of feminist ethics.[1] Her association with post-structuralism, and its perceived ethical deficit, may account for such a gap in the literature, yet even some of the prominent texts in post-structuralist feminist ethics pay scant attention to Kristeva's ethical thought.[2]

This relative neglect within the wider area of feminist ethics is out of tune with the importance accorded to her ethics in the Kristeva scholarship. For example, some commentators have identified elements of her writings as specifically ethical, such as her *Strangers to Ourselves* (see Beardsworth 2004a: 130), while others take an even broader view, suggesting that an ethics is implicit in all of Kristeva's work (Lechte and Margaroni 2004); one commentator goes as far as describing her as an 'ethical thinker par excellence' (Graybeal 1993: 32).[3] As I already suggested, the most widely discussed aspect within the feminist commentary on her work has been her attempt to develop a maternal herethics (see below), whilst her writings on the ethical dimension of immigration and multiculturalism, discussed in *Strangers to Ourselves* and *Nations without Nationalism*, have also received substantial attention. The stress on the question of a maternal ethics reflects, for obvious reasons, the wider feminist interest in issues such as care and motherhood, but it should not cloud the import of Kristeva's idea for a broader utilisation of feminist ethics. Here it is also important to emphasise that her occupation with ethical matters originates in her early work on language and language acquisition (see, for example, the essays in *Desire in Language*), and it weaves itself consistently throughout her œuvre, right up to her most recent writings on revolt, crisis and freedom; hence, I will return to questions of ethics in the remaining chapters. Moreover, whilst I give substantial consideration to the maternal aspect of a Kristevan ethics, I want to advocate a wider use of Kristeva's ethics, drawing in particular upon some of her more recent writings on revolt, violence and forgiveness.

I begin by mapping the wider philosophical commitments of Kristeva's ethics, which I want to call an ethics of traversal. This includes a brief exposition of Kristeva's concern with ethics in her early writings on language and it paves the way for a more careful consideration of the core of a Kristevan ethics, which, as I will demonstrate, is derived from her wider psychoanalytic thought. My second task in this chapter is to revisit Kristeva's conception of a maternal ethics, and to assess some of the feminist responses to it. Following this, I assess Kristeva's recent writings and their ethical linkages. Specifically, I want to engage with Kristeva's ideas for recent feminist discussions on violence, vulnerability and forgiveness. This thematic focus relates back to the discussion of revolt in the previous chapter, but it also points towards Kristeva's engagement with Hannah Arendt (see Chapter 4), with cosmopolitanism and migration, and with violence, terrorism and the 'particular other' in the figure of the Muslim (see Chapter 5). This discussion leads to a consideration of questions of forgiveness and to the wider role of psychoanalysis in Kristeva's ethics.

An Ethics of Traversal

Much of feminism's critical engagement with Kristeva has concentrated on her theory of a maternal ethics (see next section); yet it is necessary to recall that her concern with ethics is already embedded in her theory of language, articulated in some of her early writings on semiotics (see Kristeva 1969a; 1969b; 1973a) and in some of the essays published in *Desire in Language*. There, she calls for an ethics that builds upon the heterogeneity of the subject, and that draws on the subject's relationship with the other. Such an ethics is underpinned by Kristeva's commitment to the subject-in-process, and it is juxtaposed to morality, defined as a rigid code that runs counter to the idea of fluidity. Whilst the thematic application of her ethics broadens in later works, including her consideration of maternity and her concern over questions of the nation and migration, it is in these early writings that Kristeva outlines some of the key elements that continue to shape her ethical thought into the present. At the centre of this early ethical thought is her concern for the pulverisation or shattering of discourse, and of the flow of semiotic drive energy and rhythm into the symbolic (*DL*: 24). In other words, it articulates the significance that Kristeva accords to the heterogeneity of discourse and of the subject. This is an important point to make, because it establishes the parameters of Kristeva's ethical thought, and I would therefore suggest that any consideration of Kristeva's ethics needs to be mindful of this emphasis on heterogeneity. It also has two important implications: it establishes difference or otherness within the subject (I return to this point towards the end of this section), while it also articulates the wider aim of her ethics, which is to work towards establishing a relationship with the other.

These two elements, pertaining to the other within and to the relationship with the other, have led Ewa Ziarek to characterise Kristeva's thought as a 'heterology', which she defines, broadly, as an attempt, located mainly in Nietzschean and neo-Nietzschean philosophy, to think otherness (1992: 102). In her essay 'At the Limits of Discourse: Heterogeneity, Alterity, and the Maternal Body in Kristeva's Thought' (1992), Ziarek explores this idea of otherness with respect to Kristeva's discourse on maternity, but she also points up some of its underlying philosophical commitments that help to clarify, in my view, Kristeva's notion of heterogeneity and the attendant feminist concerns over the status of culture and the pre-cultural (see Chapter 1). As Ziarek suggests, heterogeneity refers to an infolding of body and language, and of the two signifying economies, the semiotic and the symbolic. Following Ziarek, I would suggest that this emphasis on heterogeneity and alterity has important and useful implications for radical theorising. For one, it challenges any attempt towards closure, in line with Kristeva's emphasis on process, keeping open the generation of subject and signification. This, essentially futural, conception of the subject is underscored by its always precarious relationship with corporeality and meaning, and their respective articulation.

Ziarek broadens the potential uses of Kristeva's ethics in her *An Ethics of Dissensus* (2001). There, she makes the case for an ethics that extends beyond care ethics and, more generally, beyond a normatively rigid account associated with morality. This opposition to morality is invoked in Ziarek's appeal to the notion of dissensus, a term that emphasises the contested nature of ethics, as opposed to morality; 'dissensus' also evokes the dual reference points of meaning and sensibility. In addition, Ziarek stresses ethics' carnal dimension, the necessity to consider questions of corporeality, and she concludes that such an ethics must, by definition, engage with racial and sexual differences. The terrain mapped out by Ziarek for such an ethics brings her to a discussion of Kristeva (who is also the subject of one of the chapters in Ziarek's book), given the importance accorded to corporeality and sensibility, meaning and language in Kristeva's ideas on ethics. Ziarek's orientation points are helpful in delineating Kristeva's ethical terrain, which include, as we have already seen, a concern with language, but also and in particular a psychoanalytic underpinning of ethics. At the centre of this psychoanalytically informed ethics, Ziarek avers, lie three psychic modalities: fantasy, abjection and the sublimation of the death drive (more on this below), which require the subject to come to terms with its own otherness. According to Ziarek, the subject's attempt to deal with the assertion, essentially ideological, of the coherence of the social order, a fantasy of fullness, can only be maintained at the cost of the expulsion and abjection of the sexualised and racialised Other. Such a traversal of fantasy requires the subject to confront its own abjection as interiorised, the Other within, in order to offset its always precarious and unstable imaginary and symbolic identifications

Corporeal Ethics

(2001: 132). Thus, the traversal of fantasy, sublimation and the encounter with the abject articulate what Ziarek considers to be Kristeva's account of the subject's 'unsettling heterogeneity': 'the acknowledgment of the internal alterity and antagonism within the subject' (2001: 127).

It is against this background that I want to describe Kristeva's ethics as an ethics of traversal.[4] To flesh this out further, the idea of traversal, and its ethical dimension, draws on the various elements of traversal that make up Kristeva's philosophy. These include a movement between affect and signification, between the semiotic and the symbolic, between the feminine and masculine, between body and discourse. This idea of traversal, or threshold, has also been highlighted by Noëlle McAfee, who points up Kristeva's contribution towards a thinking of how affective and somatic forces enter into language and culture, traversing the threshold between the pre-discursive and the discursive. Such a threshold, according to McAfee, is central to any theory of intersubjectivity; it is particularly pertinent to Kristeva's thought, given her stress on the heterogeneity of the subject, where difference and otherness are located within the subject (2005: 113–14).

Thus, building upon Kristeva's early work, which places a particular emphasis on the work of negativity in the operation of ethics and which provokes a shattering of established codes and a renewal of symbolic systems, I would identify her concern for the other, her insistence on heterogeneity and her practice of traversal as the key themes of Kristeva's ethics. These reveal themselves through her assertion of an intersubjectivity that is constituted and experienced corporeally. Moreover, this insistence on the importance of corporeality and signification operates in the wider field of sexual difference, of the feminine and the masculine, and, as we will see in the next section, it is fleshed out via her discussion of the maternal body.

Maternal Bodies, Herethics and the Feminine

The idea of an ethics of traversal is famously captured in Kristeva's discussion of maternity and of the maternal body. If motherhood, according to Kristeva, poses a challenge for representation (see below), it also raises the question of a new ethics, which Kristeva refers to as 'herethics', a pun on 'her ethics' and 'heretics' that refers to the transgression of the rigid moral codes associated with the paternal-masculine symbolic (see Kristeva 1977a).[5] This herethics encapsulates the ethical function of the maternal body as a bodily threshold, which establishes a relationship with the other whilst oscillating between the semiotic and the symbolic. Kristeva's idea of a maternal ethics, which draws upon some of her well-known essays, such as 'Stabat Mater' (1977a), 'Women's Time' (1979) and 'Motherhood according to Bellini' (included in *Desire in Language*, 1980), has received substantial critical attention within feminism. With these texts, Kristeva aims to initiate a discourse on motherhood that, in her view, is missing in feminism and, more generally, in Western discourses of representation (see 1977a; see also 2001c). Here I want to recapitulate some of Kristeva's key premises and the debates surrounding a Kristevan ethics, which have been central to the wider feminist engagement with Kristeva's thought. I want to suggest that the idea of an ethics of traversal, which I introduced in the previous section, is epitomised in the maternal body; central to this undertaking is Kristeva's insistence that ethics is grounded in corporeality.

As I discussed previously, Kristeva's important work on corporeality, including her assertion of the ethical dimension of corporeal bonds, and her stress on the centrality of abjection to the process of subjectification, has occupied much of the feminist engagement with her work. The significance of motherhood as a theme in Kristeva's writings is well known; it originates in her early work, such as *Revolution in Poetic Language*, where she establishes the maternal body, and with it the *chora*, as a reference point for the child's psycho-linguistic development, and it weaves its way through some of her most recent publications (see Chapter 1). This importance accorded to motherhood is part of Kristeva's wider contribution to psychoanalysis, which puts forward a narrative of the intersubjective relationships between the three protagonists of the Oedipal triangle (see Chapter 2). For the purpose of my argument it is important to identify a second source of Kristeva's interest in motherhood: this is her interpretation of feminism, which she criticises for its neglect of the importance of maternity. She outlines this critique in her essay 'Women's Time' (1979; see also 1977a), where she develops her account of motherhood out of her critique of the first two generations of feminism. These, according to Kristeva, regarded women's desire to be a mother as 'alienating and reactionary' (1979: 205). The alleged hostility of the first and second generations of feminists arose, according to Kristeva, out of their respective concerns with different sets of issues, pertaining to struggles for equality in the case of the first (and existentialist) generation, and the building of a female counter-symbolic in the case of the second generation (see Chapter 1). While Kristeva takes feminism to task for failing to consider women's maternal desires more fully, she hopes that a third generation will contribute to the initiation of such a discourse. Its concern should lie with the recognition of sexual difference, of which motherhood is one aspect, and with the development of a theoretical discourse on the maternal.

Kristeva's critique of the first and second generations of feminism is indicative of her wider engagement with feminism: apart from her allusion to existential feminism and its alleged hostility towards motherhood, which, without actually mentioning her, points to Simone de Beauvoir's critique of motherhood's grounding in a patriarchal context that retains women in a condition of immanence (see de Beauvoir 2009). Kristeva does not provide a detailed analysis of feminism's engagement with motherhood, but, notwithstanding her rather one-sided characterisation of feminism's position regarding motherhood, it is important to acknowledge the context of her emphasis on motherhood, as this goes some way towards explaining her ideas on maternity. Thus, a more generous interpretation might overlook the scholarly (and indeed political) shortcomings of her writings on feminism and motherhood, stressing instead her effort to counterbalance a perceived deficiency in feminist discourses on motherhood. Key to her own work on maternity, and to the feminist responses to it, is the question of the centrality of motherhood to a woman's life, which, as I will illustrate, has generated substantial discontent amongst her feminist critics.

In one of her interviews, Kristeva qualifies the importance of motherhood to a woman's life by maintaining that motherhood should not be women's exclusive domain. Work, a husband or lovers constitute potential supplements to the child (1984d). Besides, motherhood, according to Kristeva, could be understood in a non-literal sense. Asked whether a woman who chooses not have children is incomplete, Kristeva responds by advocating a 'symbolic maternity', which can be found, for example, in the teaching and caring professions, and also in a woman's personal life. Such a stress on 'symbolic maternity' is said to allow for the necessary deflection of drives on to an other, by transforming biology into signification, representation, language and thought (*Revolt*: 69–70). It is this latter aspect, the ethical encounter with the other, which is particularly important to Kristeva's conception of motherhood. This emphasis should put at ease those critics who accuse her of relegating motherhood to the only socially recognised activity in a masculine-defined symbolic order. However, even though she supports women's professional aspirations, she wonders whether women's 'double shift' of working and caring is sustainable (*Revolt*: 70). Worryingly, this concern does not lead her to rethink women's double burden by considering, for example, a redistribution of parental responsibilities or the wider sexual division of labour in the home. Although Kristeva concedes that both sexes could be involved in nurturing and separating (she is reluctant to consider the prospect of same-sex parenting, even though, as we have seen in the previous chapter, she evacuates, in *The Sense and Non-Sense of Revolt*, the triangular Oedipal structure from its heterosexual content), she fears a 'decimation' of the paternal function and the subsequent emergence of borderline children, a concern that ties in with her wider assertion of a crisis of authority (see Chapter 2).

If the paternal function is diminished, she suggests that institutions outside the family, such as the school or even the psychoanalyst, need to take over in order to ensure the child's separation from the mother and its insertion into sociality. As she ponders, 'if fathers become mothers, one may well ask oneself who will play the role of separators' (1996a: 118–19)?[6] Although not developed by Kristeva, such a displacement of the paternal function opens up the possibility of rethinking the function of sexual difference, and with it the connotation of the feminine and the masculine. In other words, is the paternal function exclusively associated with the masculine or male? Can mothers occupy the paternal function? And how is the paternal function allocated in non-heterosexual parenting arrangements? It is fair to say that Kristeva's scepticism towards alternative kinship structures beyond the heterosexual core family fails to resolve the question of the positioning of the paternal and maternal in a more radical way; it also fails to address the unequal distribution of domestic and emotional labour within the (heterosexual) home, which does not generates a rethinking of women in their traditional gender roles, connected, in the main, with motherhood.

Beyond such sociological concerns, Kristeva conceptualises motherhood as a borderline experience that oscillates between the semiotic and the symbolic, constantly transgressing the boundaries between these two signifying systems. She is at pains to emphasise mothers' essential contribution to the symbolic, their 'civilizing function' (*Crisis*: 105; see also 1977a: 183; 1996a: 10), which requires them to prepare the child for entry into the symbolic (see Chapter 1). Thus, according to Kristeva, women are connected to the symbolic in two ways: as speaking beings (see Chapter 1), and as mothers, who are tasked with '[passing] on the social norm, which one might repudiate for one's own sake but within which *one must* include the child in order to educate it along the chain of generations' (1977a: 183; italics in original). An individual woman might reject the social order for herself, but by becoming a mother she is connected to the socio-symbolic order, which she reproduces and guarantees through her contribution to the child's preparation for the rule of the law.

As Allison Weir asserts, motherhood ensures participation in the symbolic order while simultaneously maintaining women's heterogeneity; in doing so, it helps women to circumvent the fate of phallicism, being tied to the Law of the Father, but also disrupts women's exclusive association with the semiotic *chora*, and their representation as biological creatures exclusively destined for procreation (1993: 89). This importance accorded to heterogeneity, which, as I argued in the first chapter, is crucial to Kristeva's notion of the speaking subject, further unfolds in the experience of motherhood, which is also an inherently ethical experience, because it helps a woman to establish a relationship with an other:

> [W]ith the arrival of the child and the start of love (perhaps the only true love of a woman for another person ...), the woman gains the chance to form that relationship with the symbolic and ethic Other so difficult to achieve for a woman. ... [M]aternity is a bridge between singularity and ethics. Through the events of her life, a woman finds herself at the pivot of sociality – she is at once the guarantee and the threat to its stability. (1977b: 297; see also *Crisis*: 105–6)

According to Kristeva, at the heart of a woman's desire for a child lies a wish for unity and completeness. However, to prevent a descent into psychotic fusion, the symbolic must intervene. Thus, women's attachment to the Law upholds their connection with the symbolic order and constitutes a safeguard against a psychotic fusion with the child. Moreover, if pregnancy and motherhood threaten a woman with psychotic fusion in her relationship with the foetus and the child, they also provide a woman with the unique chance to enter into a renewed relationship with her own mother:

> Such an excursion to the limits of primal regression can be phantasmatically experienced as the reunion of a woman-mother with the body of *her* mother. The body of her mother is always the same Master-Mother of instinctual drive, a ruler over psychosis, a subject of biology, but also, one toward which women aspire all the more passionately simply because it lacks a penis: that body cannot penetrate her as can a man when possessing his wife. By giving birth, the woman enters into contact with her mother; she becomes, she is her own mother; they are the same continuity differentiating itself. (*DL*: 23)

Yet, unlike, for example, Irigaray (1993), Kristeva does not pursue the prospect that an ethical relationship with the mother brings to the development of a female genealogy; motherhood, for her, is a singular experience that does not translate into collective action. Neither does she translate her account of motherhood into maternal political practice, as, for example, maternal feminists such as Sara Ruddick (1989) have attempted to do. At the core of Kristeva's account of motherhood lies her emphasis on the radical and heretical nature of ethics, which requires the contribution of women. This maternal ethics, as indeed the feminine ethics more widely, is conceptualised as a transgressive practice that challenges and subverts the masculine symbolic order; hence, it is also juxtaposed against the allegedly masculine sphere of politics, characterised by its association with the symbolic and its neglect of the corporeal and affective dimensions of human life. Diagnosing the implications for women's political participation, Kristeva asserts that '[w]e cannot gain access to . . . political affairs, except by identifying with the values considered to be masculine (dominance, superego, the endorsed communicative word that institutes stable social exchange)' (CW: 37). Although it is crucial to re-emphasise that Kristeva is sympathetic to the political achievements of feminism, she is reluctant to connect (feminist) politics, always coded as masculine and symbolic, with the heterogeneity of a feminine ethics. This disconnect between politics and ethics may account for the absence of a more widespread engagement with Kristeva's ethical thought in the wider feminist scholarship on ethics. However, it has also received substantial criticism from those who did engage more fully with her ethical thought. I have already alluded to the critical reception of Kristeva's writings on motherhood and here I want to give this aspect more attention, by concentrating on three well-known critics, Nancy Fraser, Judith Butler and Drucilla Cornell.

Nancy Fraser regards Kristeva's emphasis on the maternal as proof of her conservatism and her affirmation of traditional gender roles, and she criticises Kristeva's alleged 'essentialising identification of women's femininity with maternity':

> Maternity, for [Kristeva], is the way that women, as opposed to men, touch base with the pre-Oedipal, semiotic residue. (Men do it by writing avant-garde poetry; women do it by having babies.) Here, Kristeva dehistoricises and psychologises motherhood, conflating conception, pregnancy, birthing, nursing, and childrearing, abstracting all of them from socio-political context, and erecting her own stereotype of femininity. (1992b: 190)

While Fraser, in my view, does not give due consideration to the importance that traversal and heterogeneity have in Kristeva's discussion of maternity, I would nevertheless concur with some of her reservations, specifically with her critique of Kristeva's decontextualisation of the experience of motherhood that does not acknowledge the range of different maternal experiences and that, I would add, is at odds with her insistence on plurality (see Chapter 4). Butler's critique of Kristeva's emphasis on the maternal juxtaposes the need for subversive cultural practices with Kristeva's emphasis on the maternal, and she contends that 'for Kristeva, poetry and maternity represent privileged practices within paternally sanctioned culture which permit a non-psychotic experience of that heterogeneity and dependency characteristic of the maternal terrain' (1990: 85). Butler takes particular issue with Kristeva's notion of the maternal body, which, according to Butler, together with the drives, the feminine and the semiotic, is posited as pre-cultural or natural. However, as I argued in Chapter 1, neither the (maternal) body nor (maternal) drives are unambiguously 'natural' for Kristeva; rather, they oscillate between the semiotic and the symbolic, and point to the heterogeneity of the subject.

Drucilla Cornell's (1991) analysis, while more sympathetic towards Kristeva than that of Fraser or Butler, is just as critical of the ethical implications of Kristeva's account of maternity and the maternal body. She recognises maternity's importance to feminism, because it is said to illustrate the subject's heterogeneity and irreducible alterity (see also Ziarek 1992). The feminist turn to the maternal realm, according to Cornell, is said to help uncover 'the irreducibility of the feminine as a basis for a shared female identity and also for an expression of the potential within womanliness as it is lived' (1991: 21). Such a turn towards the maternal, following Cornell, can be found in Kristeva's writings. However, she diagnoses a tension in Kristeva's writings between her work on semiotics and on maternity, which, according to Cornell, has 'ultimately been resolved in favour of the "conservative" position that rejects the value of the fantasy figure of the phallic mother as the only way to express the repression of the feminine' (1991: 22).

Cornell's critique draws on a perceived shift between Kristeva's early writings, said to invoke the phantasmatic connection between woman and Woman, between empirical women and the feminine, and a later account that, in Cornell's words, is 'obsessed with [Kristeva's] desire for the Law' (1991: 37) (see also Rose 1993). Cornell appraises Kristeva's account against what she terms 'ethical feminism', based on a futural construction of women, 'not on what women "are", but on the remembrance of the "not yet"' (1993: 59). In doing so, it draws on imagination, not description, on 'should be' and not on 'is' (see also Cornell 1995). Central to Cornell's critique of Kristeva is her claim that Kristeva, especially in her later works, collapses the feminine with empirical motherhood. While Cornell applauds Kristeva's challenge to Freud's notion that motherhood constitutes woman's accomplishment of the Oedipal crisis, advocating instead the possibility of a relation to the Other/the Mother/the child, this is said to be undermined by Kristeva's failure to hold on to the radical promise of the feminine as, potentially, other than the mother. As Cornell suggests, 'the later Kristeva can only save women by forsaking Woman' (1991: 72). This critique of Kristeva ties in with Cornell's wider attempts to free the feminine from the stranglehold of a gender hierarchy that is configured by what Butler terms a 'heterosexual matrix' (see Butler 1990), where both the feminine and the masculine are defined in accordance with heterosexual desire. Against such a move, Cornell envisages the feminine as essentially a metaphor of the other, rather than a gendered signifier in a system of sexual difference where the feminine comes to stand for 'not man' (1995: 75).

As I already argued, there are moments in Kristeva's writings that evoke such a meaning of the feminine and that chime strongly with Cornell's vision of an ethical feminism. Moreover, these moments are not, as Cornell seems to suggest, restricted to the early Kristeva; rather, they are interspersed throughout her writings, including some of her recent work on the female genius (see 2001a; 2001b; 2004c; see also Chapter 4). This recent work also challenges a further concern of Cornell's: namely, that Kristeva only ever ends up construing the feminine as the maternal, by emphasising more strongly female creation above and beyond motherhood (though it also, as I demonstrate in the next chapter, evokes the maternal). Furthermore, I also have reservations about Cornell's vision of linking the irreducible feminine to a 'shared female identity' (see above); such a linkage seems to me at odds with Kristeva's persistent challenge to identitarian logic. However, like Cornell (and indeed Fraser), I remain uncomfortable with Kristeva's wider assertions about maternity and ethics. Clearly, there is a radical account of heterogeneity at the heart of her discussion (see Ziarek 1992), which, furthermore, connects, albeit always temporarily and in a fragile bond, the corporeal with signification and representation. Yet, it is difficult to see how this radical philosophy of feminine heterogeneity, on which Kristeva's ethics is based, translates into (feminist) political efficacy. As I will illustrate in the next section, it is in the field of politics that Kristeva's feminine ethics takes a further problematic turn.

Violence and Vulnerability

While motherhood constitutes a significant reference point of a Kristevan ethics and its reception within feminism, I want to suggest that her writings pose a more fundamental ethical question: namely, that of violence, its constitutive role in the generation of the subject, and its manifestation in our relationships with (gendered and racial) others. Some of these ideas have been presented in *Strangers to Ourselves*, where Kristeva discusses the role of violence in the relationship between foreigner and political community; however, her assertion of the foundational role of violence can be traced back to her writings of the early 1970s, such as *Revolution in Poetic Language*, which draws on anthropological notions of sacrifice and on psychoanalytic notions of expulsion, separation and the theory of drives. These ideas also influence her subsequent engagement with violence, such as her discussion of abjection and her deployment of the Freudian notion of melancholia. In this section I will briefly sketch these ideas, but my main task is to attend to Kristeva's more recent consideration of the role of women as agents of violence, which is set in the context of the Middle East conflict. This focus is of particular interest, I believe, because it supplements a widespread, and necessary, focus within feminist ethics on women as victims of violence with an account of women as agents of violence. Furthermore, it illustrates some of the problems that emerge in the application of Kristeva's ethics on to politics. It also, as I suggest below, opens up a wider discussion on what I want to refer to as an ethics of forgiveness and an ethics of living. (I will discuss these in the last section of this chapter.) Separating these three components of Kristeva's ethical thought serves merely analytical and heuristic purposes; to gain a comprehensive understanding of Kristeva's ethics they need to be thought together. They also inform some of the questions that I pursue in Chapters 4 and 5.

I already stated that a concern with otherness sits at the heart of Kristeva's ethical project; this concern is underpinned by her adherence to a philosophical anthropology that posits violence as a fundamental feature of human life. It emanates from the violence of the drives, specifically the death drive, and it establishes the susceptibility of human life to vulnerability, which manifests itself, in the first instance, in the subject's fundamental dependency upon

Corporeal Ethics

an other. Violence and vulnerability constitute, paradoxically, the parameters that enable our existence, but they also pose threats and limits to human life. Kristeva's assertion of the centrality of violence builds upon anthropological claims regarding the role of sacrifice in the foundation of society (see Girard 1977; Reineke 1997), and, more specifically, on Freud's anthropological narrative of the social contract and his theory of drives. Recall that Freud, in *Totem and Taboo*, posits the murder of the father by the horde of brothers, and the displacement of the father's authority on the totemic object, as the beginning of sociality. Kristeva subscribes to these basic premises – though I will argue below that she also substantially adds to them – by stating that the sacrificial murder (of the father) initiates the socio-symbolic order. As she claims, sacrifice has 'an ambiguous function, simultaneously violent and regulatory' (*RPL*: 75). It is a violent act that ends semiotic violence, embodied in the uncontrolled flow of the drives, and that displaces this uncontrolled violence on to the symbolic. In Kristeva's own words, 'Far from unleashing violence, sacrifice shows how representing that violence is enough to stop it and to concatenate an order' (*RPL*: 75). At first glance, Kristeva's retelling of Freud's story in *Revolution in Poetic Language* seems strangely gender-neutral, possibly a testament to her emphasis on the operation of drives in the pre-Oedipal child. However, as suggested by Reineke (1997), the narrative of sacrifice is embedded in a wider framework of sexual difference that is indispensable to understanding Kristeva's account. Her coding as masculine of the symbolic order that is said to emerge from this fraternal patricide goes some way towards redressing this (as I demonstrate below, she attends to this matter in *The Sense and Non-Sense of Revolt*).[7]

Thus, *Revolution in Poetic Language* deploys an essentially Freudian account of the foundational role played by violence in the formation of subject and society. Key to Kristeva's further discussion is the violence of the drive, enacted through the process of rejection that leads to the establishment of the subject. Following Kristeva's account, the previously uncontrolled and ungendered use of violence becomes masculine once this violence transmogrifies into the symbolic. Kristeva reaffirms her position on the foundational status of violence and vulnerability in a more recent text, where she claims that

> this *I* that speaks is unveiled to itself insofar as it is constructed in a vulnerable bond with a strange *object*, or an ec-static *other*, an ab-jet: *the sexual thing* ... This vulnerable bond to the sexual thing and in it ... is no different from the heterogeneous bond ... on which our languages and our discourses depend. (2009a: 22; italics in original)

Hence, vulnerability is written into the subject, both in its relations with the other in the present, via language and the social bond, and in the originary and constitutive process of abjection and rejection. Moreover, as Kristeva has argued consistently, with reference to her notion of abjection, we remain vulnerable because we are constituted via the other, the thing. I will return to the idea of the violence of the drives in the next chapter, but for now I want to continue my survey of Kristeva's narrative of violence.

Out of Kristeva's wider œuvre, it is possibly *Powers of Horror* that is most widely associated with her claim about the foundational status of violence. As I demonstrated in Chapter 1, the expulsion of what is in between, through a process Kristeva terms 'abjection', becomes crucial to the establishment of bodily boundaries. Recounting the process of abjection, Kristeva provides a story of individual subjectification that requires the expulsion of the parents and of bodily matters.[8] Moreover, as we have seen in the first chapter, while there is some dispute within the feminist commentary over the gendered nature of abjection, it raises the spectre of the violent expulsion of the mother and the maternal body. Hence, it is perhaps unsurprising that Kristeva asserts the necessity of another act of violence, that of matricide, as indispensable to the establishment of the subject (*BS*: 27).

Whereas abjection culminates in the, always provisional, violent expulsion and externalisation of what is considered as filth, melancholia attends to an inwardly turned aggression, an internalisation of the violence of the death drive that can lead to symbolic or real death. Described by Freud as a 'mental constellation of revolt' that emerges as a result of loss (1998b), melancholia attests to the interrelated production of psychic and social life, and the internalisation of a social prohibition into the psyche, leading to the establishment of conscience and to the emergence of the subject. While this theme has received little attention in the critical commentary on Kristeva, it has attracted substantial feminist interest. Wendy Brown (1995) considers how vulnerability, or injury, forms the basis for what she calls 'politicised identities'. According to Brown, the constitution and preservation of the identity of marginalised groups, such as women, are contingent upon their attachment to their own exclusion because, Brown claims, their identity is premised on this exclusion for its very existence as identity. As she states, 'the formation of identity at the site of exclusion, as exclusion . . . installs its pain over its unredeemed history in the very foundation of its political claim, in its demand for recognition as identity' (1995: 73–4). Developing Brown's point further, Moya Lloyd asks how loss and attachment can configure feminist politics. As Lloyd suggests,

> feminists are wedded to their identity as women even as that identity is grounded in subordination and injury. It is this that gives meaning to feminism as a marginalised political grouping even as it guarantees that very marginalisation. . . . In affirming one's identity, one affirms and reiterates the hurt that constitutes that identity in the first place. To let go of the hurt is to let go of identity and to risk dissolution. (1998–9: 41)

To put it simply: there can be no identity without subjection, injury or loss, and hence violence.[9] While both Brown and Lloyd account for the generation of feminist identity via political readings of injury and violence, Kristeva's focus on art and therapy (see Beardsworth 2004a), and its seemingly attendant individualistic slant (see McAfee 2000), foreclose such a reading.[10] At best, she can hope for an aesthetic outlet of the transformation of the violence of the drive; at worst, it results in the riots of the marginalised, those affected by the society of the spectacle (see Chapter 2).

Before I move on to consider a possible application of Kristeva's discussion of violence, I want to pause for a moment and reflect upon the implications of her discussion of violence. I want to suggest that Kristeva's account of violence is a radical one; putting violence at the origin of society has profound implications, for her narration of the subject and of social formations, including the family and society, as well as for her ethical project. Thus, violence is intrinsic to the subject, and for Kristeva, there is no escaping from it (see also Lechte and Margaroni 2004: 87). Besides, for her, the question of violence is not a normative one: that is, it is not a question of whether we ought or ought not to use violence.

Rather, what occupies her ethics is how the violence constitutive of the subject can be transformed into less violent or non-violent practices. I already alluded to one such example of a constructive transformation of original violence in the previous chapter, where I pointed up the transformative role of representation, in particular in its aesthetic manifestations, in the emergence of the subject. Yet, it is also fair to state that Kristeva's overall assessment of the potential for representation is rather pessimistic. In her view, the effects of the society of the spectacle and the loss of authority in the modern world have substantially reduced the capacity for representation and have increased the risk of more violence; this becomes aggravated by the violence of the image, which she associates with the spectacle, and which further diminishes the subject's capacity to reconstruct its imaginary.[11]

I already raised the question whether Kristeva's account of violence is gendered, or, more generally, what the gendered dimension of her discussion of violence is. We have seen that an original violence, which emanates from the operation of the drives, exists prior to any conception of gender or sexual difference. Yet, the sacrifice that initiates society also founds a gendered order, a 'sexual contract' (Pateman 1988) that codes that order and its violence as masculine. By extension, the feminine becomes antithetical to violence, and this assertion also informs Kristeva's further claims about women's relationship to violence and violent acts. Such an equivalence between the feminine and non-violence is a fundamental assertion of much of feminist ethics; it underpins in particular feminist care ethics, and it also informs many debates in international relations, which have recently been challenged by feminist scholars (see Sjoberg and Gentry 2008). Here I want to turn to a recent development in Kristeva's writings, her response to the crisis in the Middle East, which offers further insight into her perspective on violence.

If a consideration of fascism accompanies Kristeva's psycho-social analysis of abjection, then her most recent writings turn on some pressing current political issues, most prominently the problem of (Islamic) terrorism, Islamic fundamentalism and the conflict in the Middle East. Kristeva's engagement with these issues is an intriguing one, especially in light of the gendered narrative that runs through her story and that connects this most recent work with some of her early writings on feminism. The violence

Corporeal Ethics

associated with global events surrounding 9/11 and the West's strategy of embarking upon a so-called 'war on terror' have occupied much of feminist discussion in this last decade. What these debates illustrate is that violence and vulnerability are not merely ontological conditions that configure the subject's existence; they are also brought upon us through others and they are distributed unevenly across racial and gendered divides (see Butler 2004; 2009).

Here it is worth exploring Kristeva's essay 'Can We Make Peace?' (2007a),[12] in which she reasserts her claim of an original violence, embodied in the workings of the death drive. This essay, originally a chapter from *La Haine et le pardon* (2005b), the third volume of her series on revolt, positions her psychoanalytic, philosophical and literary discussions of the first two revolt volumes in the context of the events in the wake of 9/11. While Kristeva, faithful to psychoanalytic thought, posits the operation of an original violence, she also seeks answers as to how to deal with it. Building upon her previous discussion, she finds the answer to this question in a strengthening of the imaginary, including analytic and aesthetic practices, as well as in an adherence to freedom (more on this below). The context for her discussion is her assertion of the need for a discourse on life on the one hand, and her concern with the political crisis in the Middle East on the other. Kristeva claims that peace is in crisis because we lack a discourse on human life.

While Kristeva connects this crisis with the regime of the spectacle already discussed (see Chapter 2), she suggests that this crisis manifests itself most clearly in a culture of death[13] that she ascribes to 'Muslim fundamentalist intransigence' (2007a: 124) and terrorism following 9/11. The explanation for violence provided by Kristeva is thus psychoanalytical on the one hand, but it also points to what is essentially described as a deeply entrenched violence of Muslim fundamentalism and what lacks any social, historical, political or economic reference points. She introduces a further dimension into her discussion, which displaces original violence even further, this time on female suicide bombers, or *shahidas*. I will further comment on her engagement with Islam in Chapter 5. For now, I want to focus on her exploration of a specifically female form of violence that she locates in the practices of so-called *shahidas*, female Palestinian suicide bombers. Here it is worth quoting Kristeva at length, as this, I believe, illuminates

105

a fundamental problematic in her approach, which, as I stated above, abstracts from context. *Shahidas*, according to Kristeva, are 'originally destined for procreation' (she supplements with reference to Arendt's distinction between bios and zoon); they are then 'sent off to sacrifice and martyrdom in imitation of the warlike man and possessor of power'. Moreover, prior to their suicidal act, they are alleged to have experienced 'amorous disasters', such as 'pregnancy outside marriage, sterility, desire for phallic equality with the man' (all references are from 2007a: 125). In short, *shahidas* are Muslim women whose life-stories, prior to their suicidal act, are said to depart from the cultural and religious expectations of their society.

Overall, it is fair to say that this essay engages in a crude generalisation that reduces complex political, ethical and cultural constellations to a question of personal tragedy, without considering the social and political contexts that generate violence; this displacement of politics on to an implicit gendered ethics is compounded by her failure to reflect on the variety of individual histories and motivations. Besides, reading Kristeva's characterisation of twenty-first-century *shahidas*, one is reminded of her depiction, in the texts from the 1970s, of the equally phallic feminist or terrorist sisters in Europe who are juxtaposed to the third-generation feminists aiming to establish the feminine. From an ethical perspective, the problem lies with a disregard of female difference and the concomitant disregard of zoon or life. Her ethics of non-violence is mapped upon a sociological account of gender and a normative conception of the feminine. If the feminisation of the foreigner, as Ziarek (2005) and Ahmed (2005) have demonstrated, constitutes one aspect of Kristeva's ethics, then it is the masculinisation of feminists and *shahidas* that stands in the way of an ethic on the other hand.

Thus, it is a rather disappointing account that lacks in social-historical analysis, relying instead on commonplace assertions and generalisations (see also Chapter 5). Moreover, it returns to the now familiar argument of the 'failure' of some women to succumb to their femininity and become masculinised. I have already commented on Kristeva's treatment of feminism in some of her texts from the 1970s, where she describes politically active women, in particular those women who seek full equality within the framework of the symbolic, including feminists, as virile, phallic, masculine and homosexual. This negative characterisation accorded to feminists, female politicians and female terrorists in the 1970s is now given to the *shahidas*. Thus, Kristeva offers a rather disturbing and facile characterisation of these women, without providing the necessary socio-cultural or historical reference points. This, I want to suggest, hinders any serious understanding of such a sensitive issue. It also impedes efforts to articulate more fully the psyche with the social. At least in this instance, Kristeva's 'psychic life of ethics' (see Ziarek 2001), which takes seriously one's ethical obligation towards the other and which reflects the heterogeneity and otherness within the subject, falls remarkably short of considering the social and political conditions of the emergence of violence.

Without referring to Kristeva, Cornell broaches this issue in a short piece, part of a wider feminist forum, published in the feminist philosophy journal *Hypatia* (2003), which seeks to establish feminist responses to 9/11. Cornell takes exception to what she considers a colonialist response to the situation in Afghanistan. Of interest to my discussion is a further claim, building upon psychoanalytic insights, which suggests that in the official discourses of Western governments, (male/Islamic) terrorism has become feminised. Moreover, this feminisation of terrorism is mirrored by what Iris Young refers to as a depiction of the masculinist protection dispensed by the security state (2003a; 2003b). This aspect has also recently been taken up by Adriana Cavarero (2009) and Kelly Oliver (2007a; see also Oliver 2007b; 2008; 2009a; 2009b), who suggest that any discussion of the violence of the *shahidas*, and of terrorism more generally, must also consider how violence, in its gendered manifestations, structures the dispensation of state violence. Thus, if in the official discourse of the West, the feminisation of non-state violence mirrors the masculinisation of state violence, then this gendered narrative continues into the analyses of the (gendered) actors who have recourse to violence. In this respect, the mirror image of the *shahidas* is those female soldiers who became associated with the widespread abuse in Abu Ghraib prison in Iraq, embodied most famously in the figure of Lyndsey England (see Oliver 2007a; 2007b).

I have yet to respond to the second point raised by Kristeva in her essay, which pertains to the question of life, the alleged lack of a discourse on life and the need for a new humanism. I turn to this point in the final section of this chapter, where I want to consider two immediate answers that Kristeva gives to the question of violence and that constitute further cornerstones of a Kristevan ethics: sublimation and forgiveness.

Sublimation, For-giveness and the Art of Living

Despite the persistence of violence and vulnerability, which, as we saw in the previous section, Kristeva posits as ontological conditions of the emergence of the human that come to frame the possibilities for ethical life, she does not give up on the prospect of a less violent world. As she claims, it is through forgiveness and sublimation that we establish a more constructive relationship with violence, and a less violent relationship with the other. Sublimation operates, in the first instance, through the transformation and displacement of drive energy, but it is also a form of work and working-through that requires psychoanalysis. Sara Beardsworth interprets Kristeva's concern with sublimation in the context of the latter's wider concern with crisis, and in particular with the absence of authority in the modern world (see Beardsworth 2004b). Sublimation allows the subject to work through this recognition of the absence of authority and, in doing so, facilitates the establishment of relationships not only with others, but also, and crucially, with oneself. It is here that the crux of Kristeva's ethics lies; it interweaves the inter- and intra-subjective relationship with the other. This relationship, as Beardsworth reminds us, includes a recognition of the irreducibility of otherness, including the alterity within (2004a: 132; see also Ziarek 2001), the central theme of Kristeva's *Strangers to Ourselves*. I return to a consideration of this book in the last chapter; for now, I want to take a closer look at Kristeva's discussion of forgiveness.

Forgiveness, for Kristeva, manifests itself in two related ways: love and transference. Already in *Black Sun*, Kristeva explores the significance of forgiveness, against the backdrop of melancholic suffering and the prospect of the atoning qualities of art. Primarily, though, forgiveness plays itself out in psychoanalytic categories, specifically in the giving of transferential love and the identification with the imaginary father or, more generally, 'an other who does not judge but hears my truth in the availability of love' (*BS*: 205) and who allows the depressed patient to begin anew, to commence a rebirth. (I return to the idea of birth and new beginnings in Chapter 4.) Kristeva pays renewed attention to forgiveness in her work on revolt, especially in *Intimate Revolt*, where she stresses the instrumental role of intimate revolt for channelling violence into liveable forms (see Chapter 2). It is worth explicating these ideas in some detail.

Whilst she states at the outset of her discussion on forgiveness in *Intimate Revolt* that forgiveness is not a psychoanalytic concept (*IR*: 14), she nevertheless establishes the idea of forgiveness firmly within psychoanalytic parameters (see also Chapter 4). Contrasting psychoanalysis with those discourses of forgiveness that are said to posit an evil requiring forgiveness external to the subject, she believes that psychoanalysis locates the guilt that is concomitant to forgiveness in the interior of the subject: to be precise, in the process of subjectification. What does this mean? Freudian theory, like the philosophy of Heidegger that Kristeva utilises in her discussion of forgiveness, posits a guilt that is coexistent with being. For Heidegger, this guilt arises from the mere fact of *Dasein*, from the fact that we are thrown into the world, whereas Freud delineates guilt in the establishment of the psychic apparatus. Guilt, according to Kristeva's reading of Freud, is internal to the structure of consciousness; it follows the internalisation of the paternal law, with its set of prohibitions, and the regulation and ordering of drives and affect that divide the psychic apparatus into consciousness and the unconscious. In essence, what will require forgiveness is associated with the re-emergence of the drives, especially the violence associated with the drives, and with their clash with conscience. Hence, the violence emanating from the drives, whilst under the control of consciousness and the super-ego, tends to resurface and needs to be channelled into non-violent forms. For Kristeva, it is not violence as such that causes hurt and that makes us vulnerable; rather, injury and vulnerability emerge whenever violence collides with conscience and consciousness. Thus, the generation of a condition that requires forgiveness is an ontological condition of human life, an ontological guilt.

However, while guilt is preceded by a primordial violence, it also entails the condition for forgiveness and thus ethics. For one, the ontological status of violence posited by Kristeva removes or displaces the notion of the victim, and the distinction between victim and perpetrator: 'we are all guilty, we are all responsible.' It is crucial to stress that Kristeva's assertion pertains to the foundational status of guilt and its ethical function in our relationship, or debt, towards others. In that sense, the displacement of the notion of victim operates prior to, or outside, the possibility of an act of evil, which does not absolve responsibility for one's actions (see also below). Here it is again helpful to invoke Kristeva's discussion of Heidegger. Drawing on the German word for guilt, 'Schuld', Kristeva, following Heidegger, establishes the possible ethical connotations of guilt. 'Schuld', in German, has two meanings, guilt and debt; Kristeva connects these two meanings by claiming that the guilty person is a person in debt, specifically towards those who facilitate our *Dasein*. This guilt-debt that we owe others contains within it the seeds of forgiveness; because we owe a debt – that is, because we are, ontologically, guilty – our guilt-debt can be cancelled by the gift of the 'par-don', the giving of the gift of for-giveness.

Although situated in a structure that differs from Heidegger's philosophy, psychoanalysis operates according to similar principles. Psychic illness is caused by the inability to connect drive energy with meaning, and it is the collapse of meaning that is the most prominent symptom of those who are ill (see Oliver 2009b). The task of psychoanalysis is to restore the capacity for signification, primarily by forgiving the sense of guilt via transference love. This in itself, according to Kristeva, helps the analysand to love and forgive him- or herself, and to begin the process of recovery. At the core of this process lies the restructuring of the psychic apparatus, a revolt leading to a rebirth and the capacity to begin anew (see Chapter 4).

The ethical relationship at the centre of this process is that between analyst and analysand, but this relationship of love and forgiveness has wider applicability, allowing for the creation of what she terms 'a new, subjective and intersubjective configuration' (*IR*: 16). Analytic experience, via transference love, facilitates the construction of an ethical position; moreover, it facilitates the emergence or re-emergence of the capacity for revolt, through permanent inquiry; and finally, analysis allows the analysand to re-establish connections, both with the other and with oneself (*IR*: 236–7). Already in *Strangers to Ourselves*, Kristeva addresses this ethical dimension at the heart of the psychoanalytic enterprise. As she states towards the end of this text, psychoanalysis teaches us to recognise the other/the foreigner within me. This ethics of psychoanalysis, based upon transference love, acquires the status of a politics that builds upon a cosmopolitanism that, furthermore, recognises this unconscious (*StO*: 192).[14]

Moreover, despite Kristeva's insistence on the ahistorical and timeless nature of forgiveness, given the alleged archaic nature of the drive and imprint of the Other (*BS*: 204), it requires a confrontation with the social nature of consciousness and with the social norms that make up the paternal law. Besides, by recognising the fundamental, albeit potentially violent, role played by drives, forgiveness entails a recognition of embodiment, which, while ideally experienced in sublimatory aesthetic activity (see also *Black Sun*), is achieved in the representation of the violence of the drives. Crucially, though, as I already stated, forgiveness does not absolve responsibility: 'Forgiveness does not cleanse actions. It raises the unconscious from beneath the actions and has it meet a living other – an other who does not judge but hears my truth in the availability of love, and for that reason allows me to be reborn' (*BS*: 205).

If Kristeva's ethics displays, as I suggested at the beginning of this chapter, an orientation towards the other, it also contains a fundamental orientation towards the self. This orientation, as we have already seen, is the result of the operation of the drives, the crossing of the threshold between drive and signification, nature and culture, feminine and masculine. Here I want to address briefly a further aspect of Kristeva's thought, what we might term her ethics of the self, or what Kristeva herself calls the art of living. In the previous chapter, on revolt, I highlighted the etymological emphasis that Kristeva places on the notion of revolt, as a return to drive, memory and unconscious. This idea of the return also influences her ethics of the self, which is performed through the practice of revolt.

Psychoanalysis plays an essential role in this revolt, as it allows the subject to engage in this return via language and transference. As she develops this further, she establishes how such a revolt-cum-return facilitates a rebirth, generating the capacity for making lives and new beginnings (see Chapter 4), and how it facilitates a freedom realised via an ethos of questioning, a questioning attitude that she posits as inherently ethical (see also Chapter 5). Of relevance to my discussion here is a further dimension to this revolt-cum-return: her claim that this could constitute the foundation for a new humanism. Kristeva alludes to this claim briefly towards the end of *Intimate Revolt*, and she returns to it in her speech accepting the Holberg Prize (2005a) and in *La Haine et le pardon* (2005b). Already in *Intimate Revolt*, Kristeva claims that we lack a positive definition of humanity. Very briefly, she asserts that the base level of humanity should be hospitality, delineated by its association with ethos, as a habitat or resting place (*IR*: 257; see also 2004c: 25). Her discussion of humanity and hospitality relates back to her discussion of foreigners, where hospitality, and hence humanity, consists of welcoming the foreigner. It is in this 'ethical and philosophical horizon of a revision of the conception of the subject itself' (2009a: 22), against the encroaching of massification, of the spectacle and the patrimonial person, that Kristeva sees the emergence of a new form of humanity, embodied by its attention to singularity and life. Thus, Kristeva's insistence on heterogeneity, embodied in the traversal of the maternal body, and on the oscillation of the drive into signification, is given a more fundamental grounding in her attention to singularity, which I will discuss in Chapter 4.

Notes

1. See, for example, Gilligan (1982) and Held (2006). Sara Ruddick makes a brief reference to Kristeva, endorsing her stress on dissidence while simultaneously equating mothering with the principle of non-violence (1989: 225). Contributions by Kristeva are not included in Gatens (1998; 2002) or Frazer et al. (1992; she is listed in the bibliography, however).
2. Some of the most prominently discussed books, such as the works by Diprose (1994) and Gatens (2002), whilst broadly sympathetic towards post-structuralist thought, pay scant attention to Kristeva. Diprose, for example, engages closely with the works of Foucault and Irigaray, relegating Kristeva to one footnote and a brief consideration of one of her commentators, Graybeal (see Graybeal 1993).
3. Edelstein (1993) describes Kristeva as a postmodern ethicist pursuing a 'poléthique' that combines ethics with politics. However, as I will argue further below, Kristeva's reluctance to embrace politics more fully is in fact one of the reasons why this potential linkage between politics and ethics is never fully fleshed out.
4. For a related argument pertaining to Kristeva's practice of traversal

Corporeal Ethics

see also Rose (1993). Mary Ann Caws (1973) locates the idea of traversal within *Tel Quel*'s, and Kristeva's, subscription to the idea of the interdiscursive and intertextual.

5. Kelly Oliver (1993a) refers to it as an outlaw ethics.
6. It also highlights the importance of the father, and more generally, of the paternal function, for the development of the child's psychic health. The father is thus always present in Kristeva's writings, and this paternal presence manifests itself not only in the father's role as a separator, but also in the mother's need for the father, as father–husband–phallus and as the imaginary father; the mother–child relationship is thus not the only sexual relationship for Kristeva, as suggested by Grosz (1990: 94). For a more detailed assessment of the role of the father in Kristeva's writings see Oliver (1993a).
7. A different version of this story of violence and sacrifice has been told by Carole Pateman (1988), who asserts that the violence enacted by the brothers against the father establishes a fraternal contract that provides the brothers with access to women.
8. *Powers of Horror* also alludes to the collective operation of such an expulsion as a mass psychological process that underpins fascism. Kristeva's notion of abjection also plays a significant role in the theorisation of a racial social contract and the policing of the boundaries of the body politic. See Young (1990).
9. See also Butler's account (1997) of the subject's attachment to subordination, through guilt and injury, which is said to reaffirm the melancholic incorporation of subordination that produces the subject in the first place. For an alternative vision of feminism beyond the subject see Zerilli's account (2005), which I discuss in Chapter 5.
10. For further political readings of the inwardly turned violence of melancholia in the context of sexual and racial-colonial politics see Butler (1997) and Bhabha (1992).
11. For a more detailed discussion of the role of the image that also draws on Kristeva see Oliver (2009b).
12. This essay was originally delivered as a contribution to the Universal Academy of Cultures at UNESCO in 2002. There is some overlap with Chapter 14 of *Intimate Revolt*. See also Kristeva (2004a; 2009a).
13. The term 'culture of death' was coined by the late John Paul II in his encyclical letter *Evangelium Vitae* from 25 March 1995. The papal reference relates, in the main, to the Catholic Church's opposition

to abortion. The notion of a culture of death is also deployed by the New Right and conservative republicans in the United States. For a discussion that engages with the suicide bombings carried out by the *shahidas* see Victor (2004).
14. I return to this aspect in Chapter 5, where I proffer a more critical assessment of Kristeva's account of strangeness that draws upon recent critical readings of the racial subtext of her argument.

4

The Singularity of Genius

> In my feminist years, I entitled a piece about the difficulty of being a woman "Un*es* femme*s*": how to preserve each woman's uniqueness within the plurality of the group.
>
> (Kristeva 2001a: 184; italics in original)

In the conclusion to her book on Kristeva, Sara Beardsworth (2004a) takes Kristeva's 1980s trilogy to task for failing to explore how lives are made. This fault is said to originate in a gap between Kristeva's emphasis on art on the one hand, and on therapy on the other. While both art and therapy are said to constitute distinctive responses to the crisis experienced by modern subjects, they fail to elucidate, Beardsworth suggests, how people make lives. This gap, according to Beardsworth, is filled with Kristeva's genius trilogy,[1] whose linkage between life and narrative, and whose focus on the exemplarity of genius, provide answers to the problem of crisis that have occupied Kristeva in much of her work since the 1980s. Thus, it is in yet another trilogy, on female genius, that the concept of life, and in particular the connection between life and discourse, take centre-stage.

The lives explored in the genius trilogy are no ordinary lives, though. They encompass three prominent female intellectuals of the twentieth century: the German–Jewish philosopher, Hannah Arendt; the psychoanalyst Melanie Klein, also German–Jewish; and the French novelist Sidonie-Gabrielle Colette. What connects these three books, and with it the lives and writings of the women who are under discussion there, is the notion of genius. Genius, as Kristeva intimates in her introduction to the first volume of the trilogy, on Hannah Arendt, describes those whose life-story is closely connected with their intellectual creations (*HA*: xi; more on this below). Although Kristeva offers a distinctly individual attraction to account for her choice of Arendt, Klein and Colette, stressing the 'personal affinities' (*HA*: xv) she feels with these women, there is more to it than individual intellectual indulgence. Rather, reading through the books, it becomes clear that her affinity draws on a substantial thematic and biographical overlap with Kristeva's background, pertaining to the respective conceptual apparatus and methodologies of her chosen geniuses, as well as to their experiences of emigration, exile and marginality. I already intimated how Melanie Klein's psychoanalytic enterprise, especially her championing of the importance of the death drive, constitutes an important influence on the development of Kristeva's psychoanalytic thought (see Chapters 1 and 3); there are also obvious parallels between Colette's sensuous and sensual style of writing, Kristeva's emphasis on the semiotic dimension of language (see Chapter 1), and its impact on the intimate (see Chapter 2).

My focus in this chapter lies with Kristeva's engagement with Hannah Arendt.[2] While the genius trilogy as a whole awaits a comprehensive analysis in the critical commentary, I want to justify my emphasis on Arendt with my own affinity with some of Arendt's ideas, especially with her agonistic account of politics, which articulates original and novel perspectives on the question of identity politics (see Disch 1995; Honig 1995b; Zerilli 2005). Moreover, whereas the import of Kristeva to Arendtian ideas has recently received attention in the Arendt scholarship (see Birmingham 2003; 2005; 2006; see also Zakin 2009),[3] I believe that it will be of interest to turn this around and to inquire into Arendt's significance to Kristeva. Hence, one of my aims in this chapter is to provide a more detailed unpacking and discussion of Kristeva's work on Arendt, and to map an, albeit tentative, feminist interpretation of these writings.

Of course, Arendt was famously dismissive of what she termed 'the woman question' and she therefore seems an unlikely object for a feminist analysis, especially one that considers her impact on Kristeva and her relationship with feminism. Furthermore, Arendt's and Kristeva's respective reference points and frameworks, including their positioning vis-à-vis politics, as well as their relationship with psychoanalysis and embodiment, seem to put them at opposite ends of the spectrum of contemporary thought. And yet, as I hope to demonstrate here, Arendtian ideas obtain an increasing prominence in Kristeva's writings since the 1990s and they inform her current thinking on politics, philosophy and ethics (see also Chapter 5 on the notion of freedom and

The Singularity of Genius

Chapter 3 on ethics and responsibility). I believe that there is a further justification for such an analysis. As I have stated repeatedly, Kristeva's wider philosophical thought, together with her critical attitude towards politics, has complicated the feminist appropriation of her ideas, especially if we understand feminism as a project aimed at social and political transformation. Yet, as I seek to demonstrate in this chapter, it is via her engagement with Arendt's ideas, which entails both an appropriation of as well as a critical departure from Arendt's work, that we can begin to map a more coherent political philosophy that resonates with Kristeva's critique of identity and with her insistence on heterogeneity, and that contributes to the formulation of a Kristevan feminism. (I will continue this task in the next chapter.) Thus, I want to suggest that it is through the writings of Arendt that Kristeva's wider political ideas are advanced, albeit in a distinctly Kristevan direction. This chapter begins the task of delineating the contours of such a Kristevan political philosophy, despite or even against her own intentions, by sketching her critical engagement with Arendt's thought, which, as I demonstrate, evolves around the themes of singularity, plurality and natality, and which draws on the topics of narrative and life, embodiment, political bonds and totalitarianism.[4]

I wish to stress emphatically, though, that I do not seek to assess the accuracy or validity of Kristeva's Arendt interpretation. In this respect, my aims are more modest; I want to identify a number of 'crystallisations', Arendt's term for the emergence and materialisation of political events, that advance Kristeva's writings and ideas. Such an approach, I believe, will further elucidate the understanding of Kristeva's critique of feminism, and it will contribute to a continuation of feminist analyses of Kristeva's thought. Thus, whereas I engage with the import of Arendt's ideas and writings for Kristeva's recent thought, I am not concerned with Kristeva's contribution to the Arendt scholarship. This entails, by necessity, a rather generous oversight of Kristeva's occasionally disappointing engagement with Arendt, including her chronological and thematic exposition of Arendt's biography and well-known texts.[5] This omission allows me, on the other hand, to focus on Kristeva's critical interventions into Arendt's writings and to develop these in the direction of feminist thought. My overall interest in this chapter could thus be summed up as follows: what does Kristeva's engagement with Arendt add to Kristeva's thought? And how could it advance a feminist reading of Kristeva?

In the first section of this chapter I consider the influence of Romanticism on Kristeva's ideas, specifically Romanticism's import for the notion of genius. This discussion is followed by three sections on Kristeva's engagement with Hannah Arendt, which explore the themes of narrative, life and rebirth; the relationship between the body and politics; and the deployment of totalitarianism, singularity and plurality. I conclude with a brief consideration of Kristeva's recent discussion of Simone de Beauvoir's work. The overall aim of this chapter, as I already intimated, is to aid the construction of a more nuanced and explicit Kristevan political philosophy, which, despite Kristeva's reluctance to embrace politics more fully, should hopefully also add to the feminist interest in her work.

Romantic Genius

In my Introduction, I alluded to a widespread reception of Kristeva's ideas, both within and beyond feminism, which subsumes her under the label of 'French theory' (see also Kristeva 2004a). As I argued there, one of the problems associated with such a label lies with the appearance it gives of a sense of coherence among a diverse body of thought that does not pay due attention to the substantial differences that exist between its alleged practitioners, a point that has been repeatedly stressed in the critical commentary on 'French feminism'. Besides, it also fails to acknowledge the wide range of reference points of Kristeva's thought: specifically, her debt towards German idealism and post-idealism, and its wider Romantic attachments.[6] Even though Hegel's relevance to Kristeva's thought is often pointed out, the latter is better known for her work on (French) modernism and the (French) avant-garde, and not often associated with the ideas of (German) Romantic philosophy.[7] This influence, however, can be detected early on in her work, and it manifests itself in particular in her attachment to the notion of singularity, which comes to bear significantly on her discussion of genius. I previously intimated that the idea of singularity is central to Kristeva's conception of the subject and that it adds force to her critical distance from feminism. The theme of singularity also runs through her genius trilogy

The Singularity of Genius

and, more specifically, through her not uncritical commitment to the ideas of Hannah Arendt, who herself was not immune to Romantic notions (see Young-Bruehl 2004). Here I want to focus on one aspect of her Romanticism that is of particular relevance to my discussion: her engagement with the idea of genius and its connotation with the female and the feminine.

As I already indicated, Kristeva justifies her selection of the three geniuses, Arendt, Klein and Colette, as personal affinity, but it is helpful to consider briefly the wider motivation for her engagement with genius, as this will elucidate the thematic emphases of her trilogy: specifically, the connection she makes between narrative and life (see next section). Kristeva proffers an outline of the concept of genius in the 'General Introduction' to her genius trilogy, included in the volume on Arendt (Kristeva 2001a), and she returns to it in the conclusion to the trilogy, which is part of the volume on Colette (2004c). In her introduction, Kristeva defines genius as

> those who force us to discuss their story because it is so closely bound up with their creations, in the innovations that support the development of thought and beings, and in the onslaught of questions, discoveries, and pleasures that their creations have inspired. (*HA*: xi)

This intrinsic connection between narrated life – that is, biography – and creation is a guiding thread of her understanding of genius, and she repeatedly returns to this theme, in her theorisation of genius as well as in her discussion of the lives of her three chosen geniuses. Crucially, Kristeva declares that it is not creation alone that defines genius; rather the hallmark of genius is the way that creative output connects with one's life. But there is still more to this. Through her discussion of female genius, Kristeva re-emphasises the main tenets of her theory of female sexuality, which, as we have already seen, constitutes one of her key contributions to psychoanalytic theory, and which seeks to recuperate the feminine, above and beyond women's concrete experience of mothering on the one hand (see Chapter 3), and feminist activism on the other. As she states in the conclusion to the trilogy, three common traits, which also run through the works of Arendt, Klein and Colette, constitute the characteristics of genius. These are, first, the intersubjective dimension of the individual, which she posits as a defining feature of female psychosexuality (see Chapter 2). The second characteristic, as already mentioned, relates to the interweaving of life and thought, while the third element is a focus on new beginnings or rebirth (see below). Taken together, these features culminate in the generation of singularity, which, according to Kristeva, is the most important characteristic of genius. As I will discuss shortly, it is through her notion of female genius that Kristeva underscores her critical distance from feminism, which she can only understand in its manifestation as a mass movement that is at odds with singularity. In other words, (female) genius allows her to rearticulate the feminine, while at the same time evacuating it from feminism.

Because this central feature of Kristeva's notion of genius ties in, rather significantly, with her wider treatment of feminism, I want to take a closer look at this. In the introduction to the trilogy, Kristeva begins by locating genius in relation to feminism. Building on some of her ideas, first articulated in the 1970s – for example, in the essay 'Women's Time' (1979) – Kristeva declares that feminism establishes sexual difference, and in that respect recognises the singularity and plurality of each man and woman; however, it is also said to tend towards the totalitarian, which only the singularity of female genius can transcend. Thus genius, according to Kristeva, simultaneously embodies and transcends feminism; it transforms feminism's alleged massification, which Kristeva detests, and in its place it brings to the fore female singularity. As I stated in previous chapters, Kristeva's depiction of feminism is curiously inattentive to feminism's plurality and heterogeneity. What's more, her celebration of the plurality of women, which is intrinsically linked with her assertion of the singularity of each woman, remains indebted to an account of women in the singular that builds substantially on psychoanalytic notions of a generalised femininity, drawing on phallic monism and the universality of the Oedipal structure (see Chapter 3). Thus, it is fair to say that Kristeva's characterisation of feminism in the genius trilogy is again emblematic of her curtailed reading of feminism. I return to her depiction of feminism as totalitarian further below in this chapter, but for now I continue with my examination of Kristeva's treatment of genius.

Whilst Kristeva's insistence on the importance of the biographical dimension of genius leads her to consider the historical context

The Singularity of Genius

of her three chosen geniuses, she does not further contextualise the concept of genius, leaving the genealogy of term and concept, and its relation to sexual difference untheorised. Thus, despite her insistence on the importance of a narrated life to the idea of genius, she pays scant attention to the social or historical context of the genius discourse; this includes an omission of the relationship of genius discourse to Romanticism and its cult of creativity. Such an omission, however, is deeply problematic. As Christine Battersby (1989) has argued, the genius discourse cannot be understood outside its historical context: specifically, the movement of the Renaissance and the Romantics. Battersby's discussion helps to detect several blind-spots in Kristeva's analysis, and I therefore want to remain with her analysis for the moment.

Battersby locates the deployment of the notion of genius in the context of the aesthetics of the Renaissance, Romanticism and modernism, all of which seek answers to the question of creativity. Through a critical genealogy of the discourse on genius, she asserts in particular the development of a close and paradoxical association between genius and femininity in the Romantic tradition. According to Battersby, the notion of genius is deeply embedded in Romanticism, whose emphasis on values such as originality, creativity, authenticity and feelings is said to capture the essence of genius. Crucially, the Romantic genius is a male, 'full of virile energy' (1989: 3), and able to transcend the constraints of his biological features. As Battersby claims, '[c]reativity was displaced male procreativity: male sexuality made sublime' (1989: 3). To be precise, male procreativity is displaced on to the feminine and turned into creativity. Hence, the creative Romantic genius is the feminine male. Women, on the other hand, are destined to fail; creative women – according to Battersby, almost a contradiction in terms for the Romantics – fail their (feminine) sexuality, while feminine women forego their creativity. It is easy to see why Battersby considers this Romantic conception of genius, and its dismissal or stifling of the development of a female aesthetics, to be harmful to women (1989: 23). What the Romantics achieved, according to Battersby, is the exclusion of women from the realm of the aesthetic and the association of (male) genius with the feminine.

Despite an occasional insistence on the importance of history, and a brief allusion to the Renaissance context of the genius discourse, Kristeva's discussion is curiously inattentive to historical context. However, her lack of attention to context should not cloud the import of Romantic conceptions of genius to Kristeva's ideas; these include the association of genius with creativity, originality and exceptionality. Thus, the Romantic emphasis on creativity, which, according to Battersby, displaces divine powers from God to modern Man, is mirrored in Kristeva's definition of genius. There, we find an equally strong emphasis on creativity that sits at the crossroads of the genius's life; as we have already seen, it is the intersection of the biographical with the creative that characterises Kristeva's female genius. The three examples chosen by Kristeva, notwithstanding their different intellectual and professional contexts, testify to this. Hannah Arendt, for example, was the first female professor at Harvard University; Colette established herself as an important writer who also set herself above the conventions of motherhood and heterosexual coupledom; whilst Melanie Klein made a significant contribution to the psychoanalytic tradition.

However, whilst Kristeva's trilogy delves into the details of the intellectual contributions of these three exceptional women, she is also at pains to advocate a conception of genius that links it with life, understood as biography, and with experience. It should be stressed, though, that Kristeva's use of the term experience acquires a very specific meaning. Experience, for Kristeva, is not a means of giving privileged status to women's lives, practices, skills or knowledges. In this respect, it differs fundamentally from the function that experience obtains in some feminist discourses, such as standpoint feminism, where its importance lies in the valuation given to previously subjugated practices, and where experience obtains the status of a privileged epistemological position. For Kristeva, experience is not an epistemological category, linked to knowledge, but an ethical one that allows the subject of experience to engage in a more meaningful relationship with the other.

This ethical aspect also allows Kristeva to include motherhood in the expression of genius. It is in the particular accomplishments of each woman, especially the accomplishment of motherhood, that Kristeva detects genius. As she declares, 'Mothers can be geniuses . . . of a certain approach to living the life of the mind. That approach to being a mother and a woman . . . bestows upon mothers a genius all their own' (*HA*: xv). She continues by establishing motherhood as 'the most essential of female vocations': 'In the future, motherhood will be desired, accepted, and carried out with the greatest blessings for the mother, the father and the child' (*HA*: xiii). We have seen in Chapter 3 that one element of this celebration is her assertion of the ethical dimension of motherhood. This idea resurfaces in her discussion of Arendt's treatment of love, which affords Kristeva an entrance point to her reinterpretation of Arendtian thought and connects it with her discussion of motherhood. Motherhood, Kristeva persists, is a 'loving concern for the other' (1997: 169), especially for the other in their vulnerability and fragility. As I will suggest below, Kristeva's insistence on human ordinariness and vulnerability, over and above the exceptionality of genius, constitutes a distinctive addition to the discourse on genius.

However, building upon my previous discussion (see Chapter 3), I would suggest that Kristeva's association of motherhood with genius is rather ambivalent in its implications for women and, more widely, for feminism. On the one hand, it broadens the concept of genius, beyond the status of the exceptional that is certified by one's intellectual or artistic creation; in that respect, it equalises and democratises genius and in doing so, it subverts and undermines genius's claim to exceptionality. It becomes profoundly problematic, though, if it elevates motherhood to the status of women's particular and unique contribution to genius. Recall my discussion in the previous chapter, on motherhood, where I considered Cornell's claim (1991) that Kristeva's treatment of the feminine always ends up returning to motherhood. As if anticipating such criticism, Kristeva defines motherhood as an expression of vulnerability, and it is on this basis that she further asserts that '[l]ife will be feminine, or not at all' (1997: 169). Moreover, this femininity, or maternity, is not exclusively linked to women or mothers. She returns to this point in the conclusion to her genius trilogy, where she asks

> Can one define, not Woman or *All* Women, but a feminine specificity that is declined differently in each sex (the feminine of woman, the feminine of man) and in a singular manner for each subject, without confining that subject within the 'other' or the 'unrepresentable'? (2004c: 408; emphasis in original)

While such an understanding of the feminine as irreducible heterogeneity should put at ease critics such as Cornell, it sits, as I stated previously, in an uncomfortable relation to Kristeva's wider assertions about motherhood.

Also unresolved in this context is the question of Oedipality, its relation to sexuality and the figure of the lesbian. As I demonstrated previously, Kristeva alludes to the possibility of Oedipus beyond heterosexual kinship structures, yet she remains committed to notions of heterosexual parenting. Declaring that '[t]hrough their love of men, too, women will continue to give birth' (*HA*: xiv), she anchors birth and motherhood in the heterosexual couple, 'the fruits of men's and women's freedom to love one another' (*HA*: 45). Paradoxically, the heterosexual couple's generation of life is predicated upon the figure of woman-as-feminine who is defined through her psychic bisexuality (*HA*: 48; see also Chapter 3). Thus, the maternal genius is a feminine – that is, psychically bisexual – woman, whose experience of maternity can be shared by those males who can tap into their feminine dispositions. Such a conception denies the prospect of lesbian mothering, and with it, access to maternal genius.

As I already stated, the two key themes that emerge repeatedly in Kristeva's discussion of genius and, by extension, in her consideration of Arendt's writings, are singularity and plurality. They play a significant role in Kristeva's critical exegesis of Arendt's work, but they take on added importance in Kristeva's critical assessment of feminism. Her main point of contention, as I already stated, is feminism's alleged neglect of the singularity of each woman and of the plurality of women. The notion of genius helps her to advance this argument further. Thus, my discussion in the following sections is underpinned by a central concern within feminist debates that resonates strongly with Kristeva's own concerns: how can we reconcile feminism, understood as an identitarian project that engages in collective action, with a concern for difference, singularity and plurality? Moreover, how do we move from Kristeva's, essentially ethical, concern for singularity towards feminism's, essentially political, project aimed at transformation? These questions guide my overall discussion in this chapter and I hope to demonstrate that Kristeva's engagement with Arendt's political philosophy will go some way towards answering them. The connection between biography and writing, or between life and narrative, which Kristeva considers to be a key element of genius, forms a central aspect of these wider considerations and it is to this issue that I turn now.

Narrative, Life and Natality

As I intimated above, exploring the possibilities that Kristeva's reading of Arendt may offer for feminist theory poses an intractable challenge. Not only do the two thinkers appear diametrically opposed in the importance they accord to the role of politics; both are also unlikely champions of feminism. How, then, does Kristeva, whose stance towards politics is ambivalent at best, openly hostile at worst, and who is often seen to favour aesthetic practices at the expense of political engagement, read the work of Arendt, the theorist of politics par excellence? Furthermore, how does Kristeva's persistent emphasis on the importance of embodiment sit alongside Arendt's admittedly impoverished account of the body? Clearly, Kristeva's engagement with Arendt's ideas engenders a series of intriguing questions that aim, directly or indirectly, at some of the key concerns of feminism, including the question of collective agency, the role of identity, the status of corporeality and affect, and the relationship between the intimate and the public. Whilst these questions foreground my exploration of Kristeva's reading of Arendt, I want to establish in particular how her deployment of Arendtian thought advances her own ideas in the direction of feminist theory. In this section, I focus on three interrelated themes that inform Kristeva's discussion of Arendt: narrative, life and natality. As I will suggest, Kristeva's Arendt interpretation subjects Arendt's explicitly political use of these concepts to an intimist interpretation that engages them, at least at times, in a pre- or anti-political way. While this may seem frustrating for the project of feminist political philosophy, it also, paradoxically, recuperates an aspect that remains underdeveloped in Arendt but is central for Kristeva and feminism; this is the intimate or psychic dimension of human life.

Kristeva's book on Arendt tracks closely the development of Arendt's life and œuvre, and is divided into three parts. Part I provides an overview of Arendt's childhood and early years, and offers an exposition of her books on Rahel Varnhagen (1997), *The Human Condition* (1958) and *Men in Dark Times* (1968). Arendt's engagement with the disasters of the twentieth century dominates the second part of the book; it includes a consideration of *The Origins of Totalitarianism* (1979), Arendt's book on the emergence and rise of Nazism and its political structure (and to a lesser extent Stalinism), and Arendt's coverage of the Eichmann trial (1992), as well as her reflections on revolution (1963). The final part turns to Arendt's unfinished philosophical work, *The Life of the Mind* (1978). Given my focus on Kristeva, I do not offer a detailed reading of Arendt; nor is it my intention to 'police' Kristeva's reading of Arendt. What interests me instead is Kristeva's utilisation of Arendt's work, which she deploys, at times in a critical fashion, to develop her own ideas. These critical interceptions, which read Arendtian thought through Kristeva's psychoanalytic lens, are crucial, though, because they advance Kristeva's thought in a number of directions and, in doing so, serve to underscore Kristeva's emphasis on the intimate, on the operation of drives and on the body.

Kristeva's notion of genius, as I suggested, draws on the connection she establishes between life and creation. Such a link, however, is not sufficient for genius to emerge; it requires that the story of one's life is told. According to Kristeva, Arendt embodies this close connection between life and work because she interweaves the story and experiences of her own life with her intellectual apparatus and philosophical ideas. Thus, Arendt's genius, as diagnosed by Kristeva, consists in the way she combines the narrative of the twentieth century with her reflections on this narrative. Arendt herself develops this theme in *The Human Condition* (1958), where she celebrates the role of narrative and narrator, and their contribution to the dissemination of the glorious deeds of political actors.[8] This function, for Arendt, is central to the flourishing of the *polis*, as it encourages political actors to excel in their contribution to their political community.

Of course, narrative is also at the heart of the psychoanalytic enterprise, which turns the psychoanalytic session into a form of story-telling. Hence, adding to Arendt's political dimension of narrative, it acquires a therapeutic-diagnostic dimension, as a 'talking cure', in Kristeva's texts and in psychoanalysis more widely. As Kelly Oliver states, 'we have a sense of ourselves, through the narratives which we prepare to tell others about our experience. Even if we do not tell our stories, we live our experience through the stories that we construct in order to "tell ourselves" to another, a loved one' (Oliver 2003: 42). This personal, or intimate, story is closely linked with the immediate family dramas, but it also connects with the wider social context. This assertion, as I discussed

The Singularity of Genius

previously, informs Kristeva's psychogenetic and socio-genetic account of crisis, generated by the society of the spectacle (see Chapter 2); hence, narrative also connects the suffering of the individual with wider social crises. Besides, the function of narrative, while clearly therapeutic, is also epistemological and ethical; for one thing, it contains a meta-narrative, a history about the present and about the way we understand, configure and conceptualise our understanding of the present. But it is also ethical, allowing for the creation of an ethical encounter with the other.

What is more, narrative is embedded in corporeality, dependent upon the inscription of drive energy that generates narrative in the first place. But, to turn this around, narrative also tells stories about bodies and, as McAfee (2005) demonstrates in her account of public testimony, it connects the somatic dimension of suffering with a therapeutic outlet and with political conflict. She commends Kristeva's work in general for the attention it pays to the affective and somatic dimension of language, but she is particularly keen to deploy Kristeva's thought to an analysis of truth commissions. The narration of the experience of violence draws on somatic and affective forces (2005: 117), but it also, rather poignantly, is said to generate the conditions for ethics by preparing the ground, at least potentially, for forgiveness that allows victim and perpetrator to work through conflict.[9] McAfee's discussion illustrates, both with and against Kristeva, how a conception of narrative that draws on soma and affect, and hence on Kristevan categories, can play a central role in political philosophising. Thus, Kristeva's intimist reading of Arendt, turned against itself, has a crucial role to play in a theory of politics.

Arendt's answer to individual narrative, as is well known, is not a therapeutic one, given her aversion to psychoanalysis. Instead, she pursues two converging paths that allow for individual as well as collective forms of life. These are, on the one hand, the life of action, the vita activa, whilst the other is the contemplative life, the life of the mind. In recent years, Kristeva has drawn in particular on this latter aspect; her book on Arendt engages in a close reading and careful exposition of Arendt's *The Life of the Mind* (1978), and she extracts several key themes that she develops in her own work. These include an emphasis on questioning and on the development of a critical attitude, and the endorsement of the importance of experience. As I suggested previously (see Chapter

2), Kristeva's emphasis on questioning as a guiding principle of revolt resonates strongly with a broader conceptualisation of feminism as a critical project; such an emphasis on feminism's critical ethos connects with the critical interrogation of key concepts and norms, including those gender norms used within feminism. (For a fuller discussion see Chapter 5.) Kristeva utilises these Arendtian themes to underscore a concern of her own, which she shares, furthermore, with Arendt: the pairing of singularity and plurality.

However, she departs from Arendt's philosophy in one important respect. Whilst Arendt places a strong emphasis on the active life of the *polis*, which she connects explicitly with the life of the mind, especially with the capacity to judge and to think (see Arendt 1958; 1978; 1992), Kristeva withdraws Arendt's emphasis on the public and active dimension of thought into the realm of the intimate. This intimist reading of Arendt's philosophy is a key feature of Kristeva's engagement with Arendt that generates a paradox for any feminist interpretation; on the one hand, it withdraws from Arendt's emphasis on politics, while on the other it is more attentive to the intimate and affective dimension of human life. Because Kristeva's intimist reading of Arendt is crucial to the further development of her thought, I want to examine it more closely.

In one of her early essays on Arendt (1997), Kristeva maps the direction of her thinking as it departs from that of Arendt. She suggests, contra Arendt's assertion in *The Human Condition* (1958), that action itself cannot guarantee a free creative life; rather, building upon Arendt's late work, she advocates an emphasis on the life of the mind (Arendt 1978). More specifically, and in response to her sensitivity to the notion of crisis (see Chapter 2), she suggests the opening up of psychic life as the privileged path towards the upholding of human freedom. The practice of writing, and in particular the sensuous style of writing that she associates with Colette, has a crucial role to play here, as it is said to constitute an important corrective to Arendt's narrow focus on the political. She further specifies this claim, again contra Arendt, by holding on to the value of the poetic and the importance of the avant-garde (Kristeva 2004c).

Central to Kristeva's further analysis is her critique of Arendt's distinction between *zoē*, the biological life and its concern with sheer physical survival, and *bios*, that part of life that can be told

The Singularity of Genius

and that is destined for the realm of the public. Against this distinction between *zoē* and *bios*, which generates Arendt's strangely somatophobic conception of life and narrative, Kristeva roots both *zoē* and *bios* firmly within the process of subjectification, which she conceptualises as intersubjective and embodied. As we have seen, narrative arises out of the actions of the drives and the separation from the mother. In other words, Kristevan narrative, whether that of the Arendtian spectator who recalls heroic actions, or that of the patient on the analytic couch, is rooted in *zoē*, in the biological life processes. Through her critique of Arendt's disembodied notion of narrative, Kristeva re-emphasises her assertion of the connection between *zoē* and *bios*. In contradistinction to Arendt, despite her stress on the Arendtian emphasis on *bios*, and in accordance with her overall thought, it is clear that for Kristeva, *bios* without *zoē* is not possible. Even though her notion of genius, as we have seen, borrows substantially from Arendtian conceptions of life and narrative, she presents into Arendtian thinking her own, psychoanalytically inflected, twist.

Her discussion of Arendt's concept of life (1997) introduces two interjections, both of which refer back to her earlier concerns with revolt and with ethics. To begin with, she is sceptical of Arendt's emphasis on action, conceding that even art can no longer provide meaning in the time of the spectacle. Instead of action, Kristeva advocates the opening up of psychic space, which, as we have already seen, is said to be essential for the individual and collective well-being of contemporary subjects. With her emphasis on the opening up of psychic space, Kristeva also aims to integrate an area of human life of which Arendt remained suspicious: the body and its drives. Thus, narrative generates prospects for representation that, in Kristeva's view, are necessary for psychic well-being. The practice of writing, through its transgression of the semiotic-symbolic threshold that introduces *jouissance* into the symbolic, is a privileged form of narration that, moreover, connects the practice of narrative directly with revolt, with the introspective and questioning return that establishes the link between the intimate and the symbolic and public dimensions of human life. Clearly, these are not Arendt's concerns; they constitute Kristeva's idiosyncratic 'intimisation' of the Arendtian project that maps Arendt's thought on Kristeva's ideas and, in the process, substantially transforms them.

It is through her consideration of a further Arendtian theme, natality, that Kristeva accentuates the importance she accords to sexual difference and reaffirms the significance of motherhood and of women's desire for motherhood. As I discussed previously, Kristeva's celebration of motherhood and her interpretation of feminism as an essentially anti-maternal movement have left many of her feminist readers puzzled. The genius trilogy restates motherhood's significant role in a woman's life and it elevates, as I outlined above, motherhood as women's contribution to genius. Drawing on assertions presented in earlier work (see, for example, Kristeva 1977a; 1980), Kristeva considers motherhood to be women's unique contribution to life at the crossroads, or threshold, between *zoē* and *bios*. Yet, the idea of natality also acquires an additional meaning, beyond its narrow association with pregnancy and motherhood; it evokes the cyclical nature of women's time and, crucially, stresses the capacity for new beginnings that Kristeva associates in particular with feminism's third generation.

It probably comes as no surprise that Arendt's celebration of birth or natality is not intended as a political celebration of motherhood. Rather, she builds upon Augustinian conceptions that suggest the possibility of new beginnings. For Arendt, natality and rebirth contain the promise of politics; this is the capacity to begin anew, which renews life and carries important ethical and political implications (see Arendt 1996). Natality allows for the foundation or refoundation of the *polis*, an indispensable condition for the revolutionary refoundation of freedom and politics, but it is also inherently ethical; it is precisely because we can start anew that we are capable of forgiving. Moreover, for Arendt, as indeed for Kristeva, natality ensures the plurality of human beings. For Arendt, such a plurality is the prerequisite for politics, because plurality creates a world, that space of 'in-between' that she defines as politics. Hence, politics, which entails acting in concert, is contingent upon the condition of plurality, which, as Arendt puts it, ensures that there is more of us than one. Kristeva's turn to plurality, on the other hand, tends to depart from politics and collective action, which she views, at least potentially, as totalitarian. This fear of the totalitarian nature of collective action emerges early on in her writings (see, for example, 1977b; 1979) and it is exemplified, as I intimated previously, in her characterisation of feminism as totalitarian, which has put her at odds with many

The Singularity of Genius

of her feminist interlocutors; against the alleged totalitarianism of political movements, Kristeva celebrates marginality, dissidence, singularity and plurality. One could plausibly argue that her endorsement of singularity, together with her suspicion of all forms of collective agency, is already contained in her earliest celebration of aesthetic practices, further evidence of her attachment to Romantic notions of exemplarity and geniality. I return to the discussion of singularity towards the end of this chapter, but for now I want to attend to Kristeva's treatment of the body and its relationship with Arendtian conceptions of politics.

Bodies, Affect and Politics

One of the central aims of *Julia Kristeva and Feminist Thought* is to assert the importance of corporeality to Kristeva's conceptions of the subject and of ethics; as I stated previously, her writings on the body constitute, without a doubt, one of her most significant contributions to contemporary feminist thought. I already outlined the importance that Kristeva accords to the body in previous chapters (see Chapters 1 and 3), where I demonstrated how she dedicates much of her writing to establishing the body within its wider social and cultural context. Given Kristeva's stress on corporeality, and its central role to psychic as well as to social and political life, it seems all the more puzzling to account for her interest in Arendt. After all, does Arendt, more explicitly and forcefully than many other contemporary thinkers, not relegate bodily matters to outside the realm of politics and philosophy? If we were to put Arendt and Kristeva into dialogue with one another, one may well imagine that the question of the body would emerge as a key point of disagreement and contention between the two. Yet, as I want to suggest here, it is paradoxically around the body that a complementary reading of Kristeva and Arendt is most beneficial; while Kristeva provides Arendt with a sophisticated understanding of the social and political significance of embodiment, which adds a corporeal dimension to Arendt's somatophobic account of politics,[10] Arendtian thought may supplement Kristeva's ideas with a more sophisticated account of civic bonds that is not at odds with Kristeva's insistence on singularity and plurality. Here I want to sketch the contours of such an embodied understanding of politics that draws on Kristeva's engagement with Arendt.

JULIA KRISTEVA AND FEMINIST THOUGHT

As is well known, the body, for Arendt, is a metaphor for need and pure life, in other words, of *zoē*, which is diametrically opposed to politics. This assertion is woven throughout Arendt's writings but illustrated starkly in *On Revolution* (1963), Arendt's account of the revolutions of the eighteenth century and of the foundation of freedom in the modern world. There, she explains the failure of the French Revolution, as opposed to the relative success of the American Revolution, by referring to the overwhelming role of poverty, need and hence the demands of the body. The revolution in France failed, according to Arendt, because revolutionary politics in France was in the thralls of the social question, Arendt's euphemistic term for poverty and the necessity of sheer physical survival. Poverty, according to Arendt, puts men 'under the absolute dictate of their bodies', and she concludes that 'freedom had to be surrendered to necessity, to the urgency of the life process itself' (1963: 60). If the French Revolution failed as a result of its admittance of the social into the public, the relative success of the American Revolution is due to its ability to evade the question of the social, helping it to succeed in the foundation of a political order based upon human singularity, common bonds and mutual promises (1963: 175).

Leaving aside Arendt's highly idiosyncratic interpretation of the two revolutions, and her disregard for bodily matters that she combines, rather paradoxically, with her deployment of corporeal metaphors, specifically the metaphor of birth, it is important to stress that Arendt recognises humans as embodied beings. Yet she is wary of the alleged danger that the body is said to pose to politics and its supreme goal: freedom (see also Chapter 5). For Arendt, politics, not the body, is the realm of freedom, of commonality and inter-esse. It is the realm of appearances and of virtuous deeds, and it is juxtaposed with the private realm as the realm of necessity, the location of the household, where humans pay attention to their needs: specifically, their bodily needs. Hence, she claims that participation in the public realm of politics is contingent upon the way that bodies are catered for adequately in the domains of the social and the private. Bodily matters and needs are relegated to the realm of the household, a realm void of freedom that, during antiquity, was populated by slaves and (non-slave) women. Arendt distinguishes this economy of the household, the *oikia*, from the *polis* as the space of politics. As is well known, many feminists have taken issue with Arendt's rigid distinction between a public and a private realm, which is mapped upon a gendered division of labour and which has been interpreted as the glorification of essentially masculine activities, at the expense of feminine activities (see Dietz 1995).

It is at this junction that Kristeva's reading of the body and, more specifically, of the politically pertinent function of bodily drives fundamentally demarcates her thought from that of Arendt. She points this up explicitly in her discussion of Arendt's distinction between *oikia* and *polis*, and proposes, contra Arendt, the need for a political anthropology that re-establishes the importance of the private sphere. Kristeva's critique of Arendt proceeds in two steps. She begins by pondering the connotation of the notion of *oikia*, the economy of the household, which she connects etymologically with the idea of the icon. This connection, Kristeva argues, allows for the representation of the divine, 'a ruse and a negotiation with immortality' (HA: 161), which, furthermore, links it with the feminine. Such a representation of the divine, an iconography, is associated in particular with the Byzantine world and Orthodox Christianity, two examples that, according to Kristeva, celebrate the intimate and the sensuous, and that she connects with the semiotic (see Chapter 5). Moreover, in addition to the household's privileged function in the representation of the divine (Kristeva's more contemporary concern is for the sacred; see Kristeva 2001c), it is also the space where bodily needs and desires, and with them the link to the maternal, are maintained. Kristeva's critique of Arendt's treatment of the *oikia* and the *polis* goes some way towards addressing the concerns of those, including Kristeva herself, who fear the glorification of the *polis* at the expense of the maternal and the feminine.

Of greater interest to my argument is Kristeva's second interjection, which further develops her critique of Arendt's conception of the body and its related neglect of psychic life and intimacy (HA: 162; see also pp. 171–84). This critique of Arendt chimes strongly with Kristeva's conception of revolt, which, as I established in Chapter 2, is displaced from the realm of politics on to the intimate and the aesthetic. Such a view is encapsulated in Kristeva's charge against Arendt's alleged undue focus on political freedom, which, according to Kristeva, neglects 'the plural and possible economies of prepolitical freedom that disclose "the social" and that are precisely what interests us today' (*HA*: 162). Against Arendt's interchangeable deployment of politics and freedom, Kristeva declares politics as, at least potentially, antithetical to freedom. For her, it is the realm of the intimate that constitutes a bulwark of freedom, which protects against the totalitarian and evasive interventions of politics. In this context, it is worth while briefly revisiting a concern I addressed previously (see Chapter 2): namely, the status of the intimate in Kristeva's thought. As we have seen, despite Kristeva's allusion to 'approaching politics from a bit of a distance' (*IR*: 1), she seems, at times, to propose a retreat from politics by emphasising intimate revolt as an alternative to politics and to political revolt (see also Keltner 2009a). This stress on the intimate as a replacement for politics is closely connected with her understanding of freedom. For example, in *Black Sun*, she asserts that

> Politics is not, as it was for Hannah Arendt, the field where human freedom is unfurled. The modern world . . . [does] not have the civilized splendour of the Greek city-state. The modern political domain is massively, in totalitarian fashion, social, levelling, exhausting. (*BS*: 235)

It is difficult to reconcile Kristeva's retreat from politics into the intimate with her call for a political anthropology that seeks to redress a perceived imbalance between politics and the intimate. She returns to this idea of an extra-, pre- or anti-political realm of freedom in *Intimate Revolt*, where human freedom is said to be generated and at its most fertile in the realm of the intimate. As she states there, politics and political revolution may stifle revolt, and hence the art of living, by prohibiting or even strangling the freedom to question (*IR*: 265–6) (see also Chapter 5). I take up Kristeva's discussion of freedom in the next chapter, where I chart her further engagement with freedom and her turn back to politics in her most recent writings, but for now I want to develop her critique of Arendt further.

As I suggested, Kristeva's call for a political anthropology draws on her concern for the role of the *oikia*, the realm of need, desire and representation, and it builds on her critique of Arendt's neglect of corporeality and, with it, of the realms of psychic life and intimacy. This request is preceded by a further demand, this time for a psychoanalytic anthropology, which in her view is also missing in Arendt (*HA*: 129). According to Kristeva, such a psychoanalytic anthropology is anchored in the theory of drives, which, as we have seen in Chapter 1, is essential to her discussion of the process of signification, her treatment of poetic language, and art more generally, and to her account of the subject-in-process. In her engagement with Arendt, she proffers a more concrete reason why she considers a theory of the drives to be central. What, in her view, is missing in Arendt's attempt to understand the violence of totalitarianism is a theory of sado-masochism, as this, according to Kristeva, provides a more fundamental explanation of totalitarian violence that goes beyond Arendt's ethico-political explanation of the banality of evil.[11] While Kristeva acknowledges Arendt's important contribution to the analysis and understanding of modern totalitarianism and its apparatus of terror and destruction, it lacks, in Kristeva's view, attention to the role played by the drives, and by sado-masochism in particular. As she asks, 'how can our individual and collective desires avoid the trap of melancholic destruction, manic fanaticism, or tyrannical paranoia?' (*HA*: 129). I already identified the relevance accorded to the drives in my discussion of violence, in the previous chapter, where I charted Kristeva's account of violence and its constitutive role in the generation of the subject and of bodily and social boundaries. Her work on abjection has also gone some way towards the development of a theory of the affective nature of politics. However, because of Kristeva's reluctance to consider the political implications of her ideas more fully, her readers are still awaiting a more detailed consideration of the relationship between affect and politics. Hence, it is mainly in the critical commentary on Kristeva that this aspect is fleshed out (see Young 1990; Ziarek 2001; Oliver 2004).

Taken together, it is fair to suggest that Kristeva's political and psychoanalytic anthropology, with its emphasis on corporeality and on affect, and its displacement of politics on to the intimate, addresses many feminist concerns over the alleged valuation of masculine activities and the masculine sphere of politics. What, though, are its implications for the building of community? How can it address the question of female or feminist agency and political efficacy? Unsurprisingly, Kristeva's turn to the intimate and the singular has at times been accused of succumbing to an individualistic streak (McAfee 2005) that, paradoxically, given her intersubjective emphasis, neglects the communal or collective dimension. Thus, which types of bonds become possible, and, crucially, which forms of community can counter the violence of the drive and the, always inevitable, threat of abjection?

Singularity, Plurality and Communal Bonds

The question of political bonds is of crucial importance to Arendt's political thought, and she offers an unequivocal answer. Despite her contempt for organised collective action, whose worst excesses she sees embodied in the manifestation of totalitarian movements, she articulates a version of the public realm that builds upon her celebration of spontaneity and rebirth, and that is contingent upon human relationships and the importance of a space between them; this emphasis on the in-between, which she refers to as an inter-esse, generates politics while at the same time leaving the plurality of its actors intact. This idea finds a poignant articulation in Arendt's acceptance speech for the Lessing Award (1968), which invokes the notion of a political friendship that transcends any claims to truth, knowledge or pre-given and pre-established identities or communities, and that establishes a blueprint for political bonds that can accommodate difference. (I return to this below.) Unsurprisingly, Kristeva is rather uneasy with the idea of political bonds. As I already pointed out, Kristeva, quite consistently, refuses to translate her conceptual tools into a more coherent political philosophy. Yet, as I also suggested previously, her notion of the drives and her account of the inter-subjective constitution of subjectivity lend themselves to a more thorough examination into the development of bonds. In fact, as I already intimated, it is out of her ethics of alterity that she articulates the prospects for the generation of bonds. (See also my discussion in Chapter 5.)

Kristeva's concern for singularity and plurality, which sits at the heart of her critique of feminism, connects her more recent works with some of her early comments on feminism (see 1979; 1981). As I already stated, this insistence on singularity and plurality chimes more broadly with her appropriation of Arendtian themes, such as Arendt's endorsement of plurality and her famous rejection of totalitarianism. How, though, does Arendt translate this concern for singularity and plurality into the language of politics?

The Singularity of Genius

Here I want to return to the consideration with which I began this section: the idea of political friendship and bonds. There, I briefly intimated how Arendt stresses the value of political friendship that she sees embedded in the 'inter-esse', the in-between of men and women, which does not rely on any pre-given notion of a shared identity. This aspect has been taken up by Lisa Disch (1995) in her reading of Arendt's acceptance speech when she was awarded the Lessing Prize. Acknowledging the import of what she refers to as radical constructivist feminism, and which she associates with a critique of identity and, more broadly, a politics of difference and diversity, Disch wonders whether new forms of collectivity are possible without having to rely on a pre-established sense of the collective self. Importantly, as she reminds her readers, this critique of identity does not deny the possibility of feminism as a collective practice; rather, it rejects the idea of a given identity as the unquestioned ground of feminism (see also Butler 1990). To facilitate such a post-identitarian feminist practice, Disch suggests a shift from unity to solidarity; according to Disch, feminist attachments to the idea of unity should not be turned into a precondition for feminist practice. In fact, any insistence on unity may well end up excluding those women who do not conform to a prescriptive account of 'woman', or whose vision of feminism clashes with pre-established criteria (see also Chapter 5). Disch also claims, again drawing upon Arendt, that solidarity must be articulated and can only arise from inter-esse, manifested in a concern for the world. Such a solidarity is embodied in what Disch terms 'vigilant partisanship', a form of political friendship that rejects the need for a sense of identity based upon abstract conceptions of womanhood or a shared orientation grounded in one's alleged moral capacities. Both presuppositions, following Disch, run counter to the very plurality that informs the radical constructionist feminist critique of identity and of the subject. I examine some of the implications of Disch's critique below; for now, I return to Kristeva's appropriation of Arendt.

As is well known, Arendt's discussion of totalitarianism (1979), which she diagnoses as the defining political phenomenon of the twentieth century, connects her historical sociology with her philosophical insistence on worldliness, appearance, judgement and plurality. Totalitarianism, according to Arendt, destroys our common world, the 'inter-esse' between the plurality of political actors with their shared responsibility for the world; in its place, totalitarianism plays on the dispersed mass society with its lack of connections and bonds. In its worst excesses, in the hell of the concentration camps, totalitarianism sets out to destruct what for Arendt is the uniquely human characteristic: the ability for spontaneity and new beginnings. Whilst not primarily concerned with the historical or sociological context and explanations that occupy Arendt's treatment of totalitarianism, Kristeva also deploys the term totalitarianism, albeit in a very specific context. She appropriates Arendtian themes, but she also, in addition to engaging directly with Arendt's discussion of totalitarianism, utilises them for her own analysis of identity and collective politics. Similar to Arendt's discussion, the context evoked by Kristeva is the crisis that is modernity and that, for her, is displayed most visibly in the new maladies of the soul. However, totalitarianism, for Kristeva, operates in a more insidious way, associated with the levelling out of difference, plurality and singularity even within the modern liberal-democratic state. Rather surprisingly, Kristeva's analysis of totalitarianism focuses in particular on those broadly left-wing political movements that are said to pursue collective practices at the expense of the singularity of the individual. One such movement is feminism. Kristeva's reasons for associating feminism with totalitarianism are as much biographical as they are conceptual. As she states,

> [p]erhaps because of my childhood and adolescence were passed in a totalitarian country, I have long mistrusted the liberation movements even of our democratic societies. I always fear they may have hidden totalitarian aims. . . . It is out of this mistrust that I have tried to dissociate myself even from mass feminism, while at the same time paying tribute to feminine creativity. (2008: 353)

If biographical factors, including her childhood spent in communist Bulgaria, constitute one element of her understanding of totalitarianism,[12] they are complemented by a philosophical concern that reverberates with her concept of genius as the epitome of singularity. Moreover, to restate a point I made previously, Kristeva's theoretical wariness of what she refers to as totalitarian, which develops through her discussion of Arendt, connects with her work from the 1970s. For example, in 'Women's Time' (1979), she criticises the inclusion of women in the power structures of modern states, including those in the former communist regimes, and she warns against women's identification with those power structures, for example, in Nazi Germany. It seems quite a distance to move from a critique of women's support or participation in totalitarian regimes, to a critique of feminism as totalitarian; yet Kristeva seems willing to make this connection. As she suggests, at the heart of such an identification lies a 'paranoid type of counter-investment in an initially denied symbolic order ... moving towards levelling, stabilization, conformism' ('WT': 201). In its place, she evokes the value of dissidence, '[t]his ruthless and irreverent dismantling of the workings of discourse, thought, and existence' ('Dissident': 299). A feminist manifestation of dissidence is probably most closely associated with feminism's third generation (see Kristeva 1979), whose openness to plurality and singularity is said to counter the totalitarian tendencies of political movements, including those of the first two generations of feminism. Ultimately, though, such a vision does not address the question of political efficacy or agency, or of political bonds. Although by no means solipsistic, the singular female genius weaves her relationships around the realm of the intimate, forever the narrator but never an actor.

From Mothers to Sisters

In her conclusion to the genius trilogy, Kristeva declares a feeling of 'sisterly proximity' with her protagonists that she experienced during the process of researching and writing the books. Without denying 'irritating differences and critical dismissals' (2004c: 403), she confesses her admiration for the genius of Arendt, Klein and Colette, which she sees embodied in the way that these three women managed to intertwine life and œuvre. This genius of singularity, as we have seen, is juxtaposed against the alleged totalising, indeed totalitarian aspirations of liberation movements, of which feminism is but one example. Thus, Kristeva can declare that her interest in singularity is 'also a way of distancing myself from feminism as a mass movement' (2004c: 404). Intriguingly, it is from her critique of feminism, which she reaffirms in her conclusion to the genius trilogy, that she turns to the figure of Simone de Beauvoir, who is embraced, in the same text, as another example of genius and singularity (in fact, it is to de Beauvoir that she dedicates her genius trilogy). This is rather surprising, as it is de Beauvoir who is the, unnamed, object of criticism in Kristeva's earlier attempts to distance herself from a conception of feminism that, she claims, rejects motherhood (Kristeva 1979). This departure in Kristeva's most recent work also requires a revision of the claim, made with some justification, that Kristeva, along with Irigaray, has 'tense theoretical relations with Beauvoir, recognizing her work as perhaps historically important but nonetheless somehow outmoded' (Zakin 2006: 31). In recognition of Kristeva's latest work, it becomes necessary, as one commentator has remarked, to challenge a perception of Kristeva and de Beauvoir as diametrically opposed thinkers (Keltner 2009b: 225).[13]

It is too early to assess the further direction and wider impact of this development in Kristeva's work. (In fact, her writings on de Beauvoir are still few in number, and a critical commentary on this aspect of her work has, at least at the time of writing, not yet emerged.) Up to now, her texts on de Beauvoir include a short section in her conclusion to the genius trilogy (2004c), as well as several speeches, delivered as part of her work on the committee of the Prix Simone de Beauvoir (more on this below), and some short articles that are published on her web site (see www.kristeva.fr).[14] At this point, one can only speculate whether the engagement with de Beauvoir will renew the feminist interest in Kristeva's work; however, what emerges in these texts is a closer engagement with de Beauvoir's ideas that could lead to a firmer formulation of a Kristevan feminism. What, then, are these ideas and how are they reformulated in Kristeva's writings?

In her essay 'Beauvoir and the Risks of Freedom' (2009b), originally delivered as the keynote address at the 2008 conference in celebration of de Beauvoir's centenary,[15] Kristeva applauds de Beauvoir for initiating an '*anthropological* revolution' that is grounded in '*transcendence* as freedom' (2009b: 226; italics in original). Kristeva draws on de Beauvoir's emphasis on equality, which she grounds in Western, and more specifically European conceptions of the universal, as embodied in republican ideals and the French Enlightenment (see also Chapter 5). As evidence of the continued relevance and appeal of de Beauvoir, Kristeva reformulates de Beauvoir's famous assertion that one is not born, but rather becomes a woman, by stating that '"One" (the impersonal body) is born a woman, but "I" (subject) am continuously becoming one' (2009b: 239).

De Beauvoir, according to Kristeva's reading, critiqued the association of women with facticity and immanence, as this was said to prevent women from gaining access to a true humanity, defined through autonomy and freedom. Moreover, she posed a conflict between the demands of every subject, seen as essential, and the imperatives of the situation, which she considered inessential. Kristeva reformulates this idea as a conflict between the condition of all women and the free realisation of every woman, in effect relating it back to her assertion of female singularity and plurality that is expressed prominently in many of her writings from the 1970s. In her analysis of de Beauvoir, Kristeva positions herself firmly on the side of singularity. In fact, she is critical of de Beauvoir's privileging of the transformation of women's condition and her alleged dismissal of the essential issue: namely, that of the singular initiative. It is this point that allows Kristeva to reinvoke the notion of genius: the 'breach through and beyond the "situation"' (2004c: 407), which is meant to free the female condition and to lead to the realisation of freedom. Her conclusion to her essay on de Beauvoir articulates a thought that captures Kristeva's own philosophical project; she applauds de Beauvoir for 'her capacity to embody a political philosophy of freedom in the microcosm of the intimate' (2009b: 229).

I began this chapter by describing Kristeva as a reluctant political philosopher; this reluctance, I suggested, lies in her unwillingness to embrace more fully the political implications of her radical account of the subject, and to connect her celebration of singularity, plurality and difference with a conception of political bonds. It is therefore perhaps unsurprising that Kristeva cannot engage with the question of political efficacy and feminist political agency. While her resistance to uniformity and her endorsement of plurality and singularity are not out of place in any understanding of feminism that builds upon difference, and that challenges conceptions of a coherent subject, I suggested that Kristeva's celebration of plurality and singularity results in a distancing from feminism, which she depicts as a totalitarian mass movement.

Yet, notwithstanding these reservations, I also want to stress that her writings are embedded in a wider set of ideas that take seriously the affective and corporeal dimension of politics and that are attentive to the question of difference. In this respect, I would like to suggest that her engagement with the work of Hannah Arendt, which evolves around the notions of narrative, singularity and plurality, and which articulates, in contradistinction to Arendt, a revaluation of the sphere of the maternal and posits a political and psychoanalytic anthropology, constitutes the foundations of a Kristevan political philosophy that has much to offer to feminist thought. A central element of such a political philosophy is Kristeva's deployment of the notion of freedom; it is this aspect that will occupy me in the final chapter of this book.

Notes

1. The title of the genius trilogy is *Female Genius: Life, Madness, Words – Hannah Arendt, Melanie Klein, Colette*. It is published in three volumes: *Hannah Arendt* (2001a), *Melanie Klein* (2001b) and *Colette* (2004c).
2. Kristeva's most comprehensive coverage can be found in her book on Arendt (Kristeva 2001a). A modified version of the first chapter of the book is presented in *Crisis of the European Subject* (2000c); for a shortened version see Kristeva (1997). See also several of her essays (2004a; 2004b; 2005a) for further references to Arendt and Arendtian ideas. The English-language version of her acceptance speech given at the 2005 Hannah Arendt Prize Award can be found in Kristeva (2008), while the responses are available at www.hannah-arendt.de/Festschriften/Festschrift_20061175498415.pdf.
3. For further discussions see also McAfee (2005), Keltner (2009a) and Sjöholm (2009).
4. I also want to flag up the centrality of the notion of freedom, which I turn to in Chapter 5.
5. Zakin has denounced Kristeva's attempt as 'cheap psychobiography' (2009: 204).
6. I should stress, though, that Kristeva has repeatedly acknowledged the range of influences on her work. See, for example, Kristeva (1996a).
7. For a recent consideration of Kristeva's Romanticism see Varsamopoulou (2009). While the focus of this chapter lies with Kristeva's discussion of genius, one could add her commitment to notions of intimacy as a further element of her Romanticism. See her *Strangers to Ourselves* (1991a) and my discussion in Chapter 2. In

The Singularity of Genius

Strangers to Ourselves, Kristeva locates the emergence of German nationalism in Herder's, essentially Romantic, connection between national genius and national language.

8. For a critique of Arendt's glorification of public deeds, which associates the public sphere with virile masculinity, see Cavarero (2000).
9. However, in order for this kind of testimonial narrative to work, it must connect affect with meaning. A simple display of images will not do (see also Oliver 2007b). Narrative without meaning remains empty or banal, as illustrated by Arendt in her study of Eichmann. See Arendt (1992).
10. Recent discussions that have utilised Kristeva's thought for an analysis of Arendt include Birmingham (2003; 2005; 2006). See also Zakin (2009) for an Arendtian critique of Kristeva.
11. See also my discussion of forgiveness in the previous chapter. Despite Kristeva's critique of Arendt's neglect of sado-masochism, Arendt manages, more successfully in my view, to connect ethics with politics.
12. One could consider Kristeva's experiences with feminist groups in the 1970s as a further biographical factor in her endorsement of singularity and her characterisation of feminism as potentially totalitarian.
13. On the question of motherhood, she does not revise her thoughts, and she charges de Beauvoir, and along with her 'a great many feminists' (2009b: 229), with a devaluation of maternity that threatens and pressures women today. The second threat, also to do with motherhood, is the reduction of maternity by a 'technicist biologism to an instinct of the species' (2009b: 229).
14. Kristeva's first novel, *The Samurai* (1992), which fictionalises the Parisian intellectual climate of the late 1960s and early 1970s, is reminiscent of de Beauvoir's *The Mandarins* (2005). Kristeva acknowledges that there are similarities, although she also declares, in an interview published initially in 1990 in the journal *L'Infini*, that she is closer to Simone Weil than to the rationalism of Simone de Beauvoir (1996a: 252). Kristeva's wider scholarly activities, including her role as chair of the annual Simone de Beauvoir Prize, are further evidence of her interest in de Beauvoir.
15. This conference also inaugurated the Prix Simone de Beauvoir, the Simone de Beauvoir Prize for Women's Freedom, which is chaired by Kristeva. For a useful summary of Kristeva's lecture see Keltner (2009b).

5

Towards a Philosophy of Freedom?

> I am increasingly skeptical about the capacity of political movements to remain places of freedom ... We saw this with the feminist movement which rapidly became a movement of chiefs where women crushed women inside the same group. The strategies of the oppressors against which women fought were reproduced in their own groups.
>
> (*Revolt*: 107–8)

The previous chapter identified the themes of singularity and plurality as key reference points of Kristeva's political philosophy, which, as I suggested, is reaffirmed through her engagement with the ideas of Hannah Arendt, and which comes to inform her recent writings on politics. While Kristeva's interpretation of Arendt's thought displays an explicit consideration for the political, it withdraws, as I demonstrated, Arendt's emphasis on 'the world' and on politics into the intimate. Even though, as I have suggested throughout *Julia Kristeva and Feminist Thought*, the idea of the political receives some considerable attention in Kristeva's writings, this is mainly implicit, and it sits uncomfortably alongside her dislike of matters pertaining to politics.[1] In this chapter I want to consider possible ways to bridge this gap between politics and the political in Kristeva's thought; my task is aided by the thematic orientation of some of her most recent writings, which have a direct bearing on politics, such as her interviews on revolt (2000b) and her essay 'Europhilia, Europhobia' (1998a) and its various modifications (2004a; 2005a), as well as some of her other more recent texts (2007a; 2007b; 2007c; 2009a; 2009d). It should be stressed again that these are not explicitly feminist writings; however, like all of Kristeva's work, they are underpinned by a psychosexual subtext that addresses the question of alterity, a core theme of Kristeva's writings. In fact, one may plausibly argue that her attention to otherness is one of the reasons why her work has received so much attention in the feminist commentary. For

Kristeva, as I argued previously, otherness constitutes an ontological condition of human life, it is there from the start, and it attests to the subject's heterogeneity; the other is always there.

This attentiveness to otherness demonstrates Kristeva's sensitivity to the social conditions of the emergence and persistence of the subject. However, given her declared focus on psychoanalysis, she has not always fully developed the political implications of the centrality of alterity in her thought. This deficit in Kristeva's writings, as I stated previously, has disappointed those readers who were looking for a more fully developed political theory in her writings. However, this gap between her, mostly implicit, consideration for the political and her general distaste for politics has also generated opportunities for a critical intervention and reinterpretation of her work, a reading against the grain, which has emerged wherever Kristeva neglects the sensitivity that she displays in her radical philosophical assertions. This chapter wants to illustrate such possibilities for a critical intervention by focusing on some recent concerns in political philosophy that also surface in Kristeva's writings, such as the idea of Europe, immigration and strangeness, and by assessing what I consider to be the psychosexual undercurrent of her geopolitical and geophilosophical considerations.

My main emphasis in this chapter lies with the interpretation and critical assessment of a crucial development in Kristeva's recent thought, which, as I want to suggest here, has paved the way for her 'return' to politics. This is her celebration of freedom, which relates directly to her writings on revolt and which is reaffirmed through her readings of Arendt and, to a lesser extent, de Beauvoir. Although there are traces of a discussion of freedom in Kristeva's work prior to the 1990s (see, for example, *Black Sun*), it is only with the series on revolt and subsequent work that she undertakes a more systematic investigation into the notion of freedom.[2] This interest in freedom also relates to a more fundamental concern of mine: how can we read Kristeva's philosophy of freedom as a feminist philosophy? More specifically, how does Kristeva's conception of freedom enhance feminism, understood as a political project?

I begin my discussion with an interpretation and critical assessment of her recent engagement with the notion of freedom, which draws in particular on the second volume of the revolt series,

Intimate Revolt. This is followed by a reflection on Kristeva's treatment of universality, particularity and cosmopolitanism, which reviews some of the assumptions initially presented in *Strangers to Ourselves* and *Nations without Nationalism*. The next two sections engage with Kristeva's discussion of the idea of Europe, focusing on her work on what I term 'Europe's others', on immigration and on 'the other Europe', her treatment of Eastern Europe. I conclude with some broader reflections on the overall usefulness of Kristeva for a feminist project.

Psychoanalysis and Freedom

Beginning with her series on revolt and developed more fully in subsequent work, Kristeva's recent writings pay considerable attention to the concept of freedom. This attention evolves broadly around the question of universality and particularity, and, as I hope to demonstrate throughout this chapter, it has a direct bearing on feminist concerns. Kristeva's treatment of the notion of freedom is already prominent in the first part of *Intimate Revolt*, where she establishes the realm of the intimate as a central locus of revolt, and where she connects her concern with the intimate with the question of freedom (*IR*: 13). Her understanding of freedom, as I want to illustrate here, derives primarily from psychoanalytic considerations, although she adds to these by pondering freedom's philosophical, ideological and geopolitical dimensions. (I discuss these in the following sections.) It is with reluctance that I would want to rank these influences according to their importance in Kristeva's work. However, one can safely assume that it is the psychoanalytic aspect of freedom that underpins the relevance and configuration of its other manifestations.

A fully-fledged engagement with freedom begins in the second part of the English-language translation of *Intimate Revolt*, entitled 'The Future of Revolt',[3] where Kristeva discusses the status of freedom in psychoanalysis. She claims that freedom is not a psychoanalytic concept, an assertion derived from her reading of Freud, who establishes an essentially Hobbesian and pre-analytic account of freedom that associates it with the unrestricted operation of the drives; these have to be subjected and sublimated to meet the demands of civilisation and community. Whereas for Freud, following Kristeva's reading, 'natural' freedom runs against the demands of culture and therefore has to be surrendered, Kristeva goes on to demonstrate the crucial role played by freedom in the maintenance or restoration of psychic life. In doing so, she claims, contra Freud, freedom as a psychoanalytic concept. The role played by prohibition, the operations of the drives and the process of sublimation allow her to establish this connection.

Central to the process of sublimation is the psychoanalytic practice of transference, which supports patients' return to their unconscious and which affirms the fragile psyche of the (transferential) love accorded by the analyst. Psychoanalytic transference thus facilitates what Kristeva calls, following Arendt, a process of rebirth (see Chapter 4); this rebirth is in fact a permanent one, putting the subject permanently in revolt and, in doing so, it provides the subject with the freedom to begin anew. Importantly, as I demonstrated in Chapter 3, it also assists the subject's capacity to establish a link to an other. Thus, at the core of the psychoanalytic enterprise, and of the rebirth and revolt that are said to be generated by it, sits a fundamentally ethical dimension; it enables the patient to develop connections. Psychoanalysis, as we have already seen, also assists the generation of narrative, which manifests itself in the capacity of analyst and analysand to articulate questions. An ethos of questioning, employing the modality of speech, allows subjects to question themselves; this practice lies at the heart of revolt. Such a working towards revolt and questioning, as Kristeva suggests, accounts for what she terms the 'implicitly political impact' (*IR*: 237) of analysis, creating a subject in revolt. She emphasises in particular that '[t]he analyzed person discovers his irreconcilable conflictuality, the dramatic splitting that constitutes him and that detaches him from any will for control, power, or even unity. This freedom distances psychoanalysis from any moralistic or blissful humanism' (*IR*: 237). Thus, to repeat a point I made previously, Kristeva envisages a type of analytic encounter that puts the subject in process, that allows for the representation of drive and affect, and in doing so, affirms the subject's heterogeneity and singularity. In short, psychoanalytic revolt works towards a decentred subject that challenges the view of a coherent, unified self.

The psychoanalytic experience of transference, coupled with philosophical considerations on nothingness by Sartre and Heidegger, lead Kristeva to assert that analytic interpretation is at its core a form of questioning; it is 'the giving of meaning in

Towards a Philosophy of Freedom?

the course of the transference/counter-transference relationship' (*IR*: 144). This assertion further illuminates her claim of the function of pardon and forgiveness that I discussed in Chapter 3. Psychoanalytic – that is, transferential – forgiveness takes the form of questioning (*IR*: 145), which originates in the separation of the subject and its accompanying frustrations and feelings of rejection that emerge in the wake of language acquisition. It becomes the task of psychoanalysis to restore the capacity for speech, and hence for questioning, putting to work affect and sensation on the one hand, and language on the other.

Kristeva's emphasis on questioning, which is central to clinical practice, also underscores her wider philosophical considerations on the concept of freedom. In her essay 'Psychoanalysis and Freedom', included in *Intimate Revolt*, Kristeva is at pains to stress the renewal and rebirth facilitated by the practice of questioning. This connection between questioning and rebirth also returns her to the issue of revolt; the practice of questioning is an act of revolt, an attack, as she states, on 'all unity, identity, norms, values' (*IR*: 233). Hence, psychoanalysis, for Kristeva, is a 'de-normalizing non-conformism' (Gratton 2007: 11; see also Chapter 2). While it attempts to restore the psychic life of the patient (and in that respect it is conservative), it also puts the subject back in process. As Kristeva puts it:

> no modern human experience aside from psychoanalysis offers man the chance to restart his psychical life and thus, quite simply, life itself, opening up choices that guarantee the plurality of an individual's capacity for connection. This version of freedom is perhaps the most precious and most serious gift that psychoanalysis has given mankind. (*IR*: 234)

It is also, as I suggested, an immensely ethical experience, which generates, through revolt and the practice of questioning, the subject's ability to create, or to recreate, links with others. This inherently ethical feature of freedom-as-questioning is central to Kristeva's psychoanalytic project because it helps the suffering subject to recuperate its bonds with others. However, what interests me further are its political implications, to which I alluded to above and which are said to contain the 'seed of politics' (*IR*: 232). It is this aspect that I explore in the following sections.

Liberty in Dark Times

Out of her overall concern with crisis, and increasingly influenced by her reading of the work of Hannah Arendt, emerges Kristeva's recent engagement with the idea of 'dark times'. This development is significant for my discussion, as it is in this context that she comes closest to an explicitly political discussion of freedom. As is probably well known, the notion of 'dark times' was used by Arendt, who in turn borrowed it from a poem by Brecht,[4] to characterise two phenomena. These are the political catastrophes of the first half of the twentieth century, specifically Nazism and Stalinism; and second, in a broader sense, the decline of the public sphere and of politics, and with it, a diminishing of the realm of freedom in the modern world (1968: ix).

Kristeva's use of the expression 'dark times' is mostly implicit and not fully fleshed out; yet, it is fair to assume that she deploys this term to give expression to her notion of crisis. In this respect, one could surmise that the idea of 'dark times' articulates her wider concern for the crisis triggered by the spectacle, the psychic afflictions of individuals and the need to restore psychic life and, with it, the realm of the intimate. We have already seen that revolt is one of Kristeva's privileged responses to the encroachment of the society of the spectacle on psychic life. Freedom is her second, and related, response, and she develops this aspect of her work in a series of essays and speeches that cover similar ground; they include the second part of *Intimate Revolt*, her acceptance speech at the Holberg Prize award ceremony (2005a), and the second part of *Crisis of the European Subject* (2000c), as well as some of her writings on Hannah Arendt (2006; 2008; see also 1998a; 2004a; 2004b). The frequency with which Kristeva turns to this topic attests to the interest and centrality it obtains in her recent work. The main thesis advanced in these publications, and my main concern in this section, draws on a conceptual and geographical distinction that Kristeva introduces into her discussion; this is the distinction between a European-philosophical and an American-instrumental conception of freedom.[5] Before I develop this point further, I want to recall briefly the significance of Kristeva's discussion of revolt, especially as it pertains to the idea of freedom, critique and feminism.

Kristeva's conception of freedom, as I already suggested,

Towards a Philosophy of Freedom?

returns us to her discussion of revolt, and more specifically, to her celebration of the intimate and its focus on contestation and questioning. It also prepares the ground for a radical contestatory practice that resonates compellingly with recent discussions in the field of radical democracy (see, for example, Lloyd and Little 2009); however, despite alluding strongly to the political potential of freedom, revolt and the radical contestatory practice associated with it, it is surprising to find that her emphasis on the intimate remains curiously removed from a political reading, focusing primarily on the role of the imaginary and of intimacy in the conception of freedom.[6] Thus, while Kristeva's writings on freedom contain the seeds of a political philosophy that, furthermore, could be highly useful for a notion of feminism conceived as a contestatory political project, she does not bridge this gap between her radical theory of the subject, her celebration of revolt and her recognition of the importance of freedom on the one hand, and the link to politics on the other. This discrepancy is particularly noteworthy because it also fails to reconnect the practice of questioning and of freedom-as-revolt with her depiction of feminism as a critical practice, which she advocated in her famous interview with *Psych et po* (1981) and which informs her conception of the feminine. Establishing more strongly the full import of Kristeva's account for a feminist political philosophy that builds upon the critique of the subject and that is attuned to the idea of difference and heterogeneity is only possible if we read her work against the grain. While questions of sexual difference become submerged in Kristeva's recent texts on freedom, they appear, albeit implicitly, through a psychosexual narrative that is mapped upon her geopolitical and geophilosophical considerations. It is to these issues that I turn now.

Already in the two volumes on revolt, Kristeva alludes to freedom's promise as a path out of crisis and as a distinctive expression of revolt. She expands upon this assertion in some of her more recent work, where she distinguishes between two manifestations of freedom, which are also given a geographical and cultural connotation. On the one hand, she refers to an American version of freedom, which she describes as instrumental, and which she associates with the logic of the calculus, the freedom of the market and with liberalism. This form of freedom, which she traces back to Kant's invocation of a 'self-beginning', is said to be essential for the emergence of the enterprising, capitalist subject, inflected as it is with its 'calculus of the market'. It is important to point out that Kristeva does not dismiss this form of freedom, but she is concerned that its dominance encroaches upon other forms of freedom and upon the creation of an intimate space. Thus, instrumental freedom is a necessary, but also a less desirable complement to a second form of freedom, described as European and traced back to the Socratic tradition, to Heidegger's notion of revelation and to Arendt's concept of disclosure. This form of freedom, which defines itself through those practices of disclosure, revelation and questioning, is epitomised in the capacity for critique. To assess Kristeva's intriguing geopolitical and philosophical connotations would lead me beyond the scope of my argument in this section, although I return to the import of Europe and its psychosexual subtext in the following sections. For the moment, it suffices to say that Kristeva does not dismiss either manifestation of freedom; rather, she seeks to champion the extension of the latter because it is said to provide us with an adequate response to crisis.[7]

While the essence of freedom-as-disclosure is captured in the practice of contestation and critique, I want to reiterate that this freedom is not primarily understood in a political sense; in fact, despite the Arendtian influence on her work, Kristeva tends to posit this form of freedom as antithetical to politics. For Arendt, as is well known, freedom becomes the raison d'être of politics (1977: 145), where 'politics' and 'freedom' can be used interchangeably.[8] Unlike Arendt, Kristeva locates freedom in the realm of the intimate. What, though, are we to make of this association between freedom, revolt and the intimate?

Freedom, for Kristeva, is revealed through revolt. Politics and political action are peripheral to this understanding; in fact, as I suggested, they could even be seen to encroach upon freedom (see Chapter 4). As Kristeva suggests, politics and political revolution may stifle revolt by prohibiting or even strangling the freedom to question (*IR*: 265–6).[9] As I intimated in the previous chapter, one may find some of the reasons for Kristeva's pre- or even antipolitical conception of freedom in her biography, specifically in the way that her dislike for what she terms totalitarian movements is reflected in her conception of freedom and, more broadly, in her conceptual apparatus, which, as we have seen, juxtaposes the singularity of the individual against collective forms of expression,

Towards a Philosophy of Freedom?

including politics. Her frequent personal interjections into her theoretical pieces support such an interpretation,[10] but, as I argued previously, her theoretical writings also display such a philosophical orientation that can be traced back, despite modifications and shifts in emphasis, to her early engagement with *Tel Quel*.[11]

And yet, as I have suggested repeatedly, there is also a strong argument to be made for a reading of revolt and freedom beyond the intimate. Sara Beardsworth (2005b) has stressed the ethical dimension of 'freedom as disclosure' and its linkage to politics via psychoanalysis. It is the sociality at the core of the psychoanalytic encounter – that is, the relationship with the other – that constitutes this ethical dimension of Kristeva's notion of freedom and revolt and which displays itself in a number of ways. To begin with, it articulates what I referred to as a concern for the care of the self (see Chapter 3). Kristeva seems to suggest as much when she describes the characteristics of her privileged form of freedom as emphasising 'the intimate, the particular, the art of living, taste/*goût*, leisure/*loisirs*, pleasure without purpose/*plaisir pour rien*' (1998a: 329; italics in original; see also *IR*: 264; 2004c: 31–2).

There is more to this, though. Taking seriously the ethical facet of freedom, Kristeva also highlights freedom's concern for the singularity and fragility of human life, including its attention to difference. Kristeva associates such an ethical concern with France, Italy, Spain and Poland: in other words, European countries that she associates with the Catholic tradition. This concern for the fragility of life and for difference resonates strongly with her engagement with the social status of the disabled, while the connection she establishes between freedom and difference is deeply embedded in her writings on foreignness and on sexual difference. Out of this ethical concern emerges, towards the end of *Intimate Revolt*, a call for a 'politics of solidarity', 'the expression of popular unity that guarantees plurality in the unity of a nation in solidarity' (*IR*: 265), whilst in a different version of the essay, in 'Europhilia, Europhobia', she advocates a 'solidarian type of freedom' (1998a: 332); in the same text she endorses the way that French *étatisme* advocates the principle of solidarity, over and above liberalism, which Kristeva codes as American. The connection Kristeva establishes between unity, solidarity and plurality is an intriguing one, which, on the surface, seems to run counter to her emphasis on singularity and its connection with plurality. Here

153

it might be helpful to recall a discussion from the previous chapter, which, drawing on Lisa Disch's reading of Arendtian thought, explored the question of identity, the constructivist critique of identitarian positions and the relation to feminist practice (Disch 1995). Recall that Disch's response, informed by Arendt's discussion of political friendship, sought to develop the idea of what she terms a 'vigilant partisanship', which generates practices based on solidarity without having to seek recourse to a pre-established subject or identity.

Disch's discussion connects, I believe, with wider questions that need to be asked of Kristeva, whose concern for freedom, as we have seen, is intimist and ethical in its aspiration, and who fails to connect this aspiration more fully with a political orientation. Is it possible to read a desire for politics into her claim, that 'politics, *strictu sensu*, can be seen as the betrayal of this freedom of thinking' (1998a: 330; italics in original)? Is Kristeva's freedom limited to an ethics of the self? Or can it translate into a feminist political practice that addresses questions of political efficacy and feminist agency? Linda Zerilli (2005), in her discussion of freedom in contemporary feminist thought, seems to suggest just that. Building upon Arendtian notions of worldliness, Zerilli rejects feminist thought based upon expediency, on the one hand, and upon the subject, on the other. According to Zerilli, a feminism based upon expediency legitimises itself through the relevance of the social, and through an insertion of social demands via a language of social justice and rights, into the fabric of the community. Such a strategy is said to presuppose an understanding of a shared set of needs, requirements and demands: in other words, of feminism as a movement of sameness. Zerilli also refutes conceptions of feminism based upon the subject, including those third-wave feminist critiques that reject the notion of a pre-established subject but that remain, through their critique, in the thrall of the subject. Instead, Zerilli advocates a feminist politics, understood as a practice of freedom, which seeks to build (upon) a common world. Such a conception, according to Zerilli, holds on to feminism, by combining feminist political practice with the idea of plurality. Zerilli's feminism of plurality, beyond expediency and subject, offers a very helpful corrective to Kristeva's invocation of totalitarianism, and it seems to me that Kristeva's account, specifically her insistence on singularity and plurality, could be developed profitably along such lines. As Zerilli points up, feminism does not require a sense of shared identity, needs, moral capabilities or biological features in order to qualify as feminism, or to articulate a feminist vision of the world. To evoke Arendt's ideas that lie at the heart of Zerilli's discussion, 'the appearance of freedom, like the manifestation of its principles, coincides with the performing act ... to *be* free and to act are the same' (Arendt 1977: 151; italics in original). What is missing in Kristeva is a more fully fleshed out engagement with the political implications of her thought, and a more honest acknowledgement of the political dimension of her intellectual enterprise that deals in a more constructive manner with the question of politics and female and feminist political agency.

As I stated at the beginning of this chapter, it is the theme of otherness that runs through Kristeva's psychoanalytic writings and that also informs her wider perspectives on ethics and politics. The following sections chart this aspect of her work further, and I begin by looking at the status of the universal and the particular in her account.

Universality, Particularity and Cosmopolitanism

Kristeva's philosophy of freedom, as I intimated in the previous section, is filtered through the lens of her conception of Europe and its relation to its other. In this section, and in the following two, I will explore this aspect further, and I begin by revisiting some of Kristeva's writings from the late 1980s and early 1990s on the idea of the nation and on nationalism (1991a; 1993). These works have received much critical commentary and it is not my intention to offer a novel interpretation of them. Rather, they provide me with some necessary context for my discussion. This context allows me to pursue some pertinent questions regarding the status of the universal and the particular in Kristeva's work. This theme has remained with Kristeva, finding its manifestation in some of her more recent work on fundamentalism and on Europe.

In *Strangers to Ourselves* (1991a), Kristeva present a narrative of the role and status of the foreigner in the history of the West and Western philosophy. It is also a vehicle for Kristeva to declare her position on the engagement with foreignness in a world that is becoming increasingly complex and intertwined. These arguments are presented again, in a more condensed form, in *Nations without*

Nationalism (1993), a collection of essays, letters and interviews on the topic of the nation and nationalism. There, Kristeva describes herself as a 'rare species': 'I am a cosmopolitan' (*NwN*: 15). This confession, along with the overall objective of her book, should be seen in the political context of late 1980s France, which saw a rise in the vote for Jean-Marie Le Pen's Front National and which witnessed, in 1988, the controversy over *l'affaire du foulard*, the so-called headscarf affair involving the expulsion and subsequent reinstatement of three schoolgirls in a French school.[12] Thus, Kristeva's self-declared position as a cosmopolitan should be seen in the first instance as an expression of her opposition to what she considers a nationalist fundamentalism, evidenced in the rise in nationalist sentiments and votes. Before continuing with this point, I want to return briefly to some of Kristeva's conclusions, presented towards the end of *Strangers to Ourselves*, where she advocates an ethical engagement with foreignness, drawing on the idea that we are all foreigners, or strangers, to ourselves. In Chapter 3, I briefly alluded to Kristeva's propagation of an ethical cosmopolitanism that is embedded in the political structure of a nation-state and that entails legal provisions for foreigners; these legal-political considerations are mapped upon her psychoanalytic discussion, which posits an ontological structure of radical strangeness within the subject and which concludes by demanding a psychoanalytic-cosmopolitan ethics of recognising the other. As I stated in Chapter 3, I am broadly sympathetic towards the central elements of Kristeva's ethical ideas, in particular her ethical orientation towards otherness. However, to repeat a claim I made previously, these ideas sit uncomfortably alongside some of her political assertions, which, as I want to demonstrate now, have invited substantial criticism (see Moruzzi 1993; Ahmed 2005).

To begin with, Kristeva's cosmopolitanism is a peculiar one, as it is embedded in her attachment to the idea of the nation and, more specifically, to the ideals of the French nation.[13] Kristeva does not reject the idea of the nation, which she considers as a, perhaps necessary, form of political organisation in our fragmented political world. There is more to this, though, than a pragmatic endorsement of the idea of the nation. Without denying the violent and problematic emergence of the nation in the context of the French Enlightenment and the French Revolution, Kristeva remains attached to the ideas of the French nation, as these are said to embody the ideals of universality. This strange mixing of the universal and particular is not just of conceptual interest. In fact, as I demonstrate in the next two sections, it has profound implications for Kristeva's thinking about immigration and about Europe. For now, though, I want to outline her treatment of cosmopolitanism and of universalism further.

Building upon her endorsement of cosmopolitanism, Kristeva rejects the critique of human rights, as expressed, in different ways, by Edmund Burke and Hannah Arendt. As is well known, Arendt, in a famous section of *The Origins of Totalitarianism* (1979), condemns a conception of human rights that is removed from any attachment to politics and citizenship. Whilst Kristeva acknowledges Arendt's critique, she declares that it is important to defend a 'universal, transnational principle of Humanity' (*NwN*: 26), what Arendt, rather disparagingly, refers to as 'naked humanity', which is removed from the concrete historical realities of the nation and of citizenship. Kristeva justifies her position, against Arendt, by suggesting that only a universal conception of humanity, grounded in cosmopolitanism, can serve as a bulwark against the contemporary fragmentation caused by nationalism and religion. She combines her attachment to the ideas of cosmopolitanism with her endorsement of the wider ideals of Enlightenment universalism, including her support for a conception of human rights, and she makes an explicit case for holding on to a universalist conception of humanity, against its potential nationalist or religious fragmentation (*NwN*: 26–7). It would be interesting to pursue her call for such a universalist project of humanity, specifically in its relationship to her insistence on the subject as heterogeneous and in-process.[14] What interests me here, instead, is to trace the further unfolding of her argument on universalism and its relationship to the particular, embodied in the French nation. Cecilia Sjöholm has described Kristeva's engagement with universalism and cosmopolitanism as 'hollow', as it is said to entail, 'not a negation of the particular, but the cut of alterity in subjectivity' (2005: 59), which, furthermore, displaces questions of politics into the realm of the intimate. While I share Sjöholm's latter diagnosis regarding Kristeva's displacement strategies, I have reservations concerning her thesis of a hollow universalism; as I want to suggest in the remainder of this section, Kristevan universalism is contaminated by the particular, embodied in the figure of the French nation.

As I already stated, Kristeva's cosmopolitanism does not entail a rejection of the nation; rather, drawing on her reading of Enlightenment universalism, she finds the most suitable expression of this cosmopolitanism in the idea of the (French) nation. Two elements are key to the further development of her argument; these include her delineation of the idea of the French nation against the backdrop of a predominantly Muslim migration into France (see next section), and her equation of the French national idea with the ideas of the Enlightenment and its legal and institutional embodiment in the French Republic (*NwN*: 40). The ideas that inform such an argument have recently been criticised by Joan Scott (2007), who contends that such a view expresses a mythical image of France that, at least in its most recent manifestation, relies upon a negative portrayal of Islam and that fails to consider the social and historical specificity and context of the emergence of the nation (2007: 7). Moreover, as several other commentators have pointed up, Kristeva's discussion of the stranger, and her reflections on the state of the nation under conditions of immigration are strangely oblivious to the racial undertone of these ethico-political reflections. Norma Claire Moruzzi, for example, takes issue with Kristeva's discussion, because it lacks, in her view, 'an acknowledgment of racial configurations' (1993: 139). Sara Ahmed (2005) critiques Kristeva's wider discussion of the stranger, including her call for an ethics based upon the recognition of strangeness. This call, expressed in *Strangers to Ourselves*, builds upon Kristeva's diagnosis of the radical alterity within the subject, which leads Kristeva to conclude that we are all strangers to ourselves; only on the basis of such radical strangeness, Kristeva suggests, can we begin to establish ethical relationships with others. However, as Ahmed argues, rightly in my view, and notwithstanding our ethical imperative to recognise others, including strangers, strangerness is unevenly distributed along racial lines; hence, the inscription of racial difference into the process of constructing some as strangers and others as hosts is an effect of power that cannot be willed away by appealing to a general, non-particular heterogeneity of the subject or a set of good intentions (Ahmed 2005: 96).

Ahmed's critique raises a further issue that has also recently been taken up by Margaroni (2007) and that I referred to previously in my discussion; this is the question of whether psychoanalytic concepts can be transposed on to an analysis of politics. As

Towards a Philosophy of Freedom?

Ahmed asks, 'Is the subject *like* the nation insofar as it requires differentiation from strangers?' (2005: 95; italics in original). Kristeva seems to answer this question in the affirmative, and her frequent allusions to what she calls a national melancholia testify to this. As I already suggested, her discussion of the nation is an intriguing one because it sits oddly alongside her insistence on the fluidity and plurality of a split subject in process; instead, it seems grounded in a conception of sovereignty that is ill at ease with her wider work. While the connection between her psychoanalytic decentring of the subject to her discussion of the nation is precarious, she deploys the psychoanalytic concept of melancholia to make sense of the contemporary national malaise, and she has stressed repeatedly, especially in some of her interviews, her concern for what she terms a widespread national depression (more on this below). Her response to this national depression is analogous to that of the melancholic suffering of the individual; the nation has to have its confidence restored.

This, however, throws up serious questions about the treatment of those at the margins of the nation. It also demands a more fundamental questioning of her thesis. Peter Gratton (2007), for example, criticises Kristeva's thesis of a national depression, which is said to be triggered by, amongst other factors, immigration, and which requires as its cure a restoration of national confidence. Such a thesis, according to Gratton, is only possible because Kristeva is blind to France's colonial history. Hence, what Kristeva diagnoses as a national depression may in fact turn out to be what Paul Gilroy (2004) refers to, with reference to Britain, as a postcolonial melancholia, triggered by a loss of colonial power and the inability to come to terms with this loss. For Gratton, France's loss of its colonies constitutes the source of the decline in national confidence amongst a section of its population, and he challenges Kristeva's reluctance to consider the colonial undercurrent of this national melancholia. While, as he further suggests, the figure of the foreigner makes a notion of the 'we' impossible, he also proposes, with and against Kristeva, to hold on to the idea of a 'paradoxical community' promised in *Strangers to Ourselves*, which is said to be truly open to the other (*StO*: 10).

Yet, as I argued, such a call leaves unanswered the question of the concrete other; it also fails to consider universalism's contamination with the particular. Because Kristeva tends to anchor the French nation in the genealogy of the (French) Enlightenment, it is perhaps unsurprising that she has been accused of proffering a conception of the nation and of cosmopolitanism that is profoundly French, even chauvinistic, and that is void of any political-historical analysis (see Varsamopoulou 2009). Her movement between the universal and the particular is particularly prominent in her discussion of Europe, where her texts display frequent elisions between 'France' and 'Europe', or 'French' and 'European' (see, for example, 1998a; 2004a; 2005a), and I want to explore concrete instances of this textual strategy in the following sections.

Europe's Others

I already alluded to the centrality that the issue of Muslim immigration occupies in Kristeva's discussion of the nation. There are obvious sociological and political reasons for this emphasis, given the geographical background and religious make-up of many of France's immigrants, and the ensuing debates over integration, particularly in relation to the role of religious symbols in the life of a state that defines itself as secular. This is an ongoing issue in contemporary French politics, and recent debates over the introduction of a ban on wearing a veil in public spaces attest to its continued relevance, but my focus lies elsewhere. Developing my arguments from the previous section, I want to examine further the psycho-sexual subtext in Kristeva's writings on the nation and on immigration. Her comments on the veil, in *Nations without Nationalism*, serve as a useful entry point to this debate. Diagnosing a 'twofold humiliation' that faces the French, coming from without, such as the erosion of national sovereignty in the face of the workings of the European Union and the re-emergence of a powerful neighbour in the wake of German unification in 1990, and from within, through immigration, Kristeva raises the spectre of the veil and its impact on the French population, which she sets against her assertion of the hard and long-fought-for values of freedom and culture: '(why accept [that daughters of Maghrebin immigrants wear] the Muslim scarf [to school]? Why change spelling? . . .)' (*NwN*: 36). Further below, she continues: 'To what libertarian, cultural, professional, or other advantage would a Muslim wish to join the French community?' (*NwN*:

37). As Sara Ahmed, in her critical reading of the same text, has pointed out, Kristeva's question proceeds on the assumption of a binary between French and Muslim, where French is defined as 'not Muslim' and Muslim signifies 'not French' (Ahmed 2005). This in itself is problematic, because it implies a racial undertone in Kristeva's discussion that undermines her subscription to what we might term civic conceptions of the nation. But there is a further comment to be made. Key to Kristeva's concept of the (French) nation is the role of culture: specifically, language and literature. This assertion, however, in addition to the racial undertone of her claim, inscribes a notion of sexual difference into 'Frenchness' and 'immigrants'. By claiming the nation as a symbolic pact, defined by language, she relegates those outside the national culture to the status of the abject feminine, engaging in an 'autistic withdrawal into their originary values' (*NwN*: 11). Moreover, the example of the veil codes the Muslim as feminine and hence as a stranger to the masculine national community.

As Ahmed asserts, '[m]odernity is understood as an empty form of universalism, one that does not take the shape of particular bodies. As such, Kristeva suggests that modernity can allow others into its community of strangers as long as they give up the visible signs of their concrete difference' (2005: 98). I already indicated that this hollow modernity comes to be filled with particular (French) content in Kristeva's further discussion, leading some of her critics to accuse her of proffering a conception of cosmopolitanism and of Europe that is profoundly French and read through a French lens. Evy Varsamopoulou (2009) contends that Kristeva conflates the idea of Europe with the ideals of France: specifically, with those ideals that, as we have already seen, Joan Scott refers to as a mythical conception of the French nation (2007). Whilst Varsamopoulou acknowledges the importance of the ethical orientation of Kristeva's discourse on foreignness, a position shared by most commentators, she faults Kristeva in particular for her lack of a historical-concrete analysis. This critique is also pertinent to Kristeva's treatment of immigration. In her letter to Harlem Désir, the figurehead of the French anti-racism organisation, *SOS Racisme*, she makes the following claim:

> It is time . . . to ask immigrant people what motivated them (beyond economic opportunities and approximate knowledge of the language

propagated by colonialism) to choose the French community ... The respect for immigrants should not erase the gratitude due the welcoming host. (*NwN*: 60)

One is tempted to answer Kristeva's question, tongue-in-cheek, with Stuart Hall's account of migration into Britain:

[T]hey had ruled the world for 300 years and, at last, when they had made up their minds to climb out of the role, at least the others ought to have stayed out there in the rim, behaved themselves, gone somewhere else, or found some other client state. But no, they had always said that this [London] was really home, the streets were paved with gold, and bloody hell, we just came to check out whether that was so or not. (quoted in Brown 1995: 52)

At worst, Kristeva's comment displays a lack of sensitivity, and indeed a lack of knowledge, towards those who migrate, often under personally difficult and indeed dangerous conditions, to France; at best, it displays a curious disconnect from her own ethical account of a hospitality that is grounded in one's own foreignness. Yet, despite my criticism of Kristeva's treatment of the subject of the stranger, I would be reluctant to dismiss this aspect of her work completely. Beyond the problematic aspects of her consideration of the concrete experience of migration, what emerges is, as I already mentioned, an ethical orientation towards otherness that is grounded in the concept of the nation and that is attentive to the affective and somatic dimensions of living together under conditions of multiculturalism. In fact, this stress on the subterranean somatic and affective aspects of the nation could be considered more widely as her effort to recapture the idea of the nation from the kind of nationalist fundamentalism that she detests. In this respect, one may regard her attempt to underpin the nation affectively as a crucial element in a hegemonic struggle towards a different conception of nationhood, based upon a pragmatic recognition of the persistence of nationhood in an era of globalisation that takes account of the porous boundaries of the nation and its subjects.

Ash Amin (2004) draws substantially on Kristeva's writings on the nation in his effort to revive the idea of Europe. He suggests that in the face of multiculturalism and diversity in Europe, where increasing numbers of Europeans trace their ancestry outside Europe, the old foundation myths of Europe, such as adherence to Roman law, a Christian-inspired ethics of solidarity, liberal individualism and Enlightenment reason, no longer have the capacity to inspire the contemporary European citizen. In their place, he proposes, building upon Kristeva, the installation of the principles of hospitality and mutuality. Hospitality, as I intimated in Chapter 3, is a central feature of Kristeva's ethics, described by her as the 'degree zero of ethos' (*IR*: 257), which, in her view, constitutes the core of the European conception of freedom. The idea of hospitality is based upon a recognition that we are all strangers in need of shelter. Such an essentially ethical commitment underlines the bond that exists between humans, between host and foreigner. However, even if we leave aside the question of its institutional implementation (Amin gives this some thought), it seems to me that Kristeva's idea of hospitality looks rather hollow, especially if it is contingent upon the condition of the recognition of the principles of French nationhood. There is indeed something rather 'thin' about Kristeva's principle of hospitality. How, though, does it fare in comparison to the second principle championed by Amin, that of mutuality? One may, in fact, consider mutuality as an important addition to the principle of hospitality; its recognition of intersubjectivity strengthens the status of those in receipt of hospitality vis-à-vis the position of the host. But even the idea of mutuality eludes the question of the particular: what kinds of concrete others share this intersubjective bond of host and guest? And, following Ahmed (2005), what kinds of racial and sexual configurations underpin the notions of hospitality and mutuality?

In *Strangers to Ourselves*, Kristeva describes women as the first foreigners; hence, their ethical stake in conceptions of welcoming otherness seems to be particularly high. Yet, in *Nations without Nationalism*, she also fears that women are particularly vulnerable to a notion of the nation grounded in *Volksgeist*, Herder's term for the mythical and mystical conception of the nation grounded in soil, blood and linguistic genius, which Kristeva rejects in favour of Montesquieu's notion of *esprit général*. Women's biological fate, including their capacity to have children and their attachment to the child and the home during nursing, according to Kristeva, ties them to such mystical conceptions of space. At the same time, women's narcissistic wound – specifically, their struggle to find a place in the symbolic – facilitates an identification with the power of the existing order. Already in 'Women's Time', Kristeva raises these issues, lamenting women's alleged tendency to become complicit with an, ultimately phallogocentric, status quo. Even though women's heterogeneity predisposes them to participate in an ethical conception of strangeness, Kristeva fears a close alliance between nationalism and feminism in its maternalist expression (*NwN*: 34).

There are two further facets to this discussion that I will address in the next section but want to highlight briefly here. First, while my emphasis so far has been with Kristeva's treatment of the question of immigration and its psychosexual and racial configuration of host and stranger, Kristeva's more recent work also raises the spectre of a colonialist or orientalist subtext that connects with some of her previous writings. Such an accusation of orientalism underpins the critique of Gayatri Spivak, who, in an influential essay published in 1981, takes issue with Kristeva's portrayal of China in her *About Chinese Women*. In addition to her staunch critique of the scholarly nature of Kristeva's argument and use of sources, Spivak accuses Kristeva of engaging in a 'colonialist benevolence' (1981: 161) that speaks from the position of 'a generalized West' (1981: 164). One can plausibly suggest that a similar colonial undertone appears in some of Kristeva's recent writings on Islamic fundamentalism. In a revised version of her 1998 essay 'Europhilia, Europhobia', Kristeva raises again the spectre of the Arab world, but this time not as the other within, embodied in the figure of the Muslim migrant, but the figure outside, resulting in a rather intriguing characterisation that is worth quoting at length:

> [T]he knowledge that we in Europe have of the Arab world, after so many years of colonialism, has made us very sensitive to Islamic culture and rendered us capable of softening, if not entirely avoiding, the 'clash of civilizations' to which I have referred. In this situation, what is at stake is our ability to offer our active support to those in the Muslim world who are now seeking to modernize Islam. At the same time, however, the insidious anti-Semitism in our countries should make us vigilant faced with the rise of new forms of anti-Semitism today. (2005a: 32; see also 2004a)

Here, Kristeva presents a highly problematic textual strategy that establishes a disturbing analogy between the terms 'Arab', 'Muslim', 'Islam' and 'anti-semitism', all of which are held together in a seemingly precarious balance by the threats posed by a clash of civilisations and underpinned by an orientalist knowledge established in the wake of colonialism. Moreover, as we have seen in Chapter 3, the spectre of violence that looms in this statement is embodied in the figure of the *shahida*, the female suicide bomber, who surfaces in some of her most recent writings. The relationship of universal to particular, which structures Kristeva's depiction of Europe's, and specifically France's, relationship with its others, returns in her discussion of the internal divisions that run through Europe and that have generated distinctive conceptions of East and West.

The Other Europe

Before delving further into Kristeva's writings on Europe, I want to recall briefly my discussion of freedom that I began in the first section of this chapter. There, I introduced Kristeva's recent emphasis on the notion of freedom that, as I sought to demonstrate, is read through the lens of psychoanalysis. As I also intimated, Kristeva's conception of freedom is distinguished by its explicit connotation with place; this, as we have seen, is introduced through her distinction between a European and an American version of freedom. She develops her discussion of freedom, in the geographical context of Europe, in subsequent writings, where she introduces a further division by opening up the possibility of a distinction between an Eastern European and Orthodox Christian tradition on the one hand, and a Western tradition of freedom on the other. In her essay 'Europe Divided: Politics, Ethics, Religion' (published in Kristeva 2000c), Kristeva demarcates a Western European version of freedom, defined as the 'desire for objects, knowledge, and production' (*Crisis*: 159), against an Eastern European and Orthodox version that embodies 'the freedom to withdraw into intimacy and mystical participation' (*Crisis*: 159–60). Both versions, according to Kristeva, are inseparable. Here I want to explore a little further what this Eastern version entails. As Kristeva suggests, the Eastern experience (which is not reducible to Orthodoxy and which is said to retain strong links to paganism) is essentially one of affectivity and of the senses. It is therefore not surprising that Kristeva links this experience with her notion of the semiotic, opposed to an association of the West with the symbolic. She suggests the necessity to connect the East with the West; after all, semiotic and symbolic modalities can only operate fully if they are connected.

Kristeva's 1998 essay, 'Europhilia, Europhobia', which I already referred to above, contains no references to the East, constructing instead a complementary transatlantic space of freedom shared between Europe and America. A revised version of this article, published under the title 'French Theory' (2004a), introduces a more nuanced conception of Europe that acknowledges differences, especially cultural and religious differences, between 'Old Europe', a term that refers to the countries of Western Europe, and 'New Europe', a shorthand for the former Soviet bloc countries in the East. This idea of two Europes recurs, in yet another version of the same article (2005a), where she considers, in several short remarks, the need to bridge the gap between East and West, especially by paying attention to the differences between the eastern and western churches. This religious dimension is indeed crucial to Kristeva's account, and is central to 'Europe Divided: Politics, Ethics, Religion', too. There, Kristeva outlines in detail her ideas for a complementary reading of two European traditions of freedom that chimes with her previous work on revolt and intimacy. Beginning from the assumption that the European subject is in crisis, Kristeva asks whether there is any prospect for a shared European cultural identity. Whilst the question of European identity remains implicit and essentially unanswered, it is her focus on the development of a new conception of freedom that interests me here. Kristeva is adamant in claiming the Eastern tradition, particularly the traditions of the Orthodox faith, since they have a central contribution to make. What would be the elements of such a contribution?

While her essay begins with some sociological observations, pertaining to the East's economic backwardness and alleged shortcomings in public morality (more on this below), Kristeva moves swiftly towards a discussion of freedom that draws on philosophy and the theology of Orthodox Christianity. Her comments on the contribution of Kant and Heidegger, and the subsequent distinction between a Protestant and a Catholic tradition of freedom, are by now familiar. What the essay brings new to my discussion is her consideration of Orthodoxy's contribution to a conception of freedom. According to Kristeva, the Orthodox faith introduces an affective or sensory dimension into culture, which she traces back to Orthodoxy's emphasis on experience and union, as opposed to the Western philosophical tradition of questioning, derived from Western Christianity. This distinction leads Kristeva to conclude that Orthodox faith is one of affect, of sensory experience, derived also from the sensory paganism that, in her view, is still widespread in Eastern Europe. Mapping this affective element of Orthodoxy on to her categorical distinction between the semiotic and the symbolic, Kristeva places Orthodoxy on the side of the semiotic, which, as she suggests, 'valorizes the preoedipal, narcissistic, depressive stage of personality' (*Crisis*: 149). This valorisation of the affective and sensory is connected, furthermore, with Orthodoxy's alleged privileging of the intimate, which, as Kristeva suggests, may go as far as resulting in a lack of attention towards the public realm (and which is said to manifest itself in widespread practices of corruption and extortion; see *Crisis*: 136). Thus, even though Kristeva identifies what she considers to be the faults and failures of Eastern Europe, she is also at pains to establish the important contribution that the countries of the East can make towards a newly configured and enlarged Europe. As we have seen in Chapter 2, intimacy and a rich psychic life are essential components of our overall psychic well-being; they are also the precondition of our capacity for revolt and hence, by extension, for freedom. In that respect, the sensory nature of Orthodoxy adds an important dimension to the conception of life and freedom that Kristeva champions. As she suggests, 'this passional and fusional subjectivity also seems to me to offer a counterweight to the exhaustion of Western freedom in pretense and the spectacular' (*Crisis*: 136–7).

There is more to this, though. The affective dimension of a conception of freedom grounded in Orthodox principles attests to the capacity to form bonds; in other words, such a freedom is inherently ethical. Kristeva says as much when she wonders whether contemporary subjects are capable of forming bonds with others without abandoning their freedom. For Kristeva, this is a difficult, though not impossible task that requires a balancing between freedom and bonds, and between understanding and the sensory

(*Crisis*: 152). Kristeva's more personal reflections on her Bulgarian background further underscore the need for such a bond, and for the crossing of the boundaries between East and West; she defines herself as a 'creature of the crossroads, between "them" and "us", belonging ultimately neither to "them" nor to "us", but perhaps to both groups' (*Crisis*: 113).

I have emphasised throughout that I am broadly sympathetic towards such a chiasmatic project[15] and in particular to Kristeva's persistent attempts at establishing bonds between the affective or sensory dimension and the symbolic. Such a traversal of boundaries, coupled with the need to create and recreate always provisional and fragile bonds with others seems to me an essential task for any feminist theory that takes seriously the critique of the subject and of identity, the assertion of the heterogeneity of the subject, and its relation to alterity: in short, a feminist theory that takes Kristevan concepts as a point of departure. However, as I have also stressed repeatedly, I remain sceptical about the concrete implementation of these radical ideas. Here I want to illustrate what I consider to be such a severance in relation to the psychosexual subtext that informs Kristeva's discussion of Europe and that stem from her psychoanalytic reading of Orthodoxy.

In order to arrive at the assertion of the passionate and affective nature of Orthodoxy, Kristeva offers a psychoanalytic reading of Orthodox faith that is based upon the idea of 'per filium', the relationship between God, the Father and the Son, which, unlike its Western Christian counterpart, is not one of equality (see also *BS*: 208). Rather, following Kristeva's reading, the authority of the Father remains untouched and the Son is left with two options: to submit or to reject the Father violently. The submissive son, as Kristeva suggests, becomes effeminate, withdrawing into a feminine position of passivity (*Crisis*: 140) that is coded as male homosexuality. Women, on the other hand, become masculinised, displaying courage, tenacity and intellectual prowess, and turning into '"hardcore-feminists"' (*Crisis*: 141).

A more sustained engagement with the theme of East and West, which, as I illustrate below, has received substantial criticism, can be found in her essay 'Bulgaria, My Suffering', also included in *Crisis of the European Subject* (2000c). 'Bulgaria, My Suffering' is Kristeva's attempt, informed by autobiography, to understand contemporary Bulgaria after the fall of the Iron Curtain. In this essay, she develops more fully what she considers to be the weaknesses of Eastern Europe, consisting of corruption and the Mafia, a certain psychopathology and the attitude towards cleanliness and filth. Perhaps unsurprisingly, she again brings into play a psychosexual context that concentrates on the maternal aspect of Bulgaria, embodied in the mother tongue and the maternal body. This attachment to the figure of the maternal-feminine is also invoked in her repeated references to the figure of Anne Comnena, a character in Kristeva's novel *Murder in Byzantium* (2004d), but also a historical figure from the Balkans whom Kristeva describes as the first female intellectual. Her assertion of female genius, represented in the figure of a Balkan woman, attests to Kristeva's self-confessed pride in the achievements of Bulgarian intellectuals in general and of women in particular. Yet, there is also a darker side to her analysis that has attracted strong criticism; if Bulgaria signifies the maternal-feminine, does it also signify the abject?

Unsurprisingly, these claims have attracted strong criticism. One commentator, Dušan I. Bjelić (2006), takes issue with Kristeva's narrative on the Balkans, and with the psychosexual imprint that is mapped upon it. His central discontent relates to Kristeva's psychoanalytic construction of geopolitics, consisting of what he terms a psychoanalytic account of the genital origin of civic subjectivity (2006: 56). What does he mean by this? Building upon his assertion that Kristeva's account is void of socio-historical context, he takes issue with her juxtaposition of French taste and Balkan filth. This juxtaposition, according to Bjelić, is a way of disavowing the violent and essentially unclean origins of nationhood, which is only sustainable if we ignore the intrinsic somatic connection between the two parts of Kristeva's discourse, where France comes to stand for vagina/mouth and the Balkans stand for anus/excrement. Of relevance to my discussion is a further aspect of Bjelić's discussion: the gendered connotations of Kristeva's East–West discourse. Bjelić points to those aspects of her writings on the Orthodox faith that identify the son with the feminine, and that, in his view, subscribe to a notion of Balkan homosexuality on the one hand, and a masculinised version of Balkan women on the other. As I indicated above, there is certainly much in Kristeva's texts that allows for such an interpretation; her distinction between a sensory and intimate generalised East on the one hand, and a questioning, critical West on the other subscribes to an idea of coherence that is at odds with her insistence on heterogeneity. However, a more generous analysis may point towards that aspect which, in my view, is essential to Kristeva's theoretical discussion: the bond between the sensory and the symbolic, which, according to her, bridges the gap between East and West.

A more nuanced criticism of Kristeva's account of Europe, and of her representation of the Balkans, can be found in Evy Varsamopoulou's essay on 'The Idea of Europe and the Ideal of Cosmopolitanism in the Work of Julia Kristeva' (2009). Like Bjelić, Varsamopoulou takes issue with Kristeva's failure to attend to a specific political-historical analysis, and, again like Bjelić, she refutes Kristeva's conflation of the idea of Europe with the ideals of France, and the conflation of the ideas of France with universalism and cosmopolitanism. Yet, Varsamopoulou also claims that the best aspects of Kristeva's work consist of 're-orientating ourselves ethically to difference' (2009: 38). This latter point returns me to my discussion at the beginning of this chapter (and indeed to a central argument of my book): that Kristeva's political philosophy, conceived as a theoretical discourse, aims at straddling the gap between the sensory and the symbolic, between psychic life and public life, and between intimate revolt and political revolution. Questioning and contestation, as we have seen, are key elements in this project, while the essence of this philosophy is freedom; I will return, one last time, to this theme in the last section of this chapter.

Towards a Kristevan Feminism?

In this chapter, I explored Kristeva's writings on freedom, which, as I have outlined, are informed by psychoanalytic, philosophical and geopolitical considerations. As I suggested, this thematic emphasis provides a new and exciting departure in her work that should stimulate the current and future Kristeva scholarship. Of particular interest is the importance she accords to the practice of questioning and critique. Although not developed by Kristeva in a distinctly feminist direction, it should influence any conception of feminism as a critical practice. However, in contradistinction to Kristeva's psychoanalytic and philosophical treatment of freedom and critique emerges her 'imaginative geography' (Said 1978), which associates Europe, and especially France, with the ideas and ideals of Enlightenment universalism, and which anchors freedom-as-contestation in the space of Western Europe. This imaginative geography, as I argued here, is underpinned by a psychosexual subtext, which establishes Europe as a subject in revolt, capable of drawing on its semiotic and symbolic capacity, and which relegates, in the main, Muslim immigrants and their descendants to the status of abject.

What, though, remains of Kristeva's overall relationship with feminism? *Julia Kristeva and Feminist Thought* examined Kristeva's relationship with feminism, which, as I stated in my Introduction, is defined as much by her ambivalence towards feminism, as it is structured by feminism's heterogeneity and plurality. Because of the diverse and plural perspectives that make up contemporary feminist thought, there exists no coherent or unified response to Kristeva's ideas, and the reception of her thought within feminism has been uneven. While her work has been welcomed by those feminist scholars who are sympathetic towards Kristeva's broad ideas, such as her critique of the subject and of identity, or her insistence on fluidity and instability, it has been rejected by others who remain attached to stable notions of the subject, who are hostile towards psychoanalysis, who question her usefulness for a feminist account of political efficacy or who turn to alternative accounts of the critique of the subject. Kristeva's relationship with feminism is further complicated because she remains ambivalent about feminism's importance. At least three responses to feminism emerge in her writings, ranging from the recognition of the importance of feminism's achievements, to an outright rejection of feminism as totalitarian, and to a transcendence of feminism through her emphasis on singularity and plurality. Thus, notwithstanding feminism's diversity and plurality, it is fair to say that Kristeva's thought does not translate easily into feminist theory. For one thing, as I already stated, she does not explicitly seek to make an impact. Moreover, her ambivalence towards politics does not connect with feminism understood as a project that aims towards social and political transformation. Hence, questions that have occupied feminist debates, such as the dispute over female or feminist political agency, political efficacy or political transformation, will struggle to find answers in Kristeva's writings.

But maybe these are the wrong questions to be asked of Kristeva's œuvre. Turning to Kristeva's wider philosophical and psychoanalytic ideas seems to me to be a more fruitful way of engaging with Kristeva's thought; a careful consideration of these ideas reveals her significant contribution to contemporary feminist theory. Such an assessment must, by necessity, consider her radical philosophy of feminine heterogeneity; it must also consider her ethics of traversal and her political anthropology, which seeks to connect the body with meaning and which stresses the affective nature of politics. One may add to this list her concern for the intimate and her insistence on the importance of revolt, as well as her celebration of singularity and plurality. Ultimately, I want to suggest, it is in her wider concern with critique, revolt and freedom that Kristeva's significance to feminism lies. This concern with critique, revolt and freedom contributes to the understanding of feminism as a critical, contestatory theory and practice that permanently negotiates and unsettles the boundaries between intimate and political revolt. Whilst conceptualising feminism in such a way can be profoundly unsettling for feminism, it also keeps feminism's heterogeneous, plural and diverse theory and practice alive.

Notes

1. I am drawing on Chantal Mouffe's distinction between politics, defined as a set of practices and institutions, and the political, which refers to the antagonism that is said to be constitutive of social life. See Mouffe (2005: 9).
2. This aspect of her writings has, as yet, not received much critical attention, and critical commentary on this work is only now beginning to emerge. See, for example, the contributions to Oliver and Keltner (2009); for an earlier, brief response see Beardsworth (2005b).
3. This part is published separately in French under the title *L'Avenir d'une révolte* (1998b).
4. The expression 'dark times' is taken from Brecht's poem 'An die Nachgeborenen' ('To Posterity') (Brecht 1990: 722–5). The connection that Arendt establishes between dark times, illumination and the singularity and biography of what Arendt terms genius lies at the heart of Kristeva's 'genius' trilogy.
5. I want to flag up at this point that this is not the only distinction Kristeva makes. As I discuss in the following sections, she opens

up two further dichotomies, between a West European and an East European conception of freedom, and between a European civilising mission, based upon Enlightenment universalism, and the Muslim world.
6. Judith Butler, like Kristeva, champions the practice of contestation as intrinsically valuable, but she develops its political import more fully. According to Butler, it is via this 'political culture of contestation' (2000b: 161) that subjectivities are made, remade and challenged.
7. Beardsworth describes Kristeva's portrayal of the two versions of freedom as a 'valuational asymmetry', which favours freedom-as-disclosure (2005b: 38).
8. However, as I discussed in the previous chapter, Arendt's celebration of politics-as-freedom goes hand in hand with her evacuation of politics from the private sphere.
9. For a similar argument see her essay on dissidence (1977b), where she celebrates various forms of dissidence, in particular the dissidence of the avant-garde, as a bulwark against a stifling symbolic. More recently, she includes female genius in the practice of dissidence, referring to Hannah Arendt and Melanie Klein as dissidents (2001b: 16).
10. Cooper (2000) makes a similar claim regarding Kristeva's preoccupation with the idea of strangeness.
11. It may be useful to recall an early article, on semiotics, that already engages with the question of critique. See Kristeva (1969b).
12. For a very useful and detailed outline, coupled with a critical assessment, see Scott (2007).
13. For a discussion of Kristeva's distinction between the idea and ideals of the nation see Ahmed (2005). I attend to Ahmed's critical reading of Kristeva below.
14. For a critique of Kristeva's 'reversion to the tenets of humanism' see Moruzzi (1993: 143). See also Ziarek (1995) for a more sympathetic reading that draws on Kristeva's deployment of the Freudian notion of the uncanny.
15. See Margaroni (2009) for an excellent analysis of the chiasmatic nature of Kristeva's thought.

Bibliography

More than forty years of scholarship, both by and on Kristeva, have generated an enormous output. This bibliography is not comprehensive; it does not consider the totality of Kristeva's output nor does it list every critical response to Kristeva's œuvre. It is limited to those texts that had an immediate impact upon my discussion. Kristeva has recently begun to make her shorter pieces available on her official web site (which can be accessed at www.kristeva.fr). Many of these texts are available in French and English; the web site also provides a comprehensive list of Kristeva's books and awards, as well as other information of use to anyone interested in her work.

Writings by Julia Kristeva

(1969a), 'Word, Dialogue and Novel', in *The Kristeva Reader*, ed. Toril Moi, Oxford: Blackwell, pp. 34–61.

(1969b), 'Semiotics: A Critical Science and/or a Critique of Science', in *The Kristeva Reader*, ed. Toril Moi, Oxford: Blackwell, pp. 74–88.

(1973a), 'The System and the Speaking Subject', in *The Kristeva Reader*, ed. Toril Moi, Oxford: Blackwell, pp. 24–33.

(1973b), 'The Subject in Process', reprinted in Patrick ffrench and Roland-François Lack (eds) (1998), *The Tel Quel Reader*, London: Routledge, pp. 133–78.

(1974a), *La Révolution du langage poétique. L'Avant-garde à la fin du XIXe siècle: Lautréamont et Mallarmé*, Paris: Seuil.

(1974b), 'About Chinese Women', in *The Kristeva Reader*, ed. Toril Moi, Oxford: Blackwell, pp. 138–59.

(1975), 'On the Women of China', *Signs: Journal of Women in Culture and Society*, vol. 1, no. 1, pp. 57–81.

(1977a), 'Stabat Mater', in *The Kristeva Reader*, ed. Toril Moi, Oxford: Blackwell, pp. 160–86.

(1977b), 'A New Type of Intellectual: The Dissident', in *The Kristeva Reader*, ed. Toril Moi, Oxford: Blackwell, pp. 292–300.

(1979), 'Women's Time', in *The Kristeva Reader*, ed. Toril Moi, Oxford: Blackwell, pp. 187–213.

(1980), *Desire in Language. A Semiotic Approach to Literature and Art*, New York: Columbia University Press.

(1981), 'Women can Never be Defined', in E. Marks and I. de Courtivron (eds), *New French Feminisms: An Anthology*, New York: Harvester & Wheatsheaf, pp. 137–41.

(1982a), *Powers of Horror. An Essay on Abjection*, New York: Columbia University Press.

(1982b), 'Approaching Abjection', *Oxford Literary Review*, vol. 5, no. 1–2, pp. 125–49.

(1983), 'Within the Microcosm of the Talking Cure', in J. H. Smith and W. Kerrigan (eds), *Interpreting Lacan*, New Haven, CT: Yale University Press, pp. 33–48.

(1984a), *Revolution in Poetic Language*, New York: Columbia University Press.

(1984b), 'My Memory's Hyperbole', *New York Literary Forum*, vols 12–13, pp. 261–76.

(1984c), 'Histoires d'amour – Love Stories', in L. Appignanensi (ed.), *Desire*, London: Institute of Contemporary Arts, pp. 18–21.

(1984d), 'Julia Kristeva in Conversation with Rosalind Coward', in L. Appignanensi (ed.), *Desire*, London: Institute of Contemporary Arts, pp. 22–7.

(1986), *About Chinese Women*, New York: Marion Boyars.

(1987a), *Tales of Love*, New York: Columbia University Press.

(1987b), *In the Beginning was Love. Psychoanalysis and Faith*, New York: Columbia University Press.

(1989a), *Black Sun. Depression and Melancholia*, New York: Columbia University Press.

(1989b), *Language the Unknown. An Initiation into Linguistics*, New York: Columbia University Press.

(1991a), *Strangers to Ourselves*, New York: Columbia University Press.

(1991b), 'Strangers to Ourselves – The "Strangers"', *Partisan Review*, vol. 58, no. 1, pp. 88–100.

(1992), *The Samurai: A Novel*, New York: Columbia University Press.

(1993), *Nations without Nationalism*, New York: Columbia University Press.

(1995), *New Maladies of the Soul*, New York: Columbia University Press.

Bibliography

(1996a), *Julia Kristeva Interviews*, ed. Ross Mitchell Guberman, New York: Columbia University Press.

(1996b), *Time and Sense: Proust and the Experience of Literature*, New York: Columbia University Press.

(1997), 'Hannah Arendt's Concept of Life', *Common Knowledge*, vol. 6, no. 2, pp. 159–69.

(1998a), 'Europhilia, Europhobia', *Constellations*, vol. 5, no. 3, pp. 321–32.

(1998b), *L'Avenir d'une révolte*, Paris: Calmann–Lévy.

(1998c), *Visions capitales*, Paris: Réunion des musées nationaux.

(2000a), *The Sense and Non-Sense of Revolt. The Powers and Limits of Psychoanalysis vol. I*, New York: Columbia University Press.

(2000b), *Revolt, She Said*, Los Angeles: Semiotext(e).

(2000c), *Crisis of the European Subject*, New York: Other.

(2001a), *Hannah Arendt*, New York: Columbia University Press.

(2001b), *Melanie Klein*, New York: Columbia University Press.

(2001c), *The Feminine and the Sacred*, with Catherine Clément, Basingstoke: Palgrave.

(2002), *Intimate Revolt. The Powers and Limits of Psychoanalysis, vol. II*, New York: Columbia University Press.

(2004a), 'French Theory', *Irish Pages: A Journal of Contemporary Writing*, Autumn/Winter, pp. 201–14.

(2004b), 'Female Genius, Freedom and Culture', *Irish Pages: A Journal of Contemporary Writing*, Autumn/Winter, pp. 214–28.

(2004c), *Colette*, New York: Columbia University Press.

(2004d), *Murder in Byzantium*, New York: Columbia University Press.

(2005a), 'Thinking about Liberty in Dark Times', *The Holberg Prize Seminar*, Bergen: Holberg, www. holbergprisen.no/images/materiell/2004_kristeva_english.pdf, pp. 21–36 (accessed 7 April 2008).

(2005b), *La Haine et le pardon. Pouvoirs et limites de la psychoanalyse III*, Paris: Arthème Fayard.

(2006), 'Hannah Arendt oder: Wiedergründen als Überleben. Festvortrag der Hannah-Arendt-Preisträgerin 2006', Festschrift zur Verleihung des Hannah-Arendt-Preises für politisches Denken 2006 an Julia Kristeva, www.hannah-arendt.de/Festschriften/Festschrift_20061175498415.pdf, pp. V–X (accessed 8 August 2008).

(2007a), 'Can We Make Peace?', in A. A. Jardine, S. Lundeen and K. Oliver (eds), *Living Attention: On Teresa Brennan*, Albany, NY: SUNY Press, pp. 117–26.

(2007b), 'My Motto is Diversity', in Centre d'Analyse et de Prévision, Collection Penser l'Europe (ed.), *Diversity and Culture/Diversité et culture*, Paris: CulturesFrance, pp. 6–23.

(2007c), 'Rethinking "Normative Conscience": The Task of the Intellectual Today', *Common Knowledge*, vol. 13, nos 2–3, pp. 219–26.

(2008), 'Refoundation as Survival: An Interrogation of Hannah Arendt', *Common Knowledge*, vol. 14, no. 3, pp. 353–64.

(2009a), 'A Meditation, a Political Act, an Art of Living', in K. Oliver and S. K. Keltner (eds) (2009), *Psychoanalysis, Aesthetics, and Politics in the Work of Kristeva*, Albany, NY: SUNY Press, pp. 19–27.

(2009b), 'Beauvoir and the Risks of Freedom', *PMLA*, vol. 124, no. 1, pp. 226–30.

(2009c), 'Decollations', in K. Oliver and S. K. Keltner (eds) (2009), *Psychoanalysis, Aesthetics, and Politics in the Work of Kristeva*, Albany, NY: SUNY Press, pp. 29–45.

(2009d), *This Incredible Need to Believe*, New York: Columbia University Press.

Secondary Literature

Ahmed, Sara (2005), 'The Skin of the Community: Affect and Boundary Formation', in T. Chanter and E. P. Ziarek (eds), *Revolt, Affect, Collectivity: The Unstable Boundaries of Kristeva's Polis*, Albany, NY: SUNY Press, pp. 95–111.

Amin, Ash (2004), 'Multi-Ethnicity and the Idea of Europe', *Theory, Culture and Society*, vol. 21, no. 2, pp. 1–24.

Arendt, Hannah (1958), *The Human Condition*, Chicago: University of Chicago Press.

— (1963), *On Revolution*, London: Penguin.

— (1968), *Men in Dark Times*, San Diego: Harcourt Brace.

— (1977), *Between Past and Future: Eight Exercises in Political Thought*, New York: Penguin.

— (1978), *The Life of the Mind*, San Diego: Harcourt Brace.

— (1979), *The Origins of Totalitarianism*, San Diego: Harcourt Brace.

— (1992), *Eichmann in Jerusalem: A Report on the Banality of Evil*, London: Penguin.

— (1996), *Love and Saint Augustine*, Chicago: University of Chicago Press.

— (1997), *Rahel Varnhagen: Lebensgeschichte einer deutschen Jüdin aus der Romantik*, Munich: Piper.

Bibliography

Banyard, Kat (2010), *The Equality Illusion: The Truth about Women and Men Today*, London: Faber & Faber.

Battersby, Christine (1989), *Gender and Genius: Towards a Feminist Aesthetics*, London: Women's Press.

Beardsworth, Sara (2004a), *Julia Kristeva: Psychoanalysis and Modernity*, Albany, NY: SUNY Press.

— (2004b), 'Kristeva's Idea of Sublimation', *Southern Journal of Philosophy*, vol. XLII, Supplement, pp. 122–36.

— (2005a), 'From Revolution to Revolt Culture', in T. Chanter and E. P. Ziarek (eds), *Revolt, Affect, Collectivity: The Unstable Boundaries of Kristeva's Polis*, Albany, NY: SUNY Press, pp. 37–56.

— (2005b), 'Freedom and Ethical Value', *The Holberg Prize Seminar*, Bergen: Holberg, www. holbergprisen.no/images/materiell/2004_kristeva_english.pdf, pp. 38–41 (accessed 7 April 2008).

Becker-Leckrone, Megan (2005), *Julia Kristeva and Literary Theory*, Basingstoke: Palgrave Macmillan.

Benhabib, Seyla, Judith Butler, Drucilla Cornell and Nancy Fraser (1995), *Feminist Contentions. A Philosophical Exchange*, New York: Routledge.

Benveniste, Emile (1971), *Problems in General Linguistics*, Coral Gables: University of Miami Press.

Bhabha, Homi K. (1992), 'Postcolonial Authority and Postmodern Guilt', in L. Grossberg, C. Nelson and P. Treichler (eds), *Cultural Studies*, London: Routledge, pp. 56–66.

Birmingham, Peg (2003), 'Holes of Oblivion: The Banality of Evil', *Hypatia*, vol. 18, no. 1, pp. 80–103.

— (2005), 'Political Affections: Kristeva and Arendt on Violence and Gratitude', in T. Chanter and E. P. Ziarek (eds), *Revolt, Affect, Collectivity: The Unstable Boundaries of Kristeva's Polis*, Albany, NY: SUNY Press, pp. 127–45.

— (2006), *Hannah Arendt and Human Rights: The Predicament of Common Responsibility*, Bloomington: Indiana University Press.

Bjelić, Dušan I. (2006), 'The Balkans: Europe's Cesspool', *Cultural Critique*, no. 62, Winter, pp. 33–66.

Boulous Walker, Michelle (1998), *Philosophy and the Maternal Body: Reading Silence*, London: Routledge.

Bové, Carol Mastrangelo (1983), 'The Text as Dialogue in Bakhtin and Kristeva', *Revue de l'Université d'Ottawa/University of Ottawa Quarterly*, vol. 53, no. 1, pp. 117–24.

— (2006), *Language and Politics in Julia Kristeva: Literature, Art, Therapy*, Albany, NY: SUNY Press.
Braidotti, Rosi (1991), *Patterns of Dissonance. A Study of Women in Contemporary Philosophy*, Cambridge: Polity.
Brandt, Joan (2005), 'Julia Kristeva and the Revolutionary Politics of *Tel Quel*', in T. Chanter and E. P. Ziarek (eds), *Revolt, Affect, Collectivity: The Unstable Boundaries of Kristeva's Polis*, Albany, NY: SUNY Press, pp. 21–36.
Brecht, Bertolt (1990), *Gedichte 2. Gesammelte Werke 9*, Frankfurt: Suhrkamp.
Brown, Wendy (1995), *States of Injury: Power and Freedom in Late Modernity*, Princeton: Princeton University Press.
— (2005), *Edgework: Critical Essays on Knowledge and Politics*, Princeton: Princeton University Press.
Burke, Carol Greenstein (1978), 'Report from Paris: Women's Writing and the Women's Movement', *Signs: Journal of Women in Culture and Society*, vol. 3, no. 4, pp. 843–55.
Butler, Judith (1990), *Gender Trouble. Feminism and the Subversion of Identity*, London: Routledge.
— (1993), *Bodies that Matter. On the Discursive Limits of 'Sex'*, New York: Routledge.
— (1997), *The Psychic Life of Power. Theories in Subjection*, Stanford: Stanford University Press.
— (2000a), *Antigone's Claim. Kinship Between Life and Death*, New York: Columbia University Press.
— (2000b), *Contingency, Hegemony, Universality: Contemporary Dialogues on the Left*, with Ernesto Laclau and Slavoj Žižek, London: Verso.
— (2004), *Precarious Life: The Powers of Mourning and Violence*, London: Verso.
— (2009), *Frames of War: When is Life Grievable?*, London: Verso.
Butler, Judith and Joan W. Scott (eds) (1992), *Feminists Theorize the Political*, New York: Routledge.
Cahill, Ann J. and Jennifer L. Hansen (eds) (2008), *French Feminists: Critical Evaluations in Cultural Theory. Vol. IV: Julia Kristeva*, London: Routledge.
Cavallaro, Dani (2003), *French Feminist Theory: An Introduction*, London: Continuum.
Cavarero, Adriana (2000), *Relating Narratives: Storytelling and Selfhood*, London: Routledge.

Bibliography

— (2009), *Horrorism: Naming Contemporary Violence*, New York: Columbia University Press.
Caws, Mary Ann (1973), '*Tel Quel*: Text and Revolution', *Diacritics*, vol. 3, no. 1, pp. 2–8.
Chanter, Tina and Ewa Płonowska Ziarek (eds) (2005), *Revolt, Affect, Collectivity: The Unstable Boundaries of Kristeva's Polis*, Albany, NY: SUNY Press.
Clark, T. J. and Donald Nicholson-Smith (1997), 'Why Art Can't Kill the Situationist International', *October*, no. 79, Winter 1997, pp. 15–31.
Coole, Diana (2000), *Negativity and Politics. Dionysus and Dialectics from Kant to Poststructuralism*, London: Routledge.
— (2005), 'Rethinking Agency: A Phenomenological Approach to Embodiment and Agentic Capacities', *Political Studies*, vol. 53, pp. 124–42.
Cooper, Sarah (2000), *Relating to Queer Theory: Rereading Sexual Self-Definition with Irigaray, Kristeva, Wittig and Cixous*, Berne: Peter Lang.
Cornell, Drucilla (1991), *Beyond Accommodation. Ethical Feminism, Deconstruction and the Law*, New York: Routledge.
— (1993), *Transformations: Recollective Imagination and Sexual Difference*, New York: Routledge.
— (1995), 'What is Ethical Feminism?', in S. Benhabib, J. Butler, D. Cornell and N. Fraser, *Feminist Contentions: A Philosophical Exchange*, New York: Routledge, pp. 75–106.
— (2003), 'Facing our Humanity', *Hypatia*, vol. 18, no. 1, pp. 170–4.
Cornell, Drucilla and Adam Thurschwell (1987), 'Feminism, Negativity, Intersubjectivity', in S. Benhabib and D. Cornell (eds), *Feminism as Critique. Essays on the Politics of Gender in Late-Capitalist Societies*, Cambridge: Polity, pp. 143–89.
Critchley, Simon (1999), 'Introduction: What is Continental Philosophy?', in S. Critchley and W. R. Schroeder (eds), *A Companion to Continental Philosophy*, Oxford: Blackwell, pp. 1–17.
Crystal, David (1992), *The Cambridge Encyclopedia of Language*, Cambridge: Cambridge University Press.
De Beauvoir, Simone (1976), *The Ethics of Ambiguity*, trans. Bernard Frechtman, New York: Citadel.
— (2005), *The Mandarins*, trans. Leonard M. Friedman, London: Harper Perennial.
— (2009), *The Second Sex*, trans. Constance Borde and Sheila Malovany-Chevallier, London: Jonathan Cape.

Debord, Guy (1994), *The Society of the Spectacle*, New York: Zone.
Delphy, Christine (2000), 'The Invention of French Feminism: An Essential Move', *Yale French Studies*, no. 97, pp. 166–97.
Dietz, Mary G. (1995), 'Feminist Receptions of Hannah Arendt', in B. Honig (ed.), *Feminist Interpretations of Hannah Arendt*, University Park: Pennsylvania State University Press, pp. 17–50.
— (2003), 'Current Controversies in Feminist Theory', *Annual Review of Political Science*, vol. 6, pp. 399–431.
Diprose, Rosalyn (1994), *The Bodies of Women: Ethics, Embodiment and Sexual Difference*, London: Routledge.
Disch, Lisa J. (1995), 'On Friendship in "Dark Times"', in B. Honig (ed.), *Feminist Interpretations of Hannah Arendt*, University Park: Pennsylvania State University Press, pp. 285–311.
Douglas, Mary (1966), *Purity and Danger. An Analysis of Concepts of Pollution and Taboo*, London: Routledge & Kegan Paul.
Duchen, Claire (1986), *Feminism in France. From May '68 to Mitterrand*, London: Routledge & Kegan Paul.
Edelstein, Marylin (1993), 'Toward a Feminist Postmodern *Poléthique*: Kristeva on Ethics and Politics', in K. Oliver (ed.), *Ethics, Politics and Difference in Julia Kristeva's Writing*, New York: Routledge, pp. 196–214.
Fanon, Frantz (2001), *The Wretched of the Earth*, London: Penguin.
Fausto-Sterling, Anne (2000), *Sexing the Body. Gender Politics and the Construction of Sexuality*, New York: Basic.
ffrench, Patrick (1995), *The Time of Theory: A History of* Tel Quel *(1960–1983)*, Oxford: Oxford University Press.
ffrench, Patrick and Roland-François Lack (eds) (1998), *The Tel Quel Reader*, London: Routledge.
Fraser, Nancy (1992a), 'Introduction: Revaluing French Feminism', in N. Fraser and S. L. Bartky (eds), *Revaluing French Feminism. Critical Essays on Difference, Agency and Culture*, Bloomington: Indiana University Press, pp. 1–24.
— (1992b), 'The Uses and Abuses of French Discourse Theories for Feminist Politics', in N. Fraser and S. L. Bartky (eds), *Revaluing French Feminism. Critical Essays on Difference, Agency and Culture*, Bloomington: Indiana University Press, pp. 177–94.
Fraser, Nancy and Sandra Lee Bartky (eds) (1992), *Revaluing French Feminism. Critical Essays on Difference, Agency and Culture*, Bloomington: Indiana University Press.

Bibliography

Frazer, Elizabeth, Jennifer Hornsby and Sabina Lovibund (eds) (1992), *Ethics: A Feminist Reader*, Oxford: Blackwell.

Freeden, Michael (2008), 'Thinking Politically and Thinking about Politics: Language, Interpretation, and Ideology', in D. Leopold and M. Stears (eds), *Political Theory: Methods and Approaches*, Oxford: Oxford University Press, pp. 196–215.

Freud, Sigmund (1994a), 'Einige psychische Folgen des anatomischen Geschlechtsunterschiedes', in *Schriften über Liebe und Sexualität*, Frankfurt: Fischer, pp. 169–88.

— (1994b), 'Über die weibliche Sexualität', in *Schriften über Liebe und Sexualität*, Frankfurt: Fischer, pp. 189–209.

— (1997), *Abriss der Psychoanalyse: Einführende Darstellungen*, Frankfurt: Fischer.

— (1998a), *Totem und Tabu. Einige Übereinstimmungen im Seelenleben der Wilden und der Neurotiker*, Frankfurt: Fischer.

— (1998b), 'Trauer und Melancholie', in *Das Ich und das Es. Metapsychologische Schriften*, Frankfurt: Fischer, pp. 171–89.

— (1998c), 'Jenseits des Lustprinzips, in *Das Ich und das Es. Metapsychologische Schriften*, Frankfurt: Fischer, pp. 191–249.

— (1998d), 'Das Ich und das Es', in *Das Ich und das Es. Metapsychologische Schriften*, Frankfurt: Fischer, pp. 251–95.

— (1998e), 'Die Weiblichkeit', in *Neue Vorlesungen zur Einführung in die Psychoanalyse*, Frankfurt: Fischer, pp. 110–32.

Gambaudo, Sylvie (2007a), *Kristeva, Psychoanalysis and Culture: Subjectivity in Crisis*, Aldershot: Ashgate.

— (2007b), 'French Feminism vs Anglo-American Feminism: A Reconstruction', *European Journal of Women's Studies*, vol. 14, no. 2, pp. 93–108.

Gatens, Moira (ed.) (1998), *Feminist Ethics*, Aldershot: Ashgate.

— (2002), *Imaginary Bodies: Ethics, Power and Corporeality*, London: Routledge.

Gilligan, Carol (1982), *In a Different Voice: Psychological Theory and Women's Development*, Cambridge, MA: Harvard University Press.

Gilroy, Paul (2004), *After Empire: Melancholia or Convivial Culture?*, Abingdon: Routledge.

Girard, René (1977), *Violence and the Sacred*, trans. P. Gregory, Baltimore: Johns Hopkins University Press.

Gratton, Peter (2007), 'What are Psychoanalysts for in a Destitute Time?', *Journal for Cultural Research*, vol. 11, no. 1, pp. 1–13.

Graybeal, Jean (1993), 'Kristeva's Delphic Proposal: Practice Encompasses the Ethical', in K. Oliver (ed.), *Ethics, Politics and Difference in Julia Kristeva's Writing*, New York: Routledge, pp. 32–40.

Gross, Elizabeth (1986), 'Philosophy, Subjectivity and the Body: Kristeva and Irigaray', in C. Pateman and E. Gross (eds), *Feminist Challenges: Social and Political Theory*, Sydney: Allen & Unwin, pp. 125–43.

— (1990), 'The Body of Signification', in J. Fletcher and A. Benjamin (eds), *Abjection, Melancholia and Love. The Work of Julia Kristeva*, London: Routledge, pp. 80–103.

Grosz, Elizabeth (1989), *Sexual Subversions. Three French Feminists*, Sydney: Allen & Unwin.

— (1990), *Jacques Lacan. A Feminist Introduction*, London: Routledge.

— (1992), 'Kristeva, Julia', in E. Wright (ed.), *Feminism and Psychoanalysis. A Critical Dictionary*, Blackwell: Oxford, pp. 194–200.

Hamilton, Edith and Huntington Cairns (1999), *The Collected Dialogues of Plato*, Princeton: Princeton University Press.

Harding, Sandra (1986), *The Science Question in Feminism*, Ithaca, NY: Cornell University Press.

Held, Virginia (2006), *The Ethics of Care: Personal, Political, and Global*, Oxford: Oxford University Press.

Hirsch, Marianne (1981), 'Review Essay: Mothers and Daughters', *Signs*, vol. 7, no. 1, pp. 200–22.

Hirschmann, Nancy J. (2003), *The Subject of Liberty: Toward a Feminist Theory of Freedom*, Princeton: Princeton University Press.

Honig, Bonnie (1995a), 'Introduction: The Arendt Question in Feminism', in B. Honig (ed.), *Feminist Interpretations of Hannah Arendt*, University Park: Pennsylvania State University Press, pp. 1–16.

— (1995b), 'Towards an Agonistic Feminism', in B. Honig (ed.), *Feminist Interpretations of Hannah Arendt*, University Park: Pennsylvania State University Press, pp. 135–66.

— (1997), 'Ruth, the Model Emigrée: Mourning and the Symbolic Politics of Immigration', *Political Theory*, vol. 25, no. 1, pp. 112–36.

hooks, bell (1984), *Feminist Theory: From Margin to Center*, Boston: South End.

Huffer, Lynne (1998), *Maternal Pasts, Feminist Futures: Nostalgia, Ethics, and the Question of Difference*, Stanford: Stanford University Press.

Hussey, Andrew and Gavin Bowd (eds) (1996), *The Hacienda Must be Built: On the Legacy of Situationist Revolt*, Huddersfield: AURA.

Irigaray, Luce (1993), *An Ethics of Sexual Difference*, London: Athlone.

Bibliography

Jardine, Alice (1981), 'Pre-texts for the Transatlantic Feminist', *Yale French Studies*, no. 62, pp. 220–36.
— (1982), 'Gynesis', *Diacritics*, vol. 12, no. 2, pp. 54–65.
Jones, Ann Rosalind (1981), 'Writing the Body', *Feminist Studies*, vol. 7, no. 2, pp. 247–63.
— (1984), 'Julia Kristeva on Femininity: The Limits of a Semiotic Politics', *Feminist Review*, no. 18, pp. 56–73.
— (1985), 'Inscribing Femininity: French Theories of the Feminine', in G. Greene and C. Kahn (eds), *Making a Difference: Feminist Literary Criticism*, London: Methuen, pp. 80–112.
Kearney, Richard (1994), 'Julia Kristeva', *Modern Movements in European Philosophy*, Manchester: Manchester University Press, pp. 332–42.
Keltner, S. K. (2009a), 'What is Intimacy?', in K. Oliver and S. K. Keltner (eds), *Psychoanalysis, Aesthetics, and Politics in the Work of Julia Kristeva*, Albany, NY: SUNY Press, pp. 163–77.
— (2009b), 'The Ambiguity of Revolt: Kristeva's Recent Turn to Beauvoir', *PMLA*, vol. 124, no. 1, pp. 224–6.
Kuykendall, Eléanor H. (1989), 'Questions for Julia Kristeva's Ethics of Linguistics', in J. Allen and I. M. Young (eds), *The Thinking Muse: Feminism and Modern French Philosophy*, Bloomington: Indiana University Press, pp. 180–94.
Lacan, Jacques (1993), *Écrits. A Selection*, London: Routledge.
— (1998), *On Feminine Sexuality. The Limits of Love and Knowledge. Encore 1972–1973: Book XX*, New York: W. W. Norton.
Lechte, John (1990), *Julia Kristeva*, London: Routledge.
Lechte, John and Maria Margaroni (2004), *Julia Kristeva: Live Theory*, London: Continuum.
Lechte, John and Mary Zournazi (eds) (2003), *The Kristeva Critical Reader*, Edinburgh: Edinburgh University Press.
Leland, Dorothy (1992), 'Lacanian Psychoanalysis and French Feminism: Toward an Adequate Political Psychology', in N. Fraser and S. L. Bartky (eds), *Revaluing French Feminism. Critical Essays on Difference, Agency and Culture*, Bloomington: Indiana University Press, pp. 113–35.
Lloyd, Moya (1998–9), 'Politics and Melancholia', *Women's Philosophy Review*, no. 20, pp. 25–43.
— (2004), 'Julia Kristeva (1941–)', in J. Simons (ed.), *Contemporary Critical Theorists: From Lacan to Said*, Edinburgh: Edinburgh University Press, pp. 135–51.

— (2005), *Beyond Identity Politics: Feminism, Power and Politics*, London: Sage.
Lloyd, Moya and Adrian Little (eds) (2009), *The Politics of Radical Democracy*, Edinburgh: Edinburgh University Press.
McAfee, Noëlle (1993), 'Abject Strangers: Towards an Ethics of Respect', in K. Oliver (ed.), *Ethics, Politics and Difference in Julia Kristeva's Writing*, New York: Routledge, pp. 116–34.
— (2000), *Habermas, Kristeva, and Citizenship*, Ithaca, NY: Cornell University Press.
— (2004), *Julia Kristeva*, London: Routledge.
— (2005), 'Bearing Witness in the *Polis*: Kristeva, Arendt, and the Space of Appearance', in T. Chanter and E. P. Ziarek (eds), *Revolt, Affect, Collectivity: The Unstable Boundaries of Kristeva's Polis*, Albany, NY: SUNY Press, pp. 113–25.
McDonough, Thomas F. (1997), 'Rereading Debord, Rereading the Situationists', *October*, no. 79, Winter 1997, pp. 3–14.
Margaroni, Maria (2005), '"The Lost Foundation": Kristeva's Semiotic *Chora* and its Ambiguous Legacy', *Hypatia*, vol. 20, no. 1, pp. 78–98.
— (2007), 'Recent Work on and by Julia Kristeva: Toward a Psychoanalytic Social Theory', *Signs: Journal of Women in Culture and Society*, vol. 32, no. 3, pp. 793–808.
— (2009), 'Julia Kristeva's Chiasmatic Journeys: From Byzantium to the Phantom of Europe and the End of the World', in K. Oliver and S. K. Keltner (eds), *Psychoanalysis, Aesthetics, and Politics in the Work of Julia Kristeva*, Albany, NY: SUNY Press, pp. 107–24.
Marks, Elaine (1978), 'Women and Literature in France', *Signs: Journal of Women in Culture and Society*, vol. 3, no. 4, pp. 832–42.
Marks, Elaine and Isabelle de Courtivron (eds) (1981), *New French Feminisms: An Anthology*, New York: Harvester & Wheatsheaf.
Maur, Cairin (no date), 'Trans-Theory and Kristeva's Adolescent Novel', produced in association with *Radical Deviance: A Journal of Transgendered Politics*, pp. 2–11.
Meyers, Diana T. (1992), 'The Subversion of Women's Agency in Psychoanalytic Feminism: Chodorow, Flax, Kristeva', in N. Fraser and S. L. Bartky (eds), *Revaluing French Feminism. Critical Essays on Difference, Agency and Culture*, Bloomington: Indiana University Press, pp. 136–61.
Mitchell, Juliet (1990), *Psychoanalysis and Feminism. A Radical Reassessment of Freudian Psychoanalysis*, London: Penguin.
— (2001), 'Psychoanalysis and Feminism at the Millennium', in

Bibliography

E. Bronfen and M. Kavka (eds), *Feminist Consequences: Theory for the New Century*, New York: Columbia University Press, pp. 3–17.

Mitchell, Juliet and Jacqueline Rose (1982) (eds), *Feminine Sexuality. Jacques Lacan and the École Freudienne*, London: MacMillan.

Moi, Toril (ed.) (1992), *French Feminist Thought: A Reader*, Oxford: Blackwell.

— (1995), *Sexual/Textual Politics*, London: Methuen.

Moruzzi, Norma Claire (1993), 'National Abjects: Julia Kristeva on the Process of Political Self-Identification', in K. Oliver (ed.), *Ethics, Politics and Difference in Julia Kristeva's Writing*, New York: Routledge, pp. 135–49.

Moses, Claire Goldberg (1998), 'Made in America: "French Feminism" in Academia', *Feminist Studies*, vol. 24, no. 2, pp. 241–74.

Mouffe, Chantal (2005), *On the Political*, Abingdon: Routledge.

Nicholson, Linda J. (ed.) (1990), *Feminism/Postmodernism*, New York: Routledge.

Okin, Susan Moller (1999), *Is Multiculturalism Bad for Women? Susan Moller Okin with Respondents*, ed. J. Cohen, M. Howard and M. C. Nussbaum, Princeton: Princeton University Press.

Oliver, Kelly (1993a), *Reading Kristeva. Unraveling the Double-Bind*, New York: Routledge.

— (ed.) (1993b), *Ethics, Politics and Difference in Julia Kristeva's Writing*, New York: Routledge.

— (ed.) (2000), *French Feminism Reader*, Lanham, MD: Rowman & Littlefield.

— (2003), 'The Crisis of Meaning', in J. Lechte and M. Zournazi (eds), *The Kristeva Critical Reader*, Edinburgh: Edinburgh University Press, pp. 36–54.

— (2004), *The Colonization of Psychic Space: A Psychoanalytic Social Theory of Oppression*, Minneapolis: University of Minnesota Press.

— (2005), 'Revolt and Forgiveness', in T. Chanter and E. P. Ziarek (eds), *Revolt, Affect, Collectivity: The Unstable Boundaries of Kristeva's Polis*, Albany, NY: SUNY Press, pp. 77–92.

— (2007a), *Women as Weapons of War: Iraq, Sex, and the Media*, New York: Columbia University Press.

— (2007b), 'Innocence, Perversion, and Abu Ghraib', *Philosophy Today*, Fall 2007, pp. 343–56.

— (2008), 'Women: The Secret Weapon of Modern Warfare?', *Hypatia*, vol. 23, no. 2, pp. 1–16.

— (2009a), 'Bodies Against the Law: Abu Ghraib and the War on Terror', *Continental Philosophy Review*, vol. 42, pp. 63–80.
— (2009b), 'Meaning against Death', in K. Oliver and S. K. Keltner (eds), *Psychoanalysis, Aesthetics, and Politics in the Work of Julia Kristeva*, Albany, NY: SUNY Press, pp. 49–63.
Oliver, Kelly and S. K. Keltner (eds) (2009), *Psychoanalysis, Aesthetics, and Politics in the Work of Julia Kristeva*, Albany, NY: SUNY Press.
Oliver, Kelly and Lisa Walsh (eds) (2004), *Contemporary French Feminism*, Oxford: Oxford University Press.
Pateman, Carole (1988), *The Sexual Contract*, Stanford: Stanford University Press.
Rajan, Tilottama (1993), 'Trans-Positions of Difference: Kristeva and Post-Structuralism', in K. Oliver (ed.), *Ethics, Politics and Difference in Julia Kristeva's Writing*, New York: Routledge, pp. 215–37.
Raunig, Gerald (2007), *Art and Revolution: Transversal Activism in the Long Twentieth Century*, Los Angeles: Semiotext(e).
Reineke, Martha J. (1997), *Sacrificed Lives: Kristeva on Women and Violence*, Bloomington: Indiana University Press.
Rich, Adrienne (1997), *Of Woman Born. Motherhood as Experience and Institution*, London: Virago.
Riley, Denise (1988), *'Am I that Name?' Feminism and the Category of 'Women' in History*, Basingstoke: Macmillan.
— (1992), 'A Short History of Some Preoccupations', in J. Butler and J. W. Scott (eds), *Feminists Theorize the Political*, New York: Routledge, pp. 121–9.
Rose, Jacqueline (1993), 'Julia Kristeva – Take Two', in K. Oliver (ed.), *Ethics, Politics and Difference in Julia Kristeva's Writing*, New York: Routledge, pp. 41–61.
Rowley, Hazel and Elizabeth Grosz (1990), 'Psychoanalysis and Feminism', in S. Gunew (ed.), *Feminist Knowledge. Critique and Construct*, London: Routledge, pp. 175–204.
Ruddick, Sara (1989), *Maternal Thinking: Towards a Politics of Peace*, Boston: Beacon.
Said, Edward (1978), *Orientalism*, New York: Random House.
Sartre, Jean-Paul (2001), 'Preface', in F. Fanon, *The Wretched of the Earth*, London: Penguin, pp. 7–26.
Scott, Joan Wallach (1996), *Only Paradoxes to Offer: French Feminism and the Rights of Man*, Cambridge, MA: Harvard University Press.
— (2007), *The Politics of the Veil*, Princeton: Princeton University Press.
Sjoberg, Laura and Caron E. Gentry (2008), 'Reduced to Bad Sex:

Narratives of Violent Women from the Bible to the War on Terror', *International Relations*, vol. 22, no. 1, pp. 5–23.

Sjöholm, Cecilia (2003), 'Kristeva and *The Idiots*', *Radical Philosophy*, no. 22, pp. 35–9.

— (2005), *Kristeva and the Political*, London: Routledge.

— (2009), 'Fear of Intimacy? Psychoanalysis and the Resistance to Commodification', in K. Oliver and S. K. Keltner (eds), *Psychoanalysis, Aesthetics, and Politics in the Work of Julia Kristeva*, Albany, NY: SUNY Press, pp. 179–94.

Smith, Anne-Marie (1998), *Julia Kristeva. Speaking the Unspeakable*, London: Pluto.

Smith, Douglas (2005), 'Giving the Game Away: Play and Exchange in Situationism and Structuralism', *Modern and Contemporary France*, vol. 13, no. 4, pp. 421–34.

Spelman, Elizabeth V. (1982), 'Woman as Body: Ancient and Contemporary View', *Feminist Studies*, vol. 8, no. 1, pp. 109–31.

Spivak, Gayatri Chakravorty (1981), 'French Feminism in an International Frame', *Yale French Studies*, no. 62, pp. 154–84.

— (1988), 'Subaltern Studies: Deconstructing Historiography', in G. C. Spivak, *In Other Worlds: Essays in Cultural Politics*, New York: Routledge, pp. 197–221.

Still, Judith (1997), 'Horror in Kristeva and Bataille: Sex and Violence', *Paragraph: Powers of Transgression/Julia Kristeva*, special issue, ed. A.-M. Smith, vol. 20, no. 3, pp. 221–39.

Stimpson, Catherine R., Joan N. Burstyn, Domna C. Stanton, Sandra M. Whisler (1975), 'Editorial', *Signs: Journal of Women in Culture and Society*, vol. 1, no. 1, pp. v–viii.

Stone, Alison (2007), *An Introduction to Feminist Philosophy*, Cambridge: Polity.

Stone, Jennifer (1983), 'The Horrors of Power: A Critique of Kristeva', in F. Barker, P. Hulme, M. Iverson, D. Loxley (eds), *The Politics of Theory*, Essex: University of Essex, pp. 39–48.

The Kulta Beats, *Julia Kristeva*, www.thekultabeats.com/julia.php (accessed 7 April 2008).

Todorov, Tzvetan (1988), 'Poetic Language: The Russian Formalists', in *Literature and its Theorists. A Personal View of Twentieth-Century Criticism*, London: Routledge, pp. 10–28.

Varsamopoulou, Evy (2009), 'The Idea of Europe and the Ideal of Cosmopolitanism in the Work of Julia Kristeva', *Theory, Culture and Society*, vol. 26, no. 1, pp. 24–44.

Victor, Barbara (2004), *Army of Roses: Inside the World of Palestinian Women Suicide Bombers*, Robinson: London.
Walter, Natasha (2010), *Living Dolls: The Return of Sexism*, London: Virago.
Weir, Alison (1993), 'Identification with the Divided Mother: Kristeva's Ambivalence', in K. Oliver (ed.), *Ethics, Politics and Difference in Julia Kristeva's Writing*, New York: Routledge, pp. 79–91.
— (1996), *Sacrificial Logics: Feminist Theory and the Critique of Identity*, London: Routledge.
Williams, Caroline (2001), *Contemporary French Philosophy. Modernity and the Persistence of the Subject*, London: Athlone.
Wollen, Peter (1989), 'The Situationist International', *New Left Review*, no. 174, pp. 1–21.
Young, Iris Marion (1990), *Justice and the Politics of Difference*, Princeton: Princeton University Press.
— (2003a), 'Feminist Reactions to the Contemporary Security Regime', *Hypatia*, vol. 18, no. 1, pp. 223–31.
— (2003b), 'The Logic of Masculinist Protection: Reflections on the Current Security State', *Signs: Journal of Women in Culture and Society*, vol. 29, no. 1, pp. 1–25.
Young-Bruehl, Elisabeth (2004), *Hannah Arendt: For Love of the World*, New Haven: Yale University Press.
Zakin, Emily (2006), 'Beauvoir's Unsettling of the Universal', in L. J. Marso and P. Moynagh (eds), *Simone de Beauvoir's Political Thinking*, Urbana: University of Illinois Press.
— (2009), 'Humanism, the Rights of Man, and the Nation-State', in K. Oliver and S. K. Keltner (eds), *Psychoanalysis, Aesthetics, and Politics in the Work of Julia Kristeva*, Albany, NY: SUNY Press, pp. 195–211.
Zerilli, Linda M. G. (1992), 'A Process without a Subject: Simone de Beauvoir and Julia Kristeva on Maternity', *Signs: Journal of Women in Culture and Society*, vol. 18, no. 1, pp. 111–35.
— (1995), 'The Arendtian Body', in B. Honig (ed.), *Feminist Interpretations of Hannah Arendt*, University Park: Pennsylvania State University Press, pp. 167–93.
— (2005), *Feminism and the Abyss of Freedom*, Chicago: University of Chicago Press.
Ziarek, Ewa (1992), 'At the Limits of Discourse: Heterogeneity, Alterity, and the Maternal Body in Kristeva's Thought', *Hypatia*, vol. 7, no. 2, pp. 91–108.
— (1993), 'Kristeva and Levinas: Mourning, Ethics, and the Feminine',

in K. Oliver (ed.), *Ethics, Politics and Difference in Julia Kristeva's Writing*, New York: Routledge, pp. 62–78.
— (1995), 'The Uncanny Style of Kristeva's Critique of Nationalism', *Postmodern Culture*, vol. 5, no. 2, http://pmc.iath.virginia.edu/text-only/issue.195/ziarek.195.
Ziarek, Ewa Płonowska (2001), *An Ethics of Dissensus: Postmodernity, Feminism, and the Politics of Radical Democracy*, Stanford: Stanford University Press.
— (2005), 'Kristeva and Fanon: Revolutionary Violence and Ironic Articulation', in T. Chanter and E. P. Ziarek (eds), *Revolt, Affect, Collectivity: The Unstable Boundaries of Kristeva's Polis*, Albany, NY: SUNY Press, pp. 57–75.

Index

abjection, 34, 44, 49–51, 90, 92, 100, 102, 104, 135–6
  abject, 50, 169
  abject feminine, 161
  abjection of women, 51
  universality of abjection, 50
aesthetics, 1, 22, 34, 40, 44, 55, 59, 72, 121
  aesthetic practices, 9, 34, 60, 65, 105, 125, 131
affect, 13, 22, 27, 62, 79, 81, 91, 109, 125, 127, 135, 148–9, 167
agency, 2–3, 6, 14, 22–3, 25, 47, 65, 72, 139
  collective agency, 75, 125, 131
  female agency, 75, 135, 155, 171
  feminist agency, 75, 135, 154
  feminist political agency, 141, 155, 171
  women's agency, 47, 75
Ahmed, S., 106, 158–9, 161, 163
alterity, 16–17, 35, 47, 90, 98, 108, 145–6, 158, 168; *see also* ethics; the other; otherness
Amin, A., 162
anthropology
  philosophical anthropology, 100
  political anthropology, 133–5, 142, 172
  psychoanalytic anthropology, 135, 142
Arendt, H., 16, 63, 65, 80–1, 88, 106, 115–19, 122–39, 142, 145–6, 148, 150, 152, 154–5, 157
art, 26, 40, 44, 61, 78, 87, 103, 108, 115, 129, 135
art of living, 111, 134
authority, 74, 78, 104, 108
  paternal authority, 61, 73–4, 76

Bakhtin, M., 9, 24, 27
Balkans, 169–70
Battersby, C., 121
Beardsworth, S., 58, 108, 115, 153
Benveniste, E., 25
biography, 14, 119, 122, 124
Bjelić, D., 169
body, 7, 22, 34, 42, 44–5, 79, 90–1, 118, 125–6, 129, 131–3, 172
  bodily boundaries, 47, 49, 50, 102, 135
  bodily disintegration, 47
  body-in-process, 44
  coherent body, 49
  maternal body, 22, 43, 48–9, 91–2, 98, 102, 112, 169
  nursing body, 48
  see also abjection; corporeality; embodiment; ethics; pregnancy
bond(s), 167–8
  civic bonds, 131
  political bonds, 17, 117, 136–7, 139, 141
  political friendship, 136–7, 154
  social bonds, 102
Boulous Walker, M., 30, 48
Brandt, J., 9
Brown, W., 102–3
Bulgaria, 138, 168–9
Butler, J., 4, 7, 9, 21, 32, 39, 45–6, 70, 80, 97–8

chora, 4, 46–8, 92, 95
Colette, S. G., 115, 119, 122, 128, 139
colonialism, 159, 164–5
contestation, 72, 74, 81, 151–2, 170
Coole, D., 30, 32, 34, 63
Cornell, D., 35, 39, 98–9, 107
corporeality, 15, 16, 22, 81, 90–2, 125, 127, 131, 134–5

corporeality (*cont.*)
  corporeal ethics, 44
  corporeal philosophy, 44
  see also body; embodiment
cosmopolitanism, 88, 111, 147, 156–8, 160–1, 170
  ethical cosmopolitanism, 156
crisis, 15, 45, 55–62, 64, 74, 76–9, 82, 88, 108, 127–8, 138, 150–2
  crisis of authority, 59, 60, 94
  crisis of paternal function, 59–61
  crisis of subject, 60, 115
  see also revolt
critique, 28, 62, 66, 74, 81–2, 150, 152, 170, 172
cultural pessimism, 61, 78
culture, 3, 7–8, 28–9, 32, 39, 46, 61, 90–1, 97, 148, 160–1, 167
culture of death, 105

De Beauvoir, S., 17, 37, 93, 118, 139–41, 146
Debord, G., 60–2, 76–7, 82; *see also* situationism; society of the spectacle
Delphy, C., 10–11
Dietz, M., 4–6
difference, 4, 6–7, 14, 35, 38–9, 81, 89, 91, 124, 136, 138, 141–2, 151, 153
Disch, L., 137, 154
discourse, 91, 115
  discourse on life, 105, 107
dissidence, 27, 48, 65, 131, 139
  female dissidence, 48
drives, 16, 24–5, 27, 30, 32–4, 45–7, 53n22, 64–5, 79, 89, 94, 98, 100–2, 111–12, 126, 129, 133, 135–6, 147, 148
  death drive, 43, 90, 100–5, 109, 116

embodiment, 2–3, 16, 43–4, 48, 55, 111, 116–17, 125; *see also* body; corporeality
Enlightenment universalism, 157–8, 171
essentialism, 3, 7, 37, 39, 46
ethics, 3, 87–91, 96–7, 99, 100, 104, 108–9, 111, 116, 127, 129, 131, 162

ethical feminism, 98–9
ethical orientation towards otherness, 162
ethics of alterity, 24, 136
ethics of forgiveness, 100
ethics of living, 100
ethics of non-violence, 106
ethics of psychoanalysis, 110–11
ethics of the self, 111, 154
feminine ethics, 96–7, 99
feminist ethics, 7, 13, 16, 87–8, 100, 104
herethics, 88, 91–2
see also corporeality; cosmopolitanism; the maternal; traversal
Europe, 4, 17, 73, 146–7, 152, 155, 157, 160–3, 165–8, 170
  Eastern Europe, 9, 147, 167
  European conceptions of the universal, 140
  European tradition of revolt, 55, 61
  Western Europe, 171
evil, 109–10, 135
exile, 116
experience, 122, 127

Fanon, F., 72–3
feminine, the, 3, 7, 10, 15–16, 22, 29, 35, 38–9, 41, 47, 57, 63–4, 66, 69, 70, 76, 81, 87, 91, 94, 98, 99, 104, 106, 111, 118–20, 133, 151, 161, 169
  feminine as force of subversion, 51
  see also ethics; heterogeneity
femininity, 7, 39, 42, 44, 68–70, 106, 120–1, 123
feminism
  as collective practice, 137
  as contestatory political project, 151, 172
  as critical practice, 81, 151, 170, 172
  as critical project, 16, 128
  as political project, 38, 74, 76
  feminism's critical ethos, 128
  see also French feminism; heterogeneity; plurality; politics; revolt; totalitarianism
foreigner(s), 100, 106, 110, 112, 155, 159, 163

Index

foreignness, 43, 153, 155–6, 161–2
forgiveness, 16, 88, 108–11, 127, 149; *see also* ethics
France, 8, 10–11, 60, 156, 158–62, 165, 169, 170
 French Enlightenment, 140, 156, 160
 French nation, 156–8, 160–1
 see also Europe; French feminism; French theory; immigration; universality
Fraser, N., 2, 9, 21, 38–9, 52n3, 97
freedom, 4, 14, 17, 88, 105, 111, 116, 128, 130, 132–4, 141–2, 146–55, 160, 165–7, 170, 172
 American conception of freedom, 150–1, 165
 Eastern European version of freedom, 165
 Ethical dimension of freedom, 167
 European freedom, 150, 152, 163, 165
 freedom as contestation, 171
 freedom as disclosure, 152–3
 freedom as questioning, 111, 149
 freedom as revolt, 151–2
 instrumental freedom, 152
 Orthodox version of freedom, 165
 Orthodoxy's contribution to conceptions of freedom, 167
 Western European version of freedom, 165
French feminism, 4, 10–11, 18n11, 19n12, 41, 118
French theory, 13, 118
Freud, S., 10, 29, 31, 34, 59, 63, 67–8, 70, 72, 98, 101–2, 109, 147–8
fundamentalism, 155
 Islamic fundamentalism, 104, 164
 Muslim fundamentalism, 8, 105
 nationalist fundamentalism, 156, 162
 see also nationalism
Futurality *see* politics; 'woman'

Gambaudo, S., 56, 59
gender, 6–8, 13, 35, 51, 56–7, 59, 70, 74, 76, 80, 104, 106

genius, 115, 118–25, 130, 138–9, 141
 female genius, 57, 99, 115, 119–20, 122, 139, 169
Gratton, P., 159
Grosz, E., 51
guilt, 109–10

Hegel, G.W.F., 28, 30–1, 34, 71, 77, 118
Heidegger, M., 109–10, 148, 152, 166
heterogeneity, 16, 89–91, 97, 99, 112, 117, 151, 170
 feminine heterogeneity, 74, 99, 123, 172
 feminism's heterogeneity, 4, 8, 14, 21, 120, 171
 heterogeneity of language, 27
 women's heterogeneity, 6, 164
hospitality, 112, 162, 163
human rights, 157
humanity, 112, 141
 new humanism, 107, 112
 universalist conception of humanity, 157

identification, 41–3, 139
 father-identification, 43
identity, 103, 125, 137–8, 154–5
 critique of identity, 2–3, 14, 37, 39, 117, 137, 168, 171
 identity politics, 116
immigration, 88, 146–7, 157–61, 164
 emigration, 116
 migration, 88–9, 162
 see also France; Muslim(s); veil
intersubjectivity, 91, 163
intertextuality, 24
intimate, the, 14, 64, 75–9, 81–2, 116, 125, 128, 133–5, 145, 147, 150–3, 167, 172
 intimacy, 80–1, 133–4, 167
 intimate revolt, 15, 56, 64, 76–80
 intimist, 57
irony, 73
 female irony, 67, 73–4
 feminine irony, 73
 women's irony, 71–2
Islam, 105, 158, 164

jouissance, 43, 52n9, 59, 62, 129

Kant, I., 151, 166
Keltner, S.K., 80–1
Klein, M., 115–16, 119, 122, 139

Lacan, J., 25–6, 28, 40–1, 67
  Lacanian, 10, 52n9, 62
  Lacanian psychoanalysis, 32, 39
language, 7, 10, 41–2, 44, 64, 67, 79, 81, 88, 90–1, 94, 102, 111, 116, 127, 161
  theory of language, 22–3, 89
life, 17, 107, 112, 115, 117–20, 122, 124–9, 132, 153, 167
  bios, 128–30
  narrated life, 121
  zoē, 128–30, 132
  see also Arendt; biography; genius
Lloyd, M., 103
love, 108, 110, 123
  transference love, 110–11

McAfee, N., 38, 91, 127
Margaroni, M., 2, 13, 33, 47
marginality, 64–5, 116, 131
  the marginalised, 65, 103
masculine, the, 7, 26, 38, 44, 69–70, 91, 94, 97, 99, 101, 104, 106, 111
masculinity, 7, 29, 42, 69, 70
maternal, the, 26, 41, 63, 87, 93–4, 97, 99, 133, 142
  maternal body, 3, 4, 22, 32, 45–7, 91, 98
  maternal ethics, 16, 92, 96
  maternal political practice, 96
  maternal semiotic, 42
  maternal suffering, 59
  maternity, 44, 89, 91–3, 97–9, 123
  symbolic maternity, 93–4
  see also motherhood
melancholia, 34, 43, 100, 102, 159
  culture of melancholy, 60
  female melancholia, 42, 59, 68
  melancholic identification, 42
  national melancholia, 159
Middle East, 100, 104–5
Moruzzi, N. C., 158
motherhood, 3, 39, 51, 88, 91–100, 124, 130, 140
  motherhood and genius, 122–3
  see also the maternal

multiculturalism, 7, 88, 162
Muslim(s), 88, 161, 164
  Muslim immigration, 160
  Muslim migrants, 164, 171
  Muslim migration, 158
  see also France; immigration
mutuality, 162

narrative, 17, 115, 117–19, 124–7, 129, 142, 148
natality, 117, 125, 130
nation, 89, 155–60, 162–3
  civic conception of the nation, 161
  nation as symbolic pact, 161
  see also France; immigration; melancholia
nationalism, 4, 155–7, 164; *see also* fundamentalism
nature and culture, 3, 22, 32–3, 47–8, 111
  nature–culture threshold, 48
negativity, 15, 22, 28, 30–2, 35, 39, 42, 45, 63, 77, 91; *see also* the semiotic

Oedipality, 26, 59, 68–9, 124
  Oedipal crisis, 28, 98
  Oedipal family, 40, 44, 45
  Oedipal triangle, 46, 92, 94
  universal applicability of Oedipal injunction, 68
  universality of Oedipal structure, 70, 120
  see also psychoanalysis
Oliver, K., 14, 39, 44, 50–1, 56, 107, 126
Orthodox Christianity, 133, 165–9
other, the, 89–90, 94–5, 99, 102, 107–8, 110–11, 122–3, 127, 146, 148, 156, 159; *see also* alterity; ethics
otherness, 30, 89–91, 100, 108, 145–6, 155–6, 163

particularity, 7, 72–3, 75, 147
  feminisation of the particular, 73
  particular, the, 72–4, 155, 157, 159–60, 163, 165
  see also universality
paternal, the, 26, 94
  paternal function, 94, 113n6

Index

phallic monism, 68–70, 72, 120
phallus, 28, 44, 46–7, 67–8, 70–2
  illusory nature of the phallus, 67, 70–1
  universality of the phallus, 69–70
plurality, 15, 17, 97, 117–18, 120, 124, 128, 130–1, 136–9, 141–2, 145, 153–4, 171–2
  female plurality, 38, 72, 141
  feminism's plurality, 4–5, 14, 21, 120, 171
  plurality of women, 37
poetic language, 26–7, 29, 135
political philosophy, 1–2, 17, 40, 63, 72, 79, 117–18, 136, 141–2, 145–6, 151, 170
  feminist political philosophy, 13, 125, 151
politics, 39–40, 65
  deterritorialisation of politics, 16, 56
  displacement of politics, 3, 15, 34, 56, 63, 106, 135
  micro-politics, 16, 56, 63
  political practice, 6, 72–3, 154
  politics, 2–3, 5–7, 10, 13–14, 38–9, 71, 97
  politics of futurality, 74, 81
  women's political participation, 96
post-structuralism, 3, 24, 35, 42, 87
pregnancy, 47, 96, 130
  pregnant body, 47
  see also the maternal; motherhood
psychic life, 44, 55–7, 60, 62, 76, 78–9, 102, 128, 133–4, 148–50, 167, 170
psychoanalysis, 1, 5, 7, 9–10, 13, 15, 24–5, 35, 37, 40, 42–5, 56–8, 64, 66, 78–80, 82, 88, 92, 108–11, 116, 127, 146–9, 165, 171
  psychoanalysis as questioning and critical practice, 66

questioning, 66, 71, 74, 111, 127–8, 148–9, 151–2, 167, 170
  ethos of questioning, 148
  practice of questioning, 81–2, 151

rebirth, 17, 79, 108, 110–11, 118, 120, 130, 136, 148–9; *see also* revolt

Reineke, M., 101
representation, 55, 59–61, 79, 83n4, 87, 91–2, 94–5, 99, 104, 111, 129, 133–4
revolt, 4, 15, 55–7, 59–68, 71–9, 82, 88, 105, 109–11, 128–9, 133, 146–51, 153, 167, 172
  culture of revolt, 63–4, 66, 77
  ethos of revolt, 71
  European tradition of revolt, 55, 61
  female revolt, 16, 56, 68, 70
  feminine revolt, 70, 72
  feminist revolt, 57, 70
  freedom as revolt, 151
  intimate revolt, 56, 76–9, 109, 134, 170
  political dimension of revolt, 57
  political revolt, 62, 65, 82, 134
  rebirth-in-revolt, 67
  see also crisis
Riley, D., 6, 38
Romanticism, 118–21
Romantic, 17
Russian Formalism, 27

sacrifice, 101
Sartre, J.-P., 72, 148
Scott, J. W., 74, 158, 161
semiotic, the, 4, 22–38, 41–2, 44–7, 49–50, 63–4, 67, 70, 79, 90–2, 95, 98, 129, 133, 166–7
  semiotic as subversive force, 29–31, 33, 39, 45, 48
  semiotic negativity, 30–2, 34, 77
  see also drives; Hegel; negativity; the symbolic; symbolic order
semiotics, 1, 10, 15, 89, 98
sexual difference, 3, 7, 15, 24–5, 38, 43, 46, 69–70, 75, 90–1, 93–4, 99, 101, 104, 120–1, 130, 151, 153, 161
sexuality, 4, 5, 7, 41, 66–70, 124
  bisexuality, 70–1
  female bisexuality, 72–3
  female psychosexuality, 120
  female sexuality, 16, 56, 67, 69, 70–3, 119
  women's constitutive bisexuality, 68, 71
  women's psychic bisexuality, 67, 70, 124

shahidas, 105–7, 165
signification, 13, 22, 27, 79, 91, 99–112, 135
singularity, 1, 15, 17, 27, 65, 75, 81, 94, 112, 117–18, 120, 124, 128, 131–2, 136, 138–42, 145, 148, 152–4, 171–2
  female singularity, 141
  singularity of women, 37–8
situationism, 60, 62; *see also* Debord; society of the spectacle
Sjöholm, C., 9, 63, 81, 157
society of the spectacle, 60–1, 64–5, 76–7, 79, 82, 103–4, 127; *see also* Debord; situationism
Spivak, G. C., 164
Still, J., 50–1
strangeness, 146, 156, 158, 164
stranger(s), 156, 158, 162–4
structuralism, 24, 27, 52n3
subject, 2–3, 5–7, 14–16, 25–7, 52n3, 79–80, 90, 100–4, 109, 111, 131, 141, 146, 148, 151, 154, 156, 159
  critique of the subject, 6, 14, 17, 25, 37–9, 137, 151, 168, 171
  decentred subject, 6, 25, 27, 28, 35, 38–9, 148, 159
  female subject, 2–3, 13
  fluidity of the subject, 15, 17, 30, 32, 35–6, 39, 42, 49, 67, 74, 77
  heterogeneity of the subject, 15, 17, 35, 38, 74, 89, 91, 98, 107, 146, 148, 157–8, 168
  instability of the subject, 2, 15, 32, 34–6, 42
  precariousness of the subject, 30, 34, 37, 50, 67, 77
  speaking subject, 22–3, 25, 95
subject in process, 6, 15, 23, 31, 34–6, 38, 42, 74, 77, 89–90, 135, 148, 157, 159
sublimation, 16, 90, 108, 148
symbolic, the, 4, 15, 22, 25–34, 36–8, 42, 45–7, 49–50, 64, 67, 70, 72–4, 77, 79, 89–92, 95, 97–8, 101, 129, 166–8, 170; *see also* semiotic
symbolic order, 29, 31, 39, 41, 43, 62, 67, 69, 71, 94–6, 101, 139

Tel Quel, 8–9, 23, 27, 153
terrorism, 88, 104–5

threshold, 48, 75, 91, 111, 129–30
  maternal body as bodily threshold, 92
totalitarianism, 117–18, 131, 135–8, 154
  collective action as totalitarian, 130
  totalitarian intervention of politics, 134
  totalitarianism of feminism, 2, 37–8, 130, 138–9, 141, 171
transference, 108, 111, 148
  transference love, 148
transformation, 22–3, 30, 56, 60, 62, 72–3, 76, 82, 124
  political transformation, 2, 6, 34, 57, 171
  social and political transformation, 57, 74, 117, 171
  social transformation, 3, 57
transgression, 27, 34, 36, 45, 49, 63, 92, 129
  transgressive practice, 24, 27, 75, 96
traversal, 22, 60, 90–2, 97, 112, 112–13n4, 168
  ethics of traversal, 16, 88–9, 91–2, 172

universality, 7, 73, 147, 157
  universal, the, 72–4, 155, 157, 160, 165
  universalism, 157, 159, 170
  see also Europe; humanity; Oedipality; particularity; phallus

Varsamopoulou, E., 161, 170
veil, 160–1; *see also* Ahmed; France; immigration; stranger(s)
violence, 16, 61, 88, 100–9, 111, 127, 135, 165; *see also* ethics
vulnerability, 88, 100–2, 105, 108–9, 123

war on terror, 105
9/11, 8, 105, 107
'woman', 5, 37–9, 98, 137
  futural construction of women, 98
writing, 9, 116, 124, 128–9

Zerilli, L., 2, 4, 21, 154–5
Ziarek, E. P., 2, 72–4, 89–91, 106